AUSTRALIA'S FERTILITY TRANSITION

A STUDY OF 19TH-CENTURY TASMANIA

AUSTRALIA'S FERTILITY TRANSITION

A STUDY OF 19TH-CENTURY TASMANIA

HELEN MOYLE

PRESS

Published by ANU Press
The Australian National University
Acton ACT 2601, Australia
Email: anupress@anu.edu.au

Available to download for free at press.anu.edu.au

ISBN (print): 9781760463366
ISBN (online): 9781760463373

WorldCat (print): 1137826491
WorldCat (online): 1137860712

DOI: 10.22459/AFT.2020

This title is published under a Creative Commons Attribution-NonCommercial-NoDerivatives 4.0 International (CC BY-NC-ND 4.0).

The full licence terms are available at creativecommons.org/licenses/by-nc-nd/4.0/legalcode

This publication was awarded a College of Arts and Social Sciences PhD Publication Prize in 2019. The prize contributes to the cost of professional copyediting.

Cover design and layout by ANU Press.

Cover photograph: NS5098/1/88, 'Woman with two children and an infant sitting outside', Tasmanian Archives.

This edition © 2020 ANU Press

Contents

Abbreviations vii
Acknowledgements ix
List of figures xi
List of tables. xv
1. Introduction: Theories of the historical fertility decline 1
2. The Australian fertility decline 27
3. Tasmania in the 19th and early 20th centuries 41
4. Research design and data sources. 63
5. Characteristics of the Tasmanian marriage cohorts. 83
6. Fertility patterns of the couples in the marriage cohorts 111
7. How, when and why did fertility decline? 145
8. Why did fertility fall in Tasmania during this period? Qualitative insights 185
9. Conclusion. 221
Appendix A: Appendix tables 231
Appendix B: Data sources used for family reconstitution. 253
Appendix C: Local history museums. 257
Appendix D: Individual stories. 259
Bibliography 265
Index 287

Abbreviations

CPA	Cohort Parity Analysis
EFP	European Fertility Project
HISCLASS	Historical International Social Class Scheme
HISCO	Historical International Classification of Occupations
NSW	New South Wales
NZ	New Zealand
TFR	total fertility rate
UK	United Kingdom
WHO	World Health Organization

Acknowledgements

I would like to thank the Humanities and Creative Arts Editorial Board of ANU Press for awarding me the 2019 CASS Publishing Prize, which enabled me to turn my PhD thesis into a published book. I would also like to thank Edith Gray, the head of the School of Demography at The Australian National University, for her support in my application for the prize. Thank you to Emily Hazlewood and her team at ANU Press for making the production of this book such a smooth process.

In regards to my original PhD thesis, I would like to thank Rebecca Kippen for her support and encouragement and for generously sharing her databases with me. The members of my supervisory panel—Rebecca, Zhongwei Zhao and David Lucas—all read my drafts and gave me helpful comments and advice. I would like to thank Teresa Neeman, from the ANU Statistical Consulting Unit, and Edith Gray for their statistical advice; Anna Reimondos for her help in preparing the dataset and for advice on STATA; and Heather Crawford and Jenny White for their help with software packages. Iwu Utomo, the PhD coordinator, was very supportive and encouraging, as were my fellow PhD students. I would also like to thank Julie Rowe for sharing her experiences of the PhD journey with me.

Janet McCalman and Trudy Cowley of the Founders and Survivors Project at the University of Melbourne/University of Tasmania generously shared their Catholic baptisms database with me. Bronwyn Meikle, who was at that time doing a PhD in history at the University of Tasmania, gave me the benefit of her extensive knowledge about 19th-century Tasmania. I would also like to thank the staff and volunteers of the Tasmanian local history museums listed in Appendix C for their time and assistance and the family history societies and genealogists who helped me try to track down some of my missing families.

I would like to thank the International Union for the Scientific Study of Population (IUSSP) Scientific Panel on Historical Demography for accepting me to participate in the workshop on 'Socioeconomic Stratification and Fertility Before, During and After the Demographic Transition' in September 2012. This was a very valuable experience and my thesis benefited from it greatly. All the participants were very helpful, but particularly Jan Van Bavel, who continued to give me advice after I returned to Australia.

I am also very grateful to George Alter for accepting me as a student in the Longitudinal Analysis of Demographic Data course at the University of Michigan summer school in August 2013. This course was invaluable and I could not have written this book if I had not participated in it. Ken Smith and Glenn Deane, who taught survival analysis, were very helpful with statistical advice after I returned to Australia.

Finally, I would like to thank my friends and family for their support and encouragement, particularly my husband, who helped me in so many ways.

List of figures

Figure 2.1 Coale's fertility indices (I_g and I_f), Australia, 1861–1921, and Tasmania, 1881–1921 28

Figure 2.2 Estimated total fertility rate (TFR) for Tasmania, 1860–1921 (three-year moving average). 29

Figure 2.3 Mean children ever born to married women, Australia and Tasmania, 1911 census 31

Figure 2.4 Mean children ever born to married women, Australia and Tasmania, 1921 census 32

Figure 2.5 Children ever born to married women by birth cohort, Australia, 1921 census 32

Figure 6.1 Proportions of families by number of children, complete group: 1860, 1870, 1880 and 1890 marriage cohorts, Tasmania 113

Figure 6.2 Proportions of women reaching each parity, complete group: 1860, 1870, 1880 and 1890 marriage cohorts, Tasmania 127

Figure 6.3 Proportions of women reaching each parity by socioeconomic status, complete group: 1860/70 marriage cohorts, Tasmania 128

Figure 6.4 Proportions of women reaching each parity by socioeconomic status, complete group: 1880 marriage cohort, Tasmania 129

Figure 6.5 Proportions of women reaching each parity by socioeconomic status, complete group: 1890 marriage cohort, Tasmania 129

Figure 6.6 White-collar workers, proportions of women reaching each parity, complete group: 1860/70, 1880 and 1890 marriage cohorts, Tasmania 130

Figure 6.7 Skilled workers, proportions of women reaching each parity, complete group: 1860/70, 1880 and 1890 marriage cohorts, Tasmania 131

Figure 6.8 Farmers, proportions of women reaching each parity, complete group: 1860/70, 1880 and 1890 marriage cohorts, Tasmania 131

Figure 6.9 Lower-skilled workers, proportions of women reaching each parity, complete group: 1860/70, 1880 and 1890 marriage cohorts, Tasmania 132

Figure 6.10 Unskilled workers, proportions of women reaching each parity, complete group: 1860/70, 1880 and 1890 marriage cohorts, Tasmania 133

Figure 6.11 Proportions of women reaching each parity by urban/rural location, complete group: 1860/70 marriage cohorts, Tasmania 134

Figure 6.12 Proportions of women reaching each parity by urban/rural location, complete group: 1880 marriage cohort, Tasmania 134

Figure 6.13 Proportions of women reaching each parity by urban/rural location, complete group: 1890 marriage cohort, Tasmania 135

Figure 6.14 Proportions of women reaching each parity for couples living in an urban area, complete group: 1860/70, 1880 and 1890 marriage cohorts, Tasmania...................... 136

Figure 6.15 Proportions of women reaching each parity for couples living in a rural area, complete group: 1860/70, 1880 and 1890 marriage cohorts, Tasmania 136

Figure 6.16 Proportions of women reaching each parity by religion, complete group: 1860/70 marriage cohorts, Tasmania 137

Figure 6.17 Proportions of women reaching each parity by religion, complete group: 1880 marriage cohort, Tasmania 138

LIST OF FIGURES

Figure 6.18 Proportions of women reaching each parity by religion, complete group: 1890 marriage cohort, Tasmania 139

Figure 6.19 Anglicans, proportions of women reaching each parity, complete group: 1860/70, 1880 and 1890 marriage cohorts, Tasmania 139

Figure 6.20 Catholics, proportions of women reaching each parity, complete group: 1860/70, 1880 and 1890 marriage cohorts, Tasmania 140

Figure 6.21 Presbyterians, proportions of women reaching each parity, complete group: 1860/70, 1880 and 1890 marriage cohorts, Tasmania 140

Figure 6.22 Methodists, proportions of women reaching each parity, complete group: 1860/70, 1880 and 1890 marriage cohorts, Tasmania 141

Figure 6.23 Other Nonconformists, proportions of women reaching each parity, complete group: 1860/70, 1880 and 1890 marriage cohorts, Tasmania. 142

Figure 7.1 Mean birth intervals by birth order (excluding last), complete group: 1860/70, 1880 and 1890 marriage cohorts, Tasmania 153

Figure 7.2 Predicted probability that a birth is the last by socioeconomic status, complete group: 1860/70, 1880 and 1890 marriage cohorts, Tasmania 169

Figure 7.3 Predicted probability that a birth is the last by socioeconomic status for women married at age 20–24 years, giving birth at 30+ years and with a husband the same age or 1–4 years older, complete group: 1860/70, 1880 and 1890 marriage cohorts, Tasmania 169

Figure 7.4 Predicted probability that a birth is the last by urban/rural location, complete group: 1860/70, 1880 and 1890 marriage cohorts, Tasmania 170

Figure 7.5 Predicted probability of women having at least a specific number of surviving children, complete group: 1860/70, 1880 and 1890 marriage cohorts, Tasmania............... 171

List of tables

Table 2.1 Age-specific marital fertility rates, New South Wales, 1871, 1881, 1891 and 1901. 30

Table 2.2 Number of children ever born to women marrying in South Australia, 1842–46, 1875–79 and 1885–89. 34

Table 2.3 Average number of children by husband's occupation group in South Australia, 1842–46, 1875–79 and 1885–89 marriage cohorts 35

Table 2.4 Average number of children ever born by birth cohort of married women by metropolitan/non-metropolitan location, Australia, 1911. 36

Table 2.5 Index of marital fertility (I_g) for urban and rural areas, selected colonies of Australia, 1871, 1881, 1891, 1901 and 1911 37

Table 2.6 Average number of children ever born to married women by religion, selected groups, Australia, 1911. 38

Table 2.7 Average number of children of married women who completed childbearing by 1901, by age at marriage and religious denomination, NSW 1901 census 38

Table 2.8 Average number of children ever born to married women by birth cohort and birthplace, Australia, 1911 39

Table 3.1 Population of Tasmania: 1822, 1832, 1842 and 1857. 48

Table 3.2 Population of Tasmania: 1861, 1870, 1881, 1891, 1901 and 1911 49

Table 3.3 Female population by age, Tasmania, 1861, 1870, 1881 and 1891 50

Table 3.4 Male population by age, Tasmania, 1861, 1870, 1881 and 1891 50

Table 3.5 Birthplace of the Tasmanian population, 1870, 1881 and 1891 52

Table 3.6 Population by religion, Tasmania, 1842, 1851, 1861, 1870 and 1891. 54

Table 3.7 State school students and attendance, Tasmania, 1870, 1881, 1891 and 1901. 56

Table 3.8 Proportion of the population who could read and write, Tasmania, 1861, 1870, 1881, 1891 and 1901 57

Table 4.1 Unregistered births and total births for children born in Tasmania, complete group: 1860, 1870, 1880 and 1890 marriage cohorts, Tasmania 77

Table 4.2 Couples with unregistered births in Tasmania as a proportion of couples with at least one birth in Tasmania, complete group: 1860, 1870, 1880 and 1890 marriage cohorts, Tasmania. 78

Table 5.1 Type of marriage: 1860, 1870, 1880 and 1890 marriage cohorts, Tasmania 84

Table 5.2 Marital status of husband and wife, complete group: 1860, 1870, 1880 and 1890 marriage cohorts, Tasmania 86

Table 5.3 Wife's age at marriage, complete group: 1860, 1870, 1880 and 1890 marriage cohorts, Tasmania. 87

Table 5.4 Husband's age at marriage, complete group: 1860, 1870, 1880 and 1890 marriage cohorts, Tasmania. 88

Table 5.5 Age difference between husband and wife at marriage, complete group: 1860, 1870, 1880 and 1890 marriage cohorts, Tasmania 89

Table 5.6 Type of religion at marriage, complete group: 1860, 1870, 1880 and 1890 marriage cohorts, Tasmania 90

Table 5.7 Whether husband and/or wife signed the marriage register, complete group: 1860, 1870, 1880 and 1890 marriage cohorts, Tasmania 91

LIST OF TABLES

Table 5.8 Husband's occupational group (HISCO) at the birth of the first child, complete group: 1860, 1870, 1880 and 1890 marriage cohorts, Tasmania 93

Table 5.9 Husband's socioeconomic status (HISCLASS) at the birth of the first child, complete group: 1860, 1870, 1880 and 1890 marriage cohorts, Tasmania 94

Table 5.10 Husband's socioeconomic status at the birth of the first child, complete group: 1860, 1870, 1880 and 1890 marriage cohorts, Tasmania 95

Table 5.11 Occupational characteristics of husbands between first and last births for couples with more than one child, complete group: 1860, 1870, 1880 and 1890 marriage cohorts, Tasmania 96

Table 5.12 Type of location of first birth, complete group: 1860, 1870, 1880 and 1890 marriage cohorts, Tasmania 98

Table 5.13 Location of all births, complete group: 1860, 1870, 1880 and 1890 marriage cohorts, Tasmania 99

Table 5.14 Changes in type of geographic location (urban, rural, outside Tasmania) during the period between the first and last births for couples with more than one child, complete group: 1860, 1870, 1880 and 1890 marriage cohorts, Tasmania 99

Table 6.1 Number of children ever born, complete group: 1860, 1870, 1880 and 1890 marriage cohorts, Tasmania 112

Table 6.2 Couples with multiple births, complete group: 1860, 1870, 1880 and 1890 marriage cohorts, Tasmania 114

Table 6.3 Mean and median numbers of children by singleton/multiple births, complete group: 1860, 1870, 1880 and 1890 cohorts, Tasmania 115

Table 6.4 Infant and child mortality rates, complete group: 1860, 1870, 1880 and 1890 marriage cohorts, Tasmania 115

Table 6.5 Proportion of families with at least one infant and/or child death, complete group: 1860, 1870, 1880 and 1890 marriage cohorts, Tasmania 117

Table 6.6 Number of deaths for families experiencing at least one death of an infant and/or young child, complete group: 1860, 1870, 1880 and 1890 marriage cohorts, Tasmania 117

Table 6.7 Mean and median numbers of children by mother's age at marriage, complete group: 1860, 1870, 1880 and 1890 marriage cohorts, Tasmania 118

Table 6.8 Mean and median numbers of children by difference in age between husbands and wives for women marrying aged 20–24 years, complete group: 1860, 1870, 1880 and 1890 marriage cohorts, Tasmania 119

Table 6.9 Mean and median numbers of children by husband's socioeconomic status at first birth, complete group: 1860, 1870, 1880 and 1890 marriage cohorts, Tasmania 121

Table 6.10 Mean and median numbers of children by location at first birth, complete group: 1860, 1870, 1880 and 1890 marriage cohorts, Tasmania 122

Table 6.11 Mean and median numbers of children by location of family births, complete group: 1860, 1870, 1880 and 1890 marriage cohorts, Tasmania 122

Table 6.12 Mean and median numbers of children by religion at marriage, complete group: 1860, 1870, 1880 and 1890 marriage cohorts, Tasmania 123

Table 6.13 Mean and median numbers of children by parents' literacy, complete group: 1860, 1870, 1880 and 1890 marriage cohorts, Tasmania 124

Table 6.14 Parity progression ratios, complete group: 1860, 1870, 1880 and 1890 marriage cohorts, Tasmania 125

Table 7.1 Age at marriage for women with children in their first marriage, complete group: 1860/70, 1880 and 1890 marriage cohorts, Tasmania 146

Table 7.2 Age at first birth, complete group: 1860/70, 1880 and 1890 marriage cohorts, Tasmania 147

Table 7.3 Age at last birth, complete group: 1860/70, 1880 and 1890 marriage cohorts, Tasmania 148

LIST OF TABLES

Table 7.4 Mean (median) age at last birth by age at marriage, complete group: 1860/70, 1880 and 1890 marriage cohorts, Tasmania 150

Table 7.5 Interval between marriage and first birth, complete group: 1860/70, 1880 and 1890 marriage cohorts, Tasmania 151

Table 7.6 First interbirth interval, complete group: 1860/70, 1880 and 1890 marriage cohorts, Tasmania 152

Table 7.7 Second interbirth interval, complete group: 1860/70, 1880 and 1890 marriage cohorts, Tasmania............... 152

Table 7.8 Last interbirth intervals, complete group: 1860/70, 1880 and 1890 marriage cohorts, Tasmania............... 154

Table 7.9 Mean overall birth interval by number of children, complete group: 1860/70, 1880 and 1890 marriage cohorts, Tasmania 155

Table 7.10 Parity of last birth, where last birth interval is six years or more, complete group: 1860/70, 1880 and 1890 marriage cohorts, Tasmania 157

Table 7.11 Length of the penultimate interval, where last birth interval is six years or more, complete group: 1860/70, 1880 and 1890 marriage cohorts, Tasmania 158

Table 7.12 Age of mother at the penultimate birth, where last birth interval is six years or more, complete group: 1860/70, 1880 and 1890 marriage cohorts, Tasmania 159

Table 7.13 Families with long last birth intervals where the gap between death of a child and last birth was less than six years (seven families), complete group: 1860/70, 1880 and 1890 marriage cohorts, Tasmania 159

Table 7.14 Mean children ever born, mean age of mother at first birth, mean age of mother at last birth and mean birth interval, complete group: 1860/70, 1880 and 1890 marriage cohorts, Tasmania 161

Table 7.15 Impact of age at first birth, age at last birth and birth intervals for children ever born, McDonald method, complete group: 1860/70, 1880 and 1890 marriage cohorts, Tasmania... 161

Table 7.16 Logistic regression of the probability that a birth is the last, complete group: 1860/70, 1880 and 1890 marriage cohorts, Tasmania 165

Table 7.17 Estimated effects (relative risks) of various characteristics on the time to the next birth (closed birth intervals), complete group: 1860/70, 1880 and 1890 marriage cohorts, Tasmania . . . 173

Table 7.18a Estimated (significant) effects (relative risks) of various characteristics on parity progression from a piecewise exponential hazard model, complete group: 1860/70, 1880 and 1890 marriage cohorts, Tasmania 178

Table 7.18b Estimated (significant) effects (relative risks) of various characteristics on parity progression from a piecewise exponential hazard model, complete group: 1860/70, 1880 and 1890 marriage cohorts, Tasmania. 179

Table A.1 Mean children ever born to married women by birth cohort, Australian censuses, 1911 and 1921 231

Table A.2 Number of children ever born by birth cohort of married women, Australian census, 1921 231

Table A.3 Number of children ever born by birth cohort of married women, Australian census, 1911 232

Table A.4 Net migration, Tasmania, 1861–1900 233

Table A.5 Female population aged 15–49 years, 1861, 1870, 1881 and 1891, Tasmania 233

Table A.6 Male population aged 15–49 years, 1861, 1870, 1881 and 1891, Tasmania 233

Table A.7 Population by occupation, 1842 and 1851, Tasmania. . . . 234

Table A.8 Population by occupation, Tasmania, 1861 and 1870. . . . 235

Table A.9 Population by occupation, Tasmania, 1881 and 1891. . . . 235

Table A.10 Population by occupation, Tasmania, 1891, 1901 and 1911 236

Table A.11 Males aged 20 years and older, occupation by class, Tasmania, 1881 237

Table A.12 Males aged 20 years and older, occupation by class, Tasmania, 1891 237

Table A.13 Males aged 20 years and older, occupation by class, Tasmania, 1901 238

Table A.14 Females by occupation and marital status, Tasmania, 1911 239

Table A.15 Major towns in Tasmania, 1881, 1891 and 1901 239

Table A.16 Marriage outcomes for incomplete group: 1860, 1870, 1880 and 1890 marriage cohorts, Tasmania 241

Table A.17 Proportion of families by number of children, complete group: 1860, 1870, 1880 and 1890 marriage cohorts, Tasmania 242

Table A.18 Infant and child mortality, incomplete group: 1860, 1870, 1880 and 1890 marriage cohorts, Tasmania 242

Table A.19 Infant and child mortality, unobserved group: 1860, 1870, 1880 and 1890 marriage cohorts, Tasmania 242

Table A.20 Age at last birth by age at marriage, complete group: 1860/70, 1880 and 1890 marriage cohorts, Tasmania 242

Table A.21 Mean birth interval by birth order, complete group: 1860/70, 1880 and 1890 marriage cohorts, Tasmania 243

Table A.22 Distribution of covariates for logistic regression (Table 7.16) 244

Table A.23 Predicted probability that a birth is the last by socioeconomic status, complete group: 1860/70, 1880 and 1890 marriage cohorts, Tasmania 245

Table A.24 Predicted probability that a birth is the last by socioeconomic status for women who married at 20–24 years, gave birth at 30+ years with a husband the same age or 1–4 years older, complete group: 1860/70, 1880 and 1890 marriage cohorts, Tasmania 246

Table A.25 Predicted probability that a birth is the last by urban/rural location, complete group: 1860/70, 1880 and 1890 marriage cohorts, Tasmania 246

Table A.26 Predicted probability that a birth is the last by urban/rural location for women who married at 20–24 years, gave birth at 30+ years with a husband the same age or 1–4 years older, complete group: 1860/70, 1880 and 1890 marriage cohorts, Tasmania 247

Table A.27 Proportion of women who have at least a specific number of surviving children, complete group: 1860/70, 1880 and 1890 marriage cohorts, Tasmania 247

Table A.28 Distribution of covariates for survival analysis (Table 7.17) 248

Table A.29 Estimated effects (relative risks) of various characteristics on the time to the next birth (closed birth intervals), interaction model, complete group: 1860/70, 1880 and 1890 marriage cohorts, Tasmania 249

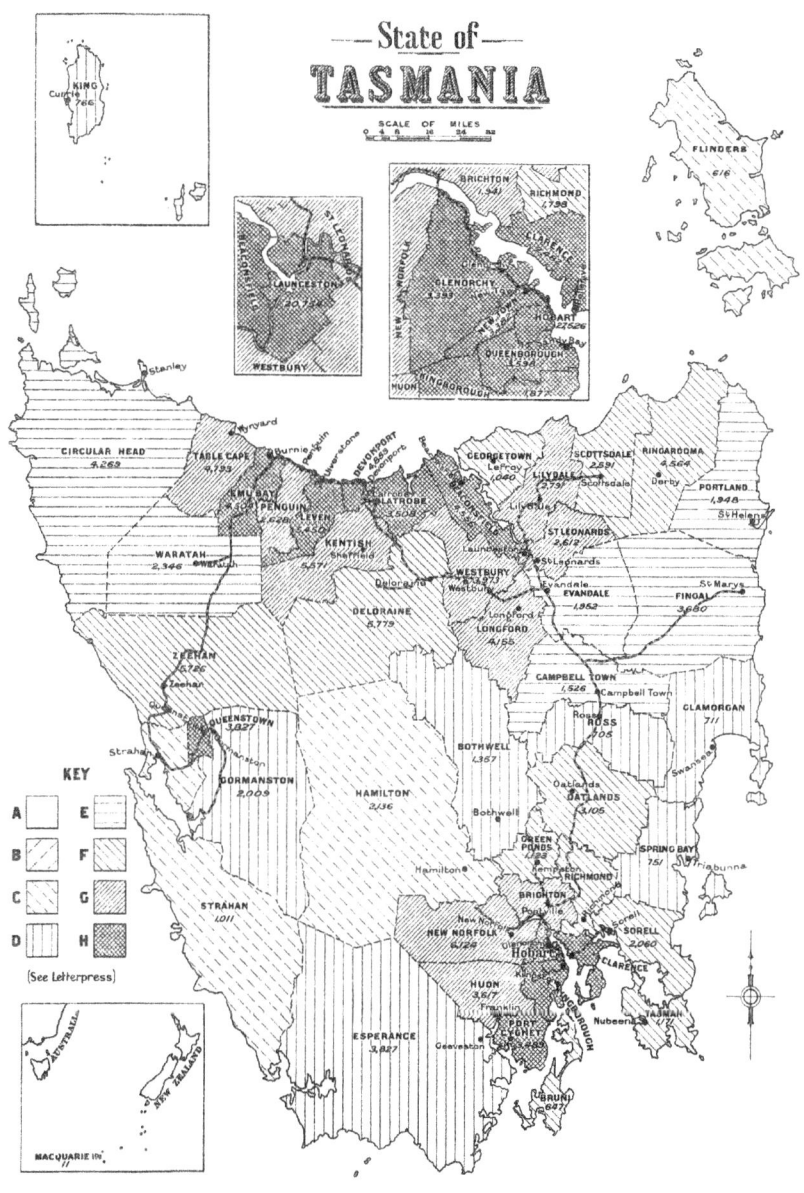

Tasmania, 1911

Persons per square mile:

A. <1 per 16
B. 1 per 16—<1 per 4
C. 1 per 4—<1 per 1
D. 1 per 1—<2 per 1
E. 2 per 1—<4 per 1
F. 4 per 1—<8 per 1
G. 8 per 1—<16 per 1
H. 16 per 1 and over

Source: Commonwealth of Australia 1914d: 431.

1
Introduction: Theories of the historical fertility decline

The historical fertility transition

In the 19th and early 20th centuries, most European countries and English-speaking countries outside Europe experienced a demographic transition.

According to McDonald:

> Demographic transition refers to the process whereby populations shift from regimes of high mortality and high fertility in approximate long-run equilibrium (zero population growth) to a new equilibrium at low levels of mortality and fertility. (McDonald 2001: 1)

Since the 1950s, many scholars have put forward theories to explain why and how the fertility transition occurred and considerable research has been undertaken to find evidence to support these theories. The European Fertility Project (EFP), for instance, which took place at the Office of Population Research at Princeton University during the 1960s and 1970s, undertook a vast amount of research into the 19th-century European fertility decline (Coale and Watkins 1986; Alter 1992).

The EFP considered that the fertility transition occurred in most European countries between 1880 and 1930, although the decline began earlier in France, from the late 18th century (Coale 1986; Cleland 2001). The project adopted a fairly conservative estimate of the timing of the decline, defining the start as the date from which marital fertility fell 10 per cent below the previous plateau and never returned to that plateau (Coale and Treadway 1986). Using this measure, fertility declined in some countries in Europe from the 1880s (Belgium and Switzerland), in England and Wales in the early 1890s and in most other European countries around 1900. Many demographers, however, disagree with the EFP criterion and consider that the fertility decline started several years earlier. For instance, according to the EFP measure, the fertility decline began in Sweden in 1902 (Coale and Treadway 1986), whereas it is now generally agreed that it began about 20 years earlier, around 1880 (Bengtsson and Dribe 2014; Dribe and Scalone 2014).

Most scholars consider that the fertility decline began in England in the 1870s and fertility fell from around the same period in other English-speaking countries (Woods 1987; Caldwell 1999). Marital fertility started to fall from about the late 1860s in the United States, from the 1870s in English-speaking Canada and New Zealand and from the 1880s in Australia (Coghlan 1903; Jones 1971; Ruzicka and Caldwell 1977; Caldwell 1999; Gauvreau and Gossage 2001; Hacker 2003). The Australian data suggest the timing of the fertility decline varied somewhat between the colonies, falling first in Victoria from the mid-1870s and from the 1880s in all other colonies except Western Australia (Jones 1971; Quiggin 1988).

The fall of marital fertility in Tasmania

The aim of this book is to examine the fall of marital fertility in Tasmania, the second settled Australian colony, in the late 19th and early 20th centuries. In this book, I use quantitative and qualitative data to examine when marital fertility fell, how it fell—that is, was the fall due to starting, stopping or spacing behaviours—and why it fell at this time. I examine how my findings support theories of why fertility fell during the fertility transition.

Total fertility consists of marital fertility and ex-nuptial fertility. In examining the historical fall in fertility, most demographers have concentrated on marital fertility. This is because ex-nuptial fertility was generally unplanned and unintended, whereas when married couples decided to limit their fertility, they made conscious decisions about their childbearing. In Australia in the late 19th and early 20th centuries, almost all births were within marriage. In New South Wales in 1891, for instance, 5.9 per cent of all births were ex-nuptial births (NSW Bureau of Statistics and Economics 1912).

In the final decades of the 20th century, some analyses were undertaken of the fertility decline in various parts of colonial Australia, as will be discussed in Chapter 2. However, about 20 years ago, a digitised database of 19th-century Tasmanian births, deaths and marriage registration information became available for research purposes, enabling much larger and more complex studies of historical demographic events to be conducted (for example, Kippen 2002c). This is the first analysis of the historical fertility decline in Tasmania using this database.

I used the Tasmanian registration data plus many other sources to reconstitute birth histories of couples marrying in Tasmania in the second half of the 19th century—specifically, in 1860, 1870, 1880 and 1890. This provided me with an individual-level database (Van Bavel 2004b), which has enabled me to use both bivariate and multivariate methods in my analysis of the fertility decline.

While some qualitative analyses have been undertaken of the historical fertility decline in Australia (Hicks 1978; Quiggin 1988; Bongiorno 2012), the findings have not been placed in any theoretical context. In this book, I examine how the historical context of Australia, and of Tasmania specifically, and historical sources—such as witness statements from the 1903 Royal Commission on the Decline of the Birth-Rate and on the Mortality of Infants in New South Wales, articles and items from the late 19th and early 20th–century Tasmanian newspapers and diaries of upper-class Tasmanian women—provide support for theories of fertility decline.

In the past five to 10 years, digitised sources, such as vital registration indexes and 19th and 20th-century Australian digitised newspapers, have become available on the internet and this has facilitated the task of reconstituting families and studying the social and economic conditions of the period. This is the largest study of reconstituted birth histories ever undertaken in Australia. Uniquely for Australia, this is the first study to examine the impacts of child mortality on fertility and to apply multivariate analysis.

Theories of the historical fertility decline

Theories as to why marital fertility declined in Western Europe and English-speaking countries in the late 19th and early 20th centuries have been reviewed by several authors (for example, Cleland and Wilson 1987; Alter 1992; Hirschman 1994; van de Kaa 1996; Mason 1997; McDonald 2001; Abbasi-Shavazi et al. 2009; Bengtsson and Dribe 2014). These theories are often difficult to test and the evidence is sometimes contradictory. This chapter examines theories of the historical fertility decline and available evidence for these theories according to the following categories: demographic transition theory, diffusion theory, economic theories, secularisation, trends in infant and child mortality, increased accessibility of artificial methods of birth control and changes in women's roles and status in society and in the family. The chapter also examines theories about how fertility declined—that is, was it through changes in age at marriage, in birth spacing or in stopping having children before the end of the reproductive lifespan?

Demographic transition theory

According to demographic transition theory, mortality declined in the 19th century in Western Europe and English-speaking countries because of 'modernisation' (Notestein 1945: 39; 1983). The decline in mortality was followed by a decline in fertility, which was a 'response to drastic changes in the social and economic setting that radically altered the motives and aims of people with respect to family size' (Notestein 1945: 40). Industrialisation and urbanisation changed the roles of the family, there was growing individualism, greater opportunities for individual social and economic advancement, large families became more expensive to maintain and parents began to concentrate more on the wellbeing of the individual child. While fairly effective means of contraception had been known for many years, they were not widely used until families had the incentive to limit their fertility.

Findings from the EFP, however, called into question demographic transition theory, since the project found the fertility decline occurred at the same time in late 19th and early 20th–century Western and Eastern European societies that were at very different stages of economic and social development (Knodel and van de Walle 1979, 1986; Cleland and

Wilson 1987). Economic and social development was measured by the following indicators: the percentage of the male labour force employed in agriculture, the percentage of the population in rural areas, the percentage of cities with more than 20,000 people and the percentage of illiterate people (Knodel and van de Walle 1979).

Demographic transition theory also states that a decline in infant and child mortality in a society is a necessary condition for marital fertility to decline (Freedman 1962; Preston 1978). The EFP findings, however, did not support this sequence, as they showed the relationship between infant mortality and fertility was not consistent (Matthiessen and McCann 1978; Knodel and van de Walle 1979; van de Walle 1986). In some countries, infant mortality declined before marital fertility; in others, the decline in marital fertility preceded the decline in infant mortality, while in others the two declines occurred around the same time (van de Walle 1986).

However, while rejected by the EFP, the demographic transition theory received renewed support from subsequent research (Schellekens and van Poppel 2012; Dribe et al. 2014). Studies on the fertility decline in two large German states, Bavaria and Prussia, using different statistical techniques to the EFP project on less highly aggregated geographic areas, concluded that economic and social factors played an important role in the fertility decline (Galloway et al. 1994; Lee et al. 1994; Brown and Guinnane 2002). More recent studies of the fertility transition in parts of Europe, Iceland, Canada and the United States also found that social and economic change was likely to have played a role in the fertility decline (Schellekens and van Poppel 2012; Dribe et al. 2014).

A re-examination of the findings of European historical studies on the relationship between infant mortality and fertility in the fertility transition and a new analysis of the fertility decline in Prussia also indicated there was a positive relationship between changes in infant mortality and changes in marital fertility (Galloway et al. 1998). A recent study of the fertility decline in Aranjuez, Spain, concluded that, in this locality, the improvement in 'child survival' was 'the key variable leading to fertility control' (Reher and Sanz-Gimeno 2007: 717).

Diffusion theories of the fertility decline

The EFP concluded that the fertility decline began and spread within and between areas that shared similar cultural characteristics, such as values and languages, because knowledge and ideas about fertility control began to spread throughout these communities (Knodel and van de Walle 1979; Cleland and Wilson 1987). This occurred independently of changes in economic and social conditions. Thus, the diffusion of ideas and values about fertility control was the reason for the decline in fertility at this time.

Linguistic and cultural boundaries were very important in explaining the fertility decline (Cleland and Wilson 1987). An analysis of the decline in Belgian fertility in the late 19th century, for instance, showed that fertility declined earlier and more quickly in French-speaking than in Dutch-speaking communities, despite similarities in their socioeconomic characteristics (Lesthaeghe 1977). Even where Dutch-speaking and French-speaking communities were located adjacent to one another and were socially and economically very similar, the two communities were 'two obviously non-interacting demographic regimes' (Lesthaeghe 1977: 112).

The EFP found that various elite groups were the 'forerunners' of the fertility decline in Europe, with fertility control practised in some areas in Europe in the 18th century (Livi-Bacci 1986: 183). Diffusion theorists argue that, in general, the highest socioeconomic status families are the first to take up any innovative behaviour and are progressively followed by groups of lower socioeconomic status, with those of the lowest status the last to change (Rogers 1983). Thus, in 19th-century Western Europe, ideas and values about fertility control spread progressively from elites to the upper and middle classes and then to the working classes (Livi-Bacci 1986).

More recent studies of the fertility transition in parts of Western Europe, Canada and the United States have shown that the upper and middle classes were the first to limit their fertility, followed by the other classes (Schellekens and van Poppel 2012; Bengtsson and Dribe 2014; Breschi et al. 2014; Dribe et al. 2014; Vézina et al. 2014). Woods (1987), however, argues that although there were differences in fertility between the occupational classes in 19th-century England and Wales, the fertility decline occurred at the same time for all classes. This finding was disputed by Haines (1989), who, using the same dataset (the 1911 England and Wales fertility survey), argued that the upper and middle classes led the fertility decline and their fertility fell more rapidly than that of the other classes.

The EFP found that couples living in urban areas in Western Europe had lower fertility than those in rural areas well before the fertility decline (Livi-Bacci 1986). According to diffusion theory, new ideas generally originate in urban settings and ideas about fertility control and information about methods of control are likely to spread more quickly within a densely populated community (Galloway et al. 1994). In Western Europe, fertility was lower in urban areas than in rural areas at the start of the fertility decline and declined more rapidly once the decline was under way (Sharlin 1986). In Canada, also, during the fertility transition couples living in urban areas were more likely to limit their fertility than those living in rural areas (Gauvreau and Gossage 2001; Vézina et al. 2014). In Utah, in the United States, on the other hand, fertility declined at the same time in rural areas and in urban areas (Bean et al. 1990). No consistent relationship has been found between urban/rural location and the decline of marital fertility in England and Wales (Woods 1987; Szreter 1996).

A study of the fertility transition in Belgium shows the diffusion of information, and ideas about fertility control from one socioeconomic group to another was facilitated by geographic propinquity. An analysis of the 19th-century fertility decline in the town of Leuven found the working-class people who lived in districts alongside upper-class people were significantly more likely to control their fertility than those who lived in predominantly working-class districts (Van Bavel 2004c).

Some authors have suggested the relationship between fertility decline and socioeconomic status is more complex than the EFP argued and stress the importance of examining the spatial context when investigating the relationship between socioeconomic status and the fertility decline (Szreter 1996; Garrett et al. 2001; Dribe and Scalone 2014). Szreter (1996) concluded from his analysis of the 1911 England and Wales fertility survey that there were important regional differences within social classes regarding the timing of the fertility decline. This led him to the view that participation in a 'communication community' was more important than social class in explaining the fertility decline (Szreter 1996: 581). A reanalysis of these data, however, challenged his findings on the importance of social class, concluding that social class accounted for around two-thirds of the differences in fertility (Barnes and Guinnane 2012). A recent study of the historical fertility declines in Canada, Iceland, Sweden, Norway and the United States using microlevel data found that socioeconomic status 'was a very important factor in the fertility transition' even after controlling for spatial heterogeneity (Dribe et al. 2014: 146).

The relationship between education and fertility has been explained using diffusion theory. This relationship is well documented in developing societies in the 1970s and 1980s, with parents with high levels of education much more likely to use birth control and have lower marital fertility (Caldwell and McDonald 1982). Education encourages people to be receptive to new ideas and behaviour and gives them the skills to access new information (Cleland 2001). Studies of the fertility decline in Spain and Italy using survey data have found a relationship between literacy and fertility, with illiterate women having higher fertility than those who are able to read and write (Baizán and Camps 2007; Breschi et al. 2014). A study of the historical decline of fertility in Verviers, Belgium, however—using the husband's and wife's signatures on birth and marriage registers as the indicator of literacy—found no evidence of a relationship between literacy and fertility (Alter 1988). In contrast, studies of the fertility decline in Quebec, Canada, have found a positive relationship between parents' literacy and their fertility, but the authors attribute this relationship to the effect of the French-Catholic schooling system on parents' value systems (Gauvreau and Gossage 2001; Vézina et al. 2014).

Casterline (2001) suggests theories relating to how ideas and values about birth control and knowledge of methods were diffused are not well developed. However, in examining how information about birth control spread through 19th-century populations, many authors argue that written material in the form of books, pamphlets and articles in newspapers and magazines was an important source of information about birth control (Seccombe 1993; Caldwell 1999).

From the 1830s, pamphlets and books on birth control methods were published and circulated in Britain. These included Francis Place's 'Diabolical Handbills', Francis Carlile's *Every Woman's Book* (1828), Charles Knowlton's *Fruits of Philosophy* (1834), George Drysdale's *The Elements of Social Science* (1861), Henry Allbutt's *The Wife's Handbook* (1886) and Annie Besant's *The Law of Population* (1877) (see also Knowlton 1878;

Besant 1887; Allbutt 1888; Branca 1975). The later publications were written in simple language, contained explanatory diagrams and were cheap to purchase. In the late 19th century, rising education levels made published information on birth control more accessible to a wider range of the population (Seccombe 1993).

Some authors consider that in the late 19th century, the publicity surrounding the trials of people distributing birth control information may have been a catalyst for the spread of birth control practices (Finch and Green 1963; Caldwell 1999; Hacker and Kippen 2007). From the 1870s, there were movements in the United States and in Britain to ban birth control books and pamphlets for reasons of obscenity. In England, for instance, in 1877, Annie Besant and Charles Bradlaugh were charged with obscenity for publishing and distributing Charles Knowles's pamphlet *Fruits of Philosophy* (Foster 1982). They were tried in the High Court and found guilty, but they appealed and the verdict was overturned. Prior to the trial, about 1,000 copies of Knowlton's book were sold every year (Bland 1995), but in the three-month period between the arrest and the conviction of Besant and Bradlaugh, around 125,000 copies were sold. Besant and Bradlaugh continued to publish the book despite being warned to stop. In the United States, however, many people were tried and imprisoned under the Comstock laws, enacted in 1873, which made it illegal to send literature about birth control methods or birth control devices through the mail (Brodie 1994).

Information about birth control methods was also disseminated in Britain through public lectures. After the Bradlaugh–Besant trial of 1877, huge crowds attended meetings to hear Besant and Bradlaugh speak about birth control (Bland 1995). In the early 1880s, Bradlaugh and Besant held meetings in many towns in the north of England advocating birth control methods and distributing literature (Elderton 1914). In the late 1880s and 1890s, female members of the Malthusian League also spoke about birth control at public meetings and gave advice to working-class women (Bland 1995).

In the decades of the late 19th century and the early 20th century, artificial contraceptive devices and abortifacients were advertised extensively in newspapers and magazines in the United Kingdom (Elderton 1914; McLaren 1990). They were also advertised widely in the United States in the 19th century, although the *Comstock Act* had some impact on the circulation of such information (Brodie 1994).

Doctors did not appear to be a major source of information about fertility control for their patients (Seccombe 1993). In Western Europe and the United Kingdom, letters and surveys about women's childbearing experiences in the late 19th and early 20th centuries indicate that doctors were unwilling to provide their working-class patients with information on how to stop further pregnancies. Contraception was not taught in medical schools and doctors were generally antagonistic to birth control devices, viewing them as injurious to health. Dr Henry Allbutt was struck off the medical register in 1887 for publishing *The Wife's Handbook* (Allbutt 1886; Foster 1982).

Seccombe (1993) argues that in 19th-century Britain and Western Europe, informal sources were more important than formal ones in spreading information about fertility control, with informal social networks important for lower-class families. 'Word of mouth was probably the principal means by which working-class people learned of contraceptives' (Seccombe 1993: 166). One working-class woman, writing to the Women's Guild in England in 1913–14 about her experiences of childbirth, explained that her friend had given her advice about contraception that had enabled her to limit the number of children she had (Llewelyn Davies 1978). A 1914 study by Elderton of working-class birth control practices in the north of England also stressed the importance of informal networks in spreading information about birth control methods:

> One correspondent reports an afternoon gathering of women, many of whom were 'good church-workers' and the subject under discussion was not the legitimacy of restriction, but the most effective means of restriction. (Elderton 1914: 34)

Elderton's report also noted that many women obtained information about birth control methods and ways of procuring abortion from midwives.

Economic theories of fertility decline

In contrast to the diffusion theory of the historical fertility decline, which explains the processes by which fertility fell, economic theories try to explain why fertility fell—that is, what couples' motivations were for controlling their fertility.

Economic demand theory asserts that the demand for children will fall when the cost of having another child is greater than the benefit of having that child (Easterlin 1975; Becker 1981; Becker et al. 1990). Fertility falls in conditions where the costs of children increase and exceed the social and psychological benefits of having an additional child (Abbasi-Shavazi et al. 2009). Becker (1981: 111) argues that, with economic development, the returns on investment in human capital (that is, education and training) increase and this shifts family expenditure 'towards quality and away from quantity' as each child becomes more expensive to rear. Additionally, in a society in which levels of human capital are high, the demand for children will be low because the 'opportunity costs' of having children are high—that is, married women experience higher returns from participating in the labour market than from childrearing (Becker et al. 1990).

The demand theory framework has also been applied by Caldwell, who argues that the introduction of mass education played a major role in the fertility decline in the late 19th century, because children became a cost rather than an economic benefit (Ruzicka and Caldwell 1977; Caldwell and Ruzicka 1978; Caldwell 1999). Once school attendance became compulsory, children became dependants and a burden on their parents rather than workers. Additionally, parents incurred expenditure in sending their children to school. Caldwell argues the decline in fertility was a response by parents to the change in the direction of 'net wealth flows' between parents and children—that is, wealth in terms of money, goods and services began to flow from parents to children, rather than from children to parents as previously (Caldwell 1976; Caldwell and Ruzicka 1978). A study of fertility decline in Ontario and Quebec found some support for Caldwell's theory in that families in Ontario whose children attended school all year had significantly lower fertility than other families (Gauvreau and Gossage 2001).

In support of economic demand theory, the timing of the fertility decline in working-class Britain and Western Europe has been linked to changes in the way children were treated in working-class families—that is, from being a 'net benefit' to a 'net cost' (Seccombe 1993). Before the fertility transition, large families were viewed as 'economically beneficial across the life-cycle', because older children could go out to work while younger children were dependent, and younger children became economically productive when parents were older and thus able to support their parents as they aged (Alter 1988: 164). In Victorian Britain even towards the end of the 19th century, working-class families could avoid sending their children to school and they were sent out to work at a relatively young age—sometimes as young as 10 or 11 years. However, in the Edwardian era, they were attending school regularly and were unable to go out to work to supplement the family income until they were considerably older. In Britain and Western Europe, respondents to surveys about childbearing experiences in the first decades of the 20th century said the main reason they wanted to stop childbearing was 'they could not afford any more children' (Seccombe 1993: 174).

A theoretical framework containing elements of both demand for and supply of children was developed by Easterlin (1975) for the analysis of marital fertility. This framework contains a number of determinants: the demand for children, which is determined by income and the cost of children relative to commodities; the 'subjective preference for children' compared with goods; the cost of fertility control, which includes attitudes towards fertility limitation, the availability of information about fertility limitation, the range of methods and their cost; and the 'potential output of children'—that is, the number of children a couple can potentially have, which depends on their natural fertility and whether or not their infants survive to adulthood (Easterlin 1975: 53–5). According to this model, couples are motivated to control their fertility when the 'supply' of children is greater than their 'demand' for children, but whether they change their behaviour by adopting fertility control methods depends on the 'costs' of fertility control (Easterlin and Crimmins 1985).

While demand theory focuses on a cross-sectional comparison of the costs and benefits of having children, another economic theory focuses on families' longer-term views of their economic future (Abbasi-Shavazi et al. 2009). According to this theory, parents began to limit their fertility because of their social and material aspirations for themselves and their children (Banks 1954; Lesthaeghe and Wilson 1986). As early as 1826, Thomas Perronet Thompson was writing about an Englishman's need to limit the number of children he had so he could support his family in the way that public opinion deemed socially acceptable (Thompson 1826). In the second half of the 19th century in English-speaking countries and many parts of Europe, there was increasing prosperity and more opportunities for social mobility because of industrialisation and a burgeoning of new occupations, particularly white-collar ones (McDonald 1974; Lesthaeghe and Wilson 1986). Education was viewed as an important factor in facilitating children's social mobility. In these circumstances, the rate at which families took up the practice of fertility control depended on their economic and social aspirations for their children.

The theory of parents' aspirations for their children explains why upper and middle-class families were the first to limit their fertility and were progressively followed by those of lower socioeconomic status, as discussed above (Banks 1954; Lesthaeghe and Wilson 1986; Seccombe 1993). Among the upper classes and the 'bourgeoisie', children were always viewed as a 'cost' and education was important for financial independence. In the 19th century, with industrialisation, workers of lower socioeconomic status began to develop aspirations for their children and saw education as the means by which these desires could be realised. In Britain, the upper strata of the working classes—the skilled workers—was the first of the working classes to limit their fertility, because of their desire for improved living standards for themselves and their children (Seccombe 1993). However, for parents in occupations such as farming, where children were important as workers and an economic benefit to their families, education beyond a basic level was not seen as an advantage. Consequently, these parents were less likely to take up fertility control.

Research into the relationship between fertility control and intergenerational social mobility has been very limited because of the availability of suitable data sources. However, Van Bavel et al. (2011) found that in Antwerp, Belgium, during the fertility transition, limiting family size was most effective as a 'defensive' strategy—for instance, when it was used by middle-class families to maintain the socioeconomic position of their children—rather than as an 'offensive' strategy. 'The effects all run in the direction of a large number of siblings increasing the odds of going down the social ladder' (Van Bavel et al. 2011: 338).

Secularisation

Some authors have argued that the spread of secularisation throughout Europe in the 19th century affected families' views on and practice of fertility limitation and was a necessary condition for the adoption of fertility control (Lesthaeghe and Wilson 1986). The basic tenet of secularisation was 'individual responsibility' and, according to this ethos, fertility, like many other aspects of life, was viewed as being under the individual's control rather than subject to 'God's will'.

The EFP found a relationship between the speed of the fertility decline and the level of secularisation in late 19th and early 20th–century Western Europe (Lesthaeghe and Wilson 1986). The fertility transition was relatively homogeneous in Protestant communities, which tended to adapt to secularisation, while in Catholic communities, there was far more variation in the start and speed of the transition. Catholic communities that experienced secularisation early were among the first of any to adopt fertility control, while those where secularisation occurred much later were the last. A more recent paper looking at the impact of secularisation on the fertility decline in Veneto, north-eastern Italy, however, found that secularisation was not important at the start of the historical fertility decline but its impact grew in importance as the decline progressed (Caltabiano and Dalla Zuanna 2015).

Many other studies have found that, in most Western European countries and in Canada during the fertility decline, religious groups such as orthodox Protestants and Catholics who were 'traditional' in outlook had higher fertility than the rest of the population who were more 'liberal' or 'modern' (Gauvreau and Gossage 2001; Van Bavel and Kok 2005; van Poppel and Derosas 2006). Jews had the lowest fertility of all religious groups and were among the 'forerunners' of the fertility decline (Livi-Bacci 1986).

Some authors have argued that the specific practices of some religious groups may have facilitated the adoption of fertility control. Van Poppel et al. (2012) suggest that in Europe, Calvinism, with its emphasis on the importance of reading the scriptures, led to high levels of literacy among its followers. Education gave them access to ideas and information about fertility control and encouraged them to take control over this aspect of their lives.

Infant and child mortality

As discussed above, demographic transition theory posits a relationship between infant and child mortality and fertility at the societal level. Four main theories have also been put forward to explain the relationship between infant and child mortality and fertility at the individual level: physiological, insurance, replacement and societal (Preston 1978; van de Walle 1986).

The 'physiological' relationship between infant mortality and fertility refers to the relationship between breastfeeding and fecundity. There is considerable evidence to show that when a child dies in infancy, a woman no longer avoids conception through breastfeeding and the space between the birth of the child who died and the subsequent child is reduced, leading to higher fertility (Knodel 1978, 1982; Wrigley et al. 1997). Knodel (1982), for instance, has shown that in several areas in pre-industrial Europe, birth intervals were shorter when the previous child had died than when the child survived, except in areas where breastfeeding was not common practice. However, he estimated that a substantial fall in infant mortality would result in only a small decline in fertility solely through the physiological mechanism, even in areas where breastfeeding was common and prolonged.

The 'insurance' relationship applies in a context of high infant mortality, in which people have as many children as possible because of their perception of the risk of their children dying. In the 'replacement' relationship, on the other hand, parents have a child to replace an infant or child who has died. Both theories imply that parents make a conscious choice to have a certain number of children or to have another child—that is, they imply a notion that parents are conscious of the ability to control their births (Knodel 1978; Preston 1978; van de Walle 1986).

Evidence for the 'replacement' effect of infant mortality on fertility was found by Knodel (1978) in his analysis of child mortality and fertility among couples in 14 German villages who married during the 18th and 19th centuries. Comparing cohorts who did not control their fertility with those who practised fertility control, Knodel concluded that families were making efforts to replace children who died in periods when family limitation had become established. Several other studies of countries in Western Europe have also found evidence for the replacement effect (Alter 1988; Alter et al. 2010; Schellekens and van Poppel 2012; Breschi et al. 2014; Vézina et al. 2014). Only a 'relatively modest' replacement effect, however, was found for the United States at the turn of the 20th century (Haines 1998: 244).

Knodel's study (1978) also found evidence for the insurance effect in that the experience of infant and child mortality within an individual family had an impact on that family's efforts to reduce their fertility. Even in a period when the general level of infant mortality remained relatively high, couples whose children survived were the most likely to adopt fertility control, while experiencing child mortality seemed to deter couples from efforts to limit their fertility. Haines (1998) also found a relatively strong insurance effect for the United States at the end of the 19th century. Another study of the fertility transition, in the Netherlands, however, found the replacement effect declined as the number of infant and child deaths increased (Schellekens and van Poppel 2012). Schellekens and van Poppel's analysis shows that the more deaths a family had, the less likely they were to have another birth, casting doubt on the insurance effect of infant mortality on fertility.

Recent research on the fertility transitions in Spain and the Netherlands has found that replacement/insurance effects can vary by socioeconomic status and, in the Netherlands, by religious affiliation (Reher and Sanz-Gimeno 2007; van Poppel et al. 2012). In the Netherlands, for instance, the number of surviving children more strongly affected parity progression ratios for the elite, middle classes and skilled workers than for other occupational groups, and more for liberal Protestants than for other religious groups (van Poppel et al. 2012). In both the Netherlands and Spain, the number of surviving children also affected birth spacing, with birth intervals longer at any given parity, the higher the number of surviving children.

Preston (1978) suggests the replacement strategy may be related to the sex of the child who dies—that is, if the parents desire a certain number of sons and the child who dies is female, they may not make efforts to 'replace' this child. Studies of fertility in Utah (Bohnert et al. 2012) and in Germany (Sandström and Vikström 2015) in the late 19th and early 20th centuries have shown families were more likely to progress to the next birth if they had only or mostly daughters. Alter et al. (2010), on the other hand, found no such relationship between sex composition and fertility in Sart in Belgium in the 19th century.

The societal strategy in relation to infant mortality and fertility refers to situations in which social norms around nuptiality or breastfeeding ensure that fertility is kept in equilibrium with mortality (Knodel 1978). For example, consistent with theories of demographic transition, scholars have argued that fertility declines because of the pressure of an increasing population due to the decline in mortality (Matthiessen and McCann 1978). In these circumstances, couples are pressured into marrying later, to limit the number of children they will have to rear. Alternatively, in societies with high infant mortality, men and women were encouraged to marry young so they could start their childbearing early (Wrigley 1978). The EFP's analysis of the patterns of nuptiality and child mortality, however, found no relationship between nuptiality and infant mortality (van de Walle 1986).

Infant mortality does not simply affect fertility; fertility can also affect infant mortality. Scholars generally agree the relationship between infant mortality and fertility is a two-way one, with higher fertility leading to higher infant mortality (van de Walle 1986; Bean et al. 1992; Haines 1998). A Swiss report published in 1878, for instance, states that medical doctors concluded that repeated pregnancies were the primary reason for high infant mortality, because mothers of high parity were weak and gave birth to unhealthy babies (Switzerland 1878, in van de Walle 1986). A study of high fertility and high infant mortality in Utah also argued that children born at high parities were at risk because of competition for resources from their siblings and because of infectious disease (Bean et al. 1992). Other scholars argue that prior to the fertility decline some babies at high parities were unwanted and their parents let them die through neglect (Scrimshaw 1978). Knodel and van de Walle (1979: 230) cite the literature of the time that shows that 'concealed infanticide' or 'infanticide by neglect' was common in most of Europe before the fertility decline. Infant mortality thus may have declined when married couples began to limit the size of their families, because they were less likely to have babies at higher parities who were at greater risk of dying during their first year of life.

Increased accessibility of artificial methods of contraception

The greater availability of artificial methods of contraception has been put forward as a reason for the decline in fertility during the late 19th century (Caldwell 1999). However, there is little written evidence from the period of the extent to which these birth control methods were used in Western Europe and in English-speaking countries other than Australia.

Histories of contraception indicate the practice of contraception and the methods used can be traced back thousands of years (Finch and Green 1963; Himes 1963). References to one of the oldest methods of contraception, *coitus interruptus* (withdrawal), can be found in the Book of Genesis in the Old Testament of the Bible, and homemade pessaries made of mud were used by the Egyptians thousands of years ago (Finch and Green 1963). Some authors argue that, prior to the Western European fertility decline, fertility was restricted mainly by forms of behaviour such as prolonged breastfeeding and/or periodic separation of spouses for economic reasons (Knodel and van de Walle 1979; Coale 1986; Cleland and Wilson 1987). Knodel and van de Walle (1979) claim many people did not know about *coitus interruptus* and its use was not widespread, but Santow (1995) argues that there is strong evidence that *coitus interruptus* was used by the general population in pre-transitional societies to increase the spacing between births. Some authors put forward the view that prior to the fertility decline artificial forms of contraception, such as condoms, were associated with immorality and were not sanctioned within marriage (Cleland 2001).

Birth control measures were not used extensively until the second half of the 19th century, since there was no effect on the general level of fertility, but some small populations, such as the Italian elite, adopted birth control measures early on (Livi-Bacci 1986). Although we do not know what methods were used, books and pamphlets published by the Freethinkers in Britain in the 1830s, such as Knowlton's *Fruits of Philosophy* (1878), described artificial methods of contraception, such as the condom, the sponge and douching with a syringe, as well as *coitus interruptus*.

From the late 19th century, artificial contraceptive devices were made more cheaply and in larger quantities (Finch and Green 1963; Himes 1963). Condoms and pessaries (such as the French *Pessaire Preventif*) had become more reliable from the 1840s, with the development of a technique for vulcanising rubber (Himes 1963; Bongiorno 2012). In 1880, London chemist Walter Rendell developed a pessary made of quinine and cocoa butter to meet the needs of the poor women in his district (Finch and Green 1963). Rendell's pessaries were so successful that, in 1886, he began to manufacture them on a large scale and was soon exporting them. A reverse-current syringe was introduced in the 1880s that improved the reliability of douching (Besant 1887). The 1887 edition of Annie Besant's *The Law of Population* contains advertisements for the 'India Rubber Check Pessary', the 'Improved Vertical and Reverse Current Syringe' and 'Rendell's Soluble Pessaries (Besant 1887: 47–8).

The spread and acceptance of ideas about birth control resulted in a greater demand for contraceptives, which led to them becoming available in more 'respectable outlets', such as chemist shops (pharmacies) (McLaren 1990; Caldwell 1999). In Britain in the later decades of the 19th century, contraceptives were also sold by mail through advertisements in newspapers and magazines, and peddled door to door in villages and working-class neighbourhoods (McLaren 1990).

As noted, advertisements for abortifacients were prevalent in the English newspapers in the late 19th and early 20th centuries. It is not possible to tell whether abortions increased during this period, but Elderton (1914) argues that abortion was a common practice by the early 20th century and her report contains numerous references to various drugs used by working-class women in the north of England to procure abortions. A report in the *British Medical Journal* of 1899 refers to the 'pestilent traffic in so-called abortifacients' (BMJ 1899: 110). Several authors argue that the number of abortions for married women increased markedly across the Western world during the later part of the 19th century (McLaren 1990; Accampo 2003, citing Sohn 1996).

It is a commonly held view that *coitus interruptus* was the most common form of birth control used during the historical fertility decline (McLaren 1990; Seccombe 1993; Szreter et al. 2003). Szreter (1996: 393), however, considers that, in England and Wales before World War I, abstinence—'reduction in the frequency of intercourse'—was the main method of reducing marital fertility. Szreter (1996: 420–1) argues that in British society withdrawal was a type of sexual abstinence, since he considers both methods are about 'sexual self-restraint'.

Many authors claim contraceptive appliances were too expensive for widespread use, their supply was low and there was hostility towards their use (McLaren 1990; Szreter 1996). McLaren (1990) argues that, although artificial contraceptives were available in the late 19th century, there is little evidence they were used widely. Brodie (1994) points out that this conclusion does not seem logical, since it is unlikely there would have been such a supply of information on contraceptive methods and contraceptive products for sale if there was only limited demand.

Evidence as to the type of birth control used during the historical fertility transition is scarce and, where available, is based on studies of highly unrepresentative populations. Mosher's survey of 47 American college-educated women undertaken around this time found a variety of methods was used to prevent conception: artificial contraceptive appliances as well as withdrawal and abstinence, with douching being the most common (MaHood and Wenburg 1980).

Changes in women's roles and status in society and within the family

Historical demographers have often ignored women's roles and their changing status in the public and private spheres as explanations for the 19th-century fertility decline (McDonald 2000). However, a few scholars have argued that attention should be paid to 'those cultural features that determine the status of women and their ability to assert their own wishes regarding childbearing' (Knodel and van de Walle 1979: 240). Seccombe (1993: 168) argues that 'women were the driving force behind family limitation', because they bore most of the burden of pregnancy, childbirth and child care. In Britain and Western Europe, surveys and letters from working-class women who underwent childbearing in the late 19th century and the first two decades of the 20th century show many women were motivated to adopt fertility control because of health concerns (Llewelyn Davies 1978; Seccombe 1993). They recounted difficult pregnancies and horrific experiences in confinement, which made them dread having more children.

Some authors argue that it should be impossible to study fertility transition without considering the part played by changing power relations between husbands and wives (Folbre 1983; McDonald 2000). McDonald (2000) has characterised power relations in the family as a component of 'gender equity', which is itself a characteristic of a society's gender system. The gender system is 'the socially constructed expectations for male and female behaviour that are found (in variable form) in every known human society' and applies to both the public and the private spheres (Mason 1997: 158). In societies with high fertility, for example, women experience 'gender inequity' in the private sphere (the family) when they are dissatisfied with the 'constant round of childbearing and childrearing imposed by spousal, familial, and societal expectations' (McDonald 2000: 428). In societies undergoing fertility transition, it is possible to have gender equity in the private sphere (the family), but not the public sphere (wider society), and vice versa.

According to McDonald (2000), gender equity within the family is a necessary condition for fertility to decline and is facilitated through women's education. Not only do educated women become receptive to new ideas, but also education improves their autonomy and power within the family (Breschi et al. 2014). As noted above, studies of the fertility decline in Europe have found that more educated women were more likely to control their fertility.

Some authors have noted the importance of gender equity in the family as an explanation of the fertility decline in late 19th-century Britain and Western Europe. Szreter (1996), for instance, regards the difference in power relations between husbands and wives as one explanation for the low fertility of textile workers compared with the very high fertility of mining families in late 19th-century England. He argues that, among textile workers, relations between husbands and wives were relatively equal because of the wife's income and employment outside the home. In contrast, men had the power within mining families, because miners had high wages and their wives did not work outside the home.

The power relations between husband and wife may be affected by the difference in their ages and this may impact on their fertility preferences and use of contraceptive methods (Casterline et al. 1986). The association between a couple's fertility and the difference in age of the husband and wife is difficult to disentangle. Wives or husbands who are older than their spouse may have more influence on the couple's fertility behaviour (Tsuya et al. 2010), but their fecundity may be lower because of their age (McDonald 1984; Casterline et al. 1986). Studies of fertility in some areas of 19th-century Western Europe have found that couples among whom husbands were six or more years older than their wives had significantly lower fertility than couples among whom the wife was up to five years younger, but there were no significant differences where a wife was older than her husband (Feng et al. 2010). A study of the fertility transition in Alghero, Sardinia, however, found no significant differences in fertility according to the age difference between husband and wife (Breschi et al. 2014).

The feminist movement in Britain was viewed as important in influencing women to adopt birth control methods. Although feminism was primarily a middle-class movement in 19th-century Britain, feminist ideas had spread to working-class women by the early 20th century and strengthened these women in their decision to limit their families (Seccombe 1993).

Letters from working-class women about their childbearing experiences sent to the Women's Cooperative Guild just before World War I show many women had adopted a feminist position on several issues (Llewelyn Davies 1978).

The two methods scholars have put forward as the main methods of birth control used during the historical fertility decline—withdrawal and abstinence—are both within the control of men. McDonald and Moyle (2018) argue that women played an important role in the fertility transition and female methods of contraception were more important in Britain and Western Europe than many scholars have acknowledged.

Birth control pamphlets published and distributed in Britain were directed to women and recommended female methods of contraception, some of which could 'be used by the woman without inconvenience or knowledge of the husband' (Allbutt 1888: 49). Female contraceptive appliances and abortifacients were advertised and sold widely in Britain and the United States. Women in England actively sought information on birth control by attending lectures on the topic; some of these lectures were for 'women only' (Elderton 1914; Bland 1995). As noted previously, women had an important role in spreading information about methods of contraception through their informal networks.

Models of fertility decline: 'Adjustment' or 'innovation' or both

Since the middle of the 20th century, there has been an ongoing debate in historical demography as to whether the fertility decline was caused primarily by 'adjustment' to new social and economic conditions or by 'innovation'—that is, the diffusion and acceptance of innovative ideas and behaviours (Carlsson 1966; Cleland and Wilson 1987). It is now generally agreed, however, that the 'two sets of explanations are complementary, not competing' (Casterline 2001: 3). As McDonald (2001: 1) concludes, 'both adaptation and innovation are necessarily involved because people cannot change their behaviour without the necessary knowledge (innovation) nor do they do so without reason (adaptation)'. This reflects Coale's three major preconditions for a decline in marital fertility:

> Fertility must be within the calculus of conscious choice … perceived social and economic circumstances must make reduced fertility seem advantageous to individual couples … [and] effective techniques of fertility reduction must be available. (Coale 1973: 65)

Cleland (2001: 45) has proposed a 'blended' version of innovation–diffusion theory: 'Under the blended theory, the engine of demographic change is the structural transformation of societies, and diffusion is the lubricant.'

How did fertility decline: Starting, stopping or spacing?

There has been a major debate among demographers as to the extent to which fertility declined in the late 19th century through changes in 'starting', 'spacing' or 'stopping' behaviours (Okun 1995). Most of the debate has concerned the relative importance of 'stopping' and 'spacing' behaviour, which relates to the debate about the importance of the 'innovation' theory versus the 'adjustment' theory (van Poppel et al. 2012). 'Stopping' is viewed as an innovative form of behaviour that incorporates ideas that were unthinkable in pre-transition societies (Knodel and van de Walle 1979; Coale 1986; Cleland and Wilson 1987). 'Spacing' behaviour, on the other hand, is viewed as an extension of behaviour that was practised before the fertility decline, but became a way by which couples adjusted to new economic and social conditions during the decline (Anderton and Bean 1985; Santow 1995; Szreter 1996; Van Bavel 2004a; Van Bavel and Kok 2004).

The younger a woman is at marriage, the longer are her potential childbearing years (Wrigley et al. 1997). Scholars have argued that the timing of marriage—either delaying marriage or encouraging couples to marry earlier—was a fertility strategy for many centuries in Western Europe and English-speaking societies (McDonald 1981). In the early 19th century, Malthus (1798) viewed late marriage as a preventive check on population growth and suggested people exercise 'moral restraint' and delay their marriage to curb fertility. Although theories about the relationship between marriage and fertility are primarily applied to pre-transition societies (Freedman 1963), some authors have claimed it also applied to some societies during the 19th-century fertility decline (Spengler 1968, cited in McDonald 1981; Matras 1965; Ruzicka and Caldwell 1977). McDonald (1981, 1984), however, argues that in both pre-transitional and transitional societies, the timing of marriage relates to economic, social and psychological factors, not to fertility preferences. In both pre-transitional and transitional societies, people married late so they would be in a better economic position to marry, rather than with the intention of curtailing their fertility. In the past 25 years, comparatively little attention has been paid to 'starting' behaviour in analyses of the 19th-century fertility decline in Western Europe and English-speaking countries. More recent studies of marriage in parts of Western Europe, Japan and China, however, support McDonald's view, finding that the risk of marriage in pre-transitional and transitional societies was 'influenced by socioeconomic status, household context, and local economic and demographic conditions' (Lundh and Kuroso 2014: 8).

In the mid-20th century, an influential group of demographers argued that, in late 19th-century Western Europe, couples began to deliberately limit their fertility through 'stopping' behaviour (Henry 1961; Coale 1986). This was an entirely new behaviour that was taken up to such an extent it initiated the fertility decline (Knodel and van de Walle 1979). According to this theory, first put forward by Henry (1961), couples use contraceptive methods—such as withdrawal, artificial methods or abortion—to avoid having more births after they have had a certain number of children and have decided they do not want any more. Henry contrasted this with behaviours such as prolonged breastfeeding, which increased birth intervals but are not parity related. Birth-spacing strategies can be used after any parity, including the first, and couples do not change their behaviour once they have reached a specific family size. Henry termed fertility that is deliberately controlled through 'stopping' at a specific parity as 'controlled fertility' and fertility where people practise non-parity-limiting behaviours as 'natural fertility'.

Coale (1986: 9) argues that fertility fell in Western Europe because of a change from 'spacing' behaviour to 'stopping' behaviour, with couples changing from non-parity-specific fertility-limiting behaviours to parity-specific limiting behaviours. Some authors have interpreted the theory of 'stopping' behaviour to mean that parents have in mind a preferred family size—that is, 'they become conscious of a desirable size of the family and set for themselves a target number of children, which they do not want to exceed' (van de Walle 1986: 205). Neither Henry nor Coale, however, specifically introduced the concept of a 'desired family size' into their theory, arguing instead that parents proceeded to have children until they decided they had as many as they wanted. While this may not seem an important distinction, as shown in the quantitative analysis, it has implications for identifying stopping and spacing behaviours in birth patterns.

Other demographers have argued that deliberate birth spacing—that is, intentionally lengthening the time between births early in marriage—played an important role in the fertility decline (Anderton and Bean 1985; Bean et al. 1990; Santow 1995; Szreter 1996; Hionidou 1998). Analyses of fertility in 19th-century Utah show that stopping behaviour was an important fertility control strategy during the fertility decline, but birth spacing was also used as a strategy to limit fertility (Anderton and Bean 1985; Bean et al. 1990). Studies of populations in parts of Western Europe have shown that some families used spacing behaviour to control their fertility prior to the fertility decline, particularly in times of economic stress (Van Bavel 2004a; Dribe and Scalone 2010; Tsuya et al. 2010; Van Bavel and Kok 2010; Kolk 2011).

Nowadays, as with the associated 'innovation/adaptation' debate, most scholars agree that both stopping and spacing behaviours played a part in the 19th-century fertility decline, but the extent to which these behaviours were responsible for the decline within a society is a matter for investigation (van Poppel et al. 2012).

The use of theories in this book

In this book, I examine how findings from the quantitative and qualitative analysis of the fertility decline in Tasmania support the various theories outlined in this chapter and how they compare with findings from studies of Western Europe and other English-speaking countries. In the qualitative analysis, I pay particular attention to areas where the quantitative evidence is not available—that is, how ideas and values about fertility control and knowledge of methods were diffused; what methods of contraception were used during the fertility decline; and what the role of women was in the decline.

2
The Australian fertility decline

In this chapter, I examine the current state of knowledge about the historical fertility decline in Australia. Analyses of the fertility decline have mainly used population census data of the period, retrospective data from the 1911 and 1921 population censuses and vital registration data (Jones 1971; Ruzicka and Caldwell 1977; Quiggin 1988; Larson 1994; Anderson 1999). The colonial statistics offices did not publish data on births by age of the mother, although this information was available on birth certificates in some colonies (Larson 1994). Age-specific fertility rates and age-specific marital fertility rates are available only for New South Wales (NSW), as discussed below. No census forms are available for any period in Australia's history, so the 'own child' method cannot be used to estimate age-specific fertility rates and age-specific marital fertility rates (Cho et al. 1986).

Most analyses of the Australian historical fertility decline have relied on retrospective census data from the 1911 and 1921 Australian censuses to look at trends in the number of children ever born to various birth cohorts of married women (Jones 1971; Ruzicka and Caldwell 1977; Quiggin 1988). These data are available only in the form of published tables (for example, Commonwealth of Australia 1914c, 1921). There is also a number of small studies that have used vital registration data from specific colonies or regional areas (Grimshaw et al. 1985; Carmichael 1996; Mackinnon et al. 2007). The two largest are Anderson's study of the 19th-century fertility decline in South Australia, with a total of 836 families in three marriage cohorts (1842–46, 1875–79 and 1885–89), and Larson's study of the 19th-century fertility decline in Melbourne using a sample of 3,592 registered births for 1871, 1881, 1891 and 1900 (Larson 1994; Anderson 1999).

Coale's fertility indices

Jones (1971) used data on the number of births in a year, the population of women in five-year age groups and the population of married women in each age group to calculate Coale's fertility indices for Australia from 1861 to 1921 and for Tasmania from 1881 to 1921 (Figure 2.1). These indices show fertility fell in the Australian colonies overall from around the 1880s. Coale's index of marital fertility (I_g) ranged from 0.69 to 0.74 between 1861 and 1881, but then fell steadily from 1881, until it reached 0.45 in 1921. The level of marital fertility was slightly higher in Tasmania in 1881 than in the Australian colonies overall (0.76 compared with 0.74), but fell over the same period until it reached 0.50 in 1921 (Jones 1971). The index of overall fertility (I_f) fell from 1861 for Australia as a whole and from 1891 for Tasmania but levelled off after 1901. As the trends in marital fertility for Tasmania are very similar to those for Australia, findings in this book in relation to Tasmania are likely to be indicative of the situation in Australia as a whole.

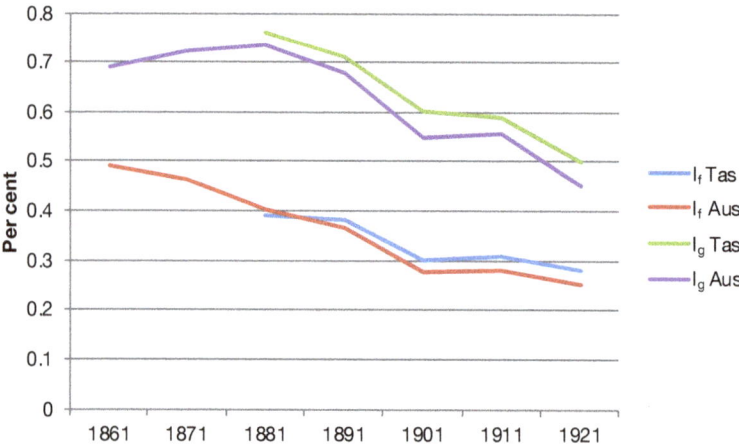

Figure 2.1 Coale's fertility indices (I_g and I_f), Australia, 1861–1921, and Tasmania, 1881–1921

Source: Jones (1971: 326–7).

Tasmania: Estimated total fertility rate

I have estimated the total fertility rate (TFR) for Tasmania (Figure 2.2) by indirect standardisation, using data for the estimated female population by five-year age group (Kippen 2002b) and the annual number of registered births (ABS 2008) adjusted for under-registration (Kippen 2002c). I applied the age-specific fertility rates for New South Wales for 1891 (NSW Bureau of Statistics and Economics 1912) to the five-year age groups to give an expected number of births for each year and divided the actual number of Tasmanian births by the expected number to obtain an index. I multiplied this index by the 1891 TFR for New South Wales to obtain estimated fertility rates for Tasmania and calculated a three-year moving average to smooth out the trend. These data show the estimated TFR for Tasmania fluctuated between 5.8 and 5.2 between 1860 and 1884, but began to fall steadily, from 5.77 in 1885 to 4.08 in 1898, and then remained fairly flat until about 1914, when it began to fall again, reaching 3.69 in 1921.

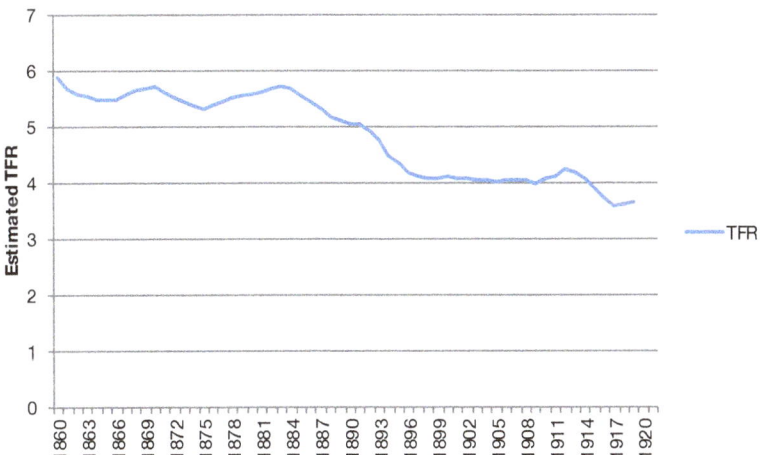

Figure 2.2 Estimated total fertility rate (TFR) for Tasmania, 1860–1921 (three-year moving average)

Source: Author's calculations.

Age-specific marital fertility rates

As noted above, the only Australian age-specific marital fertility rates available for the fertility transition period are for New South Wales. Coghlan, who was the NSW statistician between 1886 and 1905, prepared and presented data on NSW age-specific marital fertility rates for 1871, 1881, 1891 and 1901 to the 1903 Royal Commission on the Decline of the Birth-Rate and on the Mortality of Infants in New South Wales (NSW 1904a, 1904b). In New South Wales, age-specific marital fertility rates declined from the 1880s, with the decline greater in the 1890s than in the previous decade (Table 2.1). The relative fall in fertility was larger at older ages, suggesting women may have been stopping their childbearing after several births (Jones 1971).

Table 2.1 Age-specific marital fertility rates, New South Wales, 1871, 1881, 1891 and 1901

	1871	1881	1891	1901
Age (years)	Birth rates per 1,000			
15–19	501.0	516.0	471.1	556.6
20–24	441.5	457.9	416.3	397.0
25–29	407.5	405.2	353.7	298.7
30–34	336.7	338.6	292.2	226.8
35–39	270.4	273.6	236.3	172.5
40–44	134.1	128.9	118.4	88.1

Source: NSW (1904a: 90).

Looking at the data by birth cohort of married women shows an alternative picture (Quiggin 1988). The cohort born in 1847–51, who were 30–34 years of age in 1881, had about the same fertility as the 1837–41 cohort in 1871, but by 1891, when they were aged 40–44 years, their marital fertility rates were 8 per cent lower than the 1837–41 cohort 10 years previously (Quiggin 1988: 30). Similarly, the 1852–56 cohort, who were aged 25–29 years in 1881, had similar fertility to the 1842–46 cohort in 1871, but by the time they were aged 35–39 years in 1891, their fertility was 14 per cent lower than the earlier cohort at that age. This again suggests successive birth cohorts of married women were stopping having children towards the end of their childbearing years.

Children ever born

Data from the 1911 Australian census on children ever born show married women born in the 1830s and early 1840s had, on average, seven children during their childbearing years, but the mean number of children ever born fell to 6.75 for the 1847–51 birth cohort and then fell steadily to 5.25 for the cohort born in 1862–66 (Figure 2.3). The mean number of children ever born for married women in Tasmania was slightly higher for the earlier and later cohorts but fell over the same period.

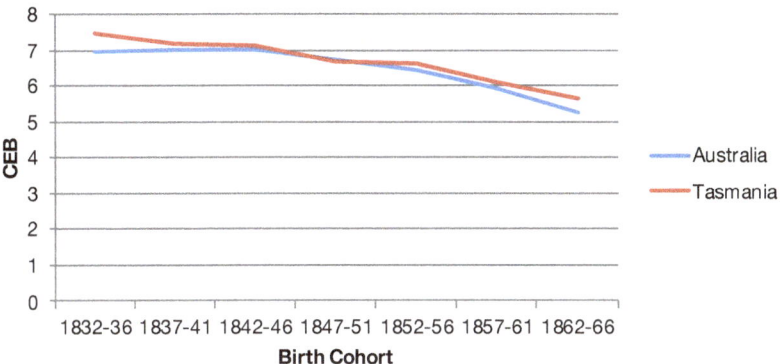

Figure 2.3 Mean children ever born to married women, Australia and Tasmania, 1911 census
Source: Appendix A: Table A.1 (this volume).

Equivalent data from the 1921 census show fertility continued to fall for the 1867–71 and 1872–76 birth cohorts, reaching a mean of 4.19 for the 1872–76 birth cohort in Australia as a whole and 4.56 for Tasmania (Figure 2.4). Once again, the trends for Tasmania are very similar to those for Australia.

It is important to note, however, that these data refer to women living in Tasmania in 1911 and 1921; some women who had children in Tasmania in the 19th century may have left the state before or after they completed childbearing. Similarly, Australia is a nation of immigrants and women living in Australia in the 1910s and 1920s may not have been living there during their childbearing years.

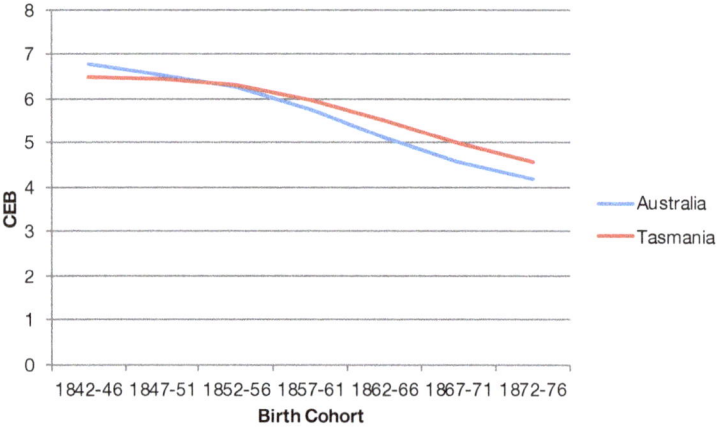

Figure 2.4 Mean children ever born to married women, Australia and Tasmania, 1921 census

Source: Appendix A: Table A.1 (this volume).

Examining the distribution of the number of children ever born to women who were married at the time of the 1921 census indicates that there were marked falls in the proportions of large families and a marked increase in the proportions of small families during the Australian fertility decline (Figure 2.5). The proportion of couples with seven or more children fell from 55 per cent for the 1842–46 cohort to 21.8 per cent for the 1872–76 cohort, while the proportion with one to three children increased from 12.4 per cent for the earliest cohort to 34.6 per cent for the latest cohort.

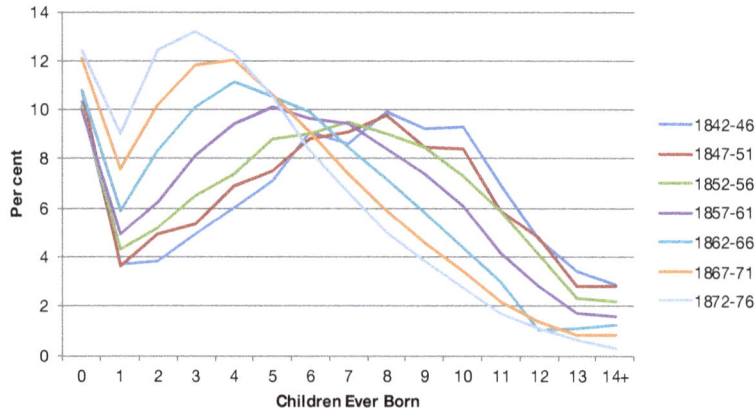

Figure 2.5 Children ever born to married women by birth cohort, Australia, 1921 census

Source: Appendix A: Table A.1 (this volume).

It is important to note that the census data for 1911 and 1921 do not include those who were widowed or divorced at the time of the census. However, the 1911 census data show the average number of children ever born to currently married women was very similar to that of all women who had ever married (Quiggin 1988).

Additionally, still-married women who were still alive at the time of the census may not be representative of the entire cohort who had completed their childbearing—that is, there may be a positive or negative relationship between fertility and longevity. A study of couples marrying in Utah in the second half of the 19th century, among whom both husband and wife survived the wife's childbearing years, found that women who had fewer children lived longer after completing childbearing than other women with children (Smith et al. 2002).

The 1911 and 1921 Australian censuses indicate that these retrospective data on children ever born may underestimate completed marital fertility for the birth cohorts for this reason (Appendix A: Tables A.2, A.3). For each identical birth cohort, the average numbers of children ever born are lower in the 1921 census than the 1911 census and the proportions of married women without any children are higher. This suggests a negative relationship between fertility and longevity, with husbands and/or wives with no children or with fewer children more likely to survive than those with more children. Thus, the apparent increase in childlessness across the birth cohorts may be at least partly due to differential longevity.

Anderson's (1999) study of families in three marriage cohorts in 19th-century South Australia, reconstituted from vital registration data, shows similar trends to the retrospective census data (Table 2.2). The mean number of births of women from all marriages dropped between the 1842–46 and the 1875–79 cohorts, from 8 to 6.9, and then fell more sharply, to 5.2, for the 1885–89 cohort. The proportion of women without children fluctuated between 4 per cent and 6.9 per cent for the three cohorts, but the proportion with one to three children increased markedly, from 5.3 per cent to 24.3 per cent, while the proportion with 10 or more children fell sharply, from 34.6 per cent to 8 per cent.

Table 2.2 Number of children ever born to women marrying in South Australia, 1842–46, 1875–79 and 1885–89

	1842–46	1875–79	1885–89
No. of births	Percentage		
None	5.9	4.0	6.9
1–3	5.3	13.8	24.3
4–5	15.0	17.5	25.8
6–9	39.3	38.2	35.0
10+	34.6	26.5	8.0
Total (%)	100.0	100.0	100.0
Total (no.)	153	325	349
Mean/median	No. of births		
Mean	8.0	6.9	5.2
Median	8	7	5

Note: Includes a small number of illegitimate births.
Source: Anderson (1999: 252).

Fertility and family characteristics

There have been several analyses of the relationship between 19th-century Australian fertility and different family characteristics—particularly husband's occupation, geographic location, religion and mother's birthplace (Jones 1971; Ruzicka and Caldwell 1977; Quiggin 1988; Larson 1994; Anderson 1999). These studies are mainly descriptive, however, and do not place their findings in a theoretical context.

Such studies have used retrospective census data or vital registration data. Regarding the retrospective census data, it is important to note that husband's occupation, religion and geographic location were measured at the time of the census and these were not necessarily the same as at the birth of the children. Caution must be taken in drawing conclusions from census data for the oldest cohorts because of the relatively small numbers in some of the cells.

Husband's occupation

Australian data on children ever born and husband's occupation suggest an inverse relationship between socioeconomic status and fertility.

Jones (1971) and Ruzicka and Caldwell (1977) used retrospective data from the 1911 and 1921 censuses to look at the relationship between the average number of children ever born and husband's occupation. Jones (1971), using data from the 1911 census, found that for every cohort of married men: primary producers had the highest fertility; professional, domestic and commercial workers had the lowest fertility; and transport, communication and industrial workers fell between the two. Ruzicka and Caldwell (1977) compared data from the 1911 and 1921 censuses to examine the relationship between 'occupational status' and fertility decline, finding that in most occupational groupings during the late 19th and early 20th centuries, 'employers' and 'husbands working on own account, but not employing labour' had larger reductions in family size than 'wage-earners'.

Anderson (1999) and Larson (1994) looked at the relationship between the fertility decline and occupational status using colonial vital registration data. Anderson found that fertility fell for the three marriage cohorts in all occupational categories across the cohorts (Table 2.3). She suggests families of gentlemen and professionals may have started adopting fertility control as early as the 1850s or 1860s and they were followed by the families of white-collar workers in the 1870s, with families in the remaining occupational groups progressively adopting these practices. She found marked differences in family size by occupational status for the 1885–89 marriage cohort. In this cohort, groups that Anderson describes as 'middle-class'—gentlemen, professionals, merchants, white-collar workers, small businessmen and skilled tradesmen—were more likely to have smaller families (that is, fewer than seven children) than farmers and unskilled labourers.

Table 2.3 Average number of children by husband's occupation group in South Australia, 1842–46, 1875–79 and 1885–89 marriage cohorts

	1842–46	1875–79	1885–89
Occupation group	Mean number of children ever born		
Gentlemen, professionals	4.9	5.4	3.8
Small businessmen	6.6	6.7	4.6
White-collar	7.9	5.2	5.0
Skilled trades	8.0	6.9	5.2
Other labourers	8.0	7.3	5.5
Farmers	7.9	7.0	5.8

Source: Anderson (1999: 254).

Larson (1994), using Melbourne birth registration data, found there was an increase in birth spacing between 1871 and 1900, with the percentage of births for which the previous sibling was three or more years old increasing from 17 per cent to 35 per cent over the period. Professionals, businessmen and skilled manual workers were significantly more likely to space their births, particularly during the 1890s. White-collar workers also tended to have longer birth intervals over the years, but the differences were not statistically significant. In contrast, the proportions of semi-skilled workers and labourers with long birth intervals, while fluctuating, did not increase between 1871 and 1900.

Geographic location

Analyses of the relationship between fertility and geographic location suggest there was a strong relationship between fertility and urban/rural residence, with families in urban areas having fewer children than those in rural areas.

There were marked differences in the overall level of fertility and the timing of the fertility decline between women living in rural (ex-metropolitan) areas and those in urban (metropolitan) areas, according to the 1911 census (Table 2.4). The average number of children ever born was greater for women living in rural areas for every birth cohort. Fertility started to fall earlier for women in urban areas than for those in rural areas, falling for the 1842–46 birth cohort in urban areas and for the 1852–56 cohort in rural areas (Larson 1994).

Table 2.4 Average number of children ever born by birth cohort of married women by metropolitan/non-metropolitan location, Australia, 1911

Birth cohort	1832–36	1837–41	1842–46	1847–51	1852–56	1857–61	1862–66
Place of residence	Mean number of children ever born						
Metropolitan	6.58	6.59	6.36	6.04	5.71	5.16	4.57
Non-metropolitan	7.21	7.30	7.48	7.27	6.99	6.49	7.21

Source: Commonwealth of Australia (1914c: 1143).

Jones (1971) used statistical information for the period (including the censuses) to calculate Coale's fertility indices separately for urban and rural areas of a selection of the colonies in the late 19th and early 20th centuries. This shows a slightly different picture from the 1911 census data (Table 2.5). While marital fertility was already lower in urban areas than in rural areas in 1871, it began to fall in both areas in the 1880s. However, it fell more sharply in urban areas than in rural areas, plateauing in the rural areas in the first decade of the 20th century.

Table 2.5 Index of marital fertility (I_g) for urban and rural areas, selected colonies of Australia, 1871, 1881, 1891, 1901 and 1911

Year	1871	1881	1891	1901	1911
Place of residence			I_g		
Urban	0.63	0.66	0.59	0.46	0.51
Rural	0.76	0.77	0.72	0.59	0.59

Notes: Data for 1871 include only New South Wales and Victoria. For 1881, 1891 and 1901, data include New South Wales, Victoria, Queensland and South Australia. Data for 1911 include New South Wales, Victoria, Queensland, South Australia and Western Australia.
Source: Jones (1971: 328).

In South Australia, there were no significant differences in fertility by geographic location at the time of marriage for the 1842–47 marriage cohort (Anderson 1999). However, rural couples had significantly larger families than urban families in both the 1875–79 and the 1885–89 cohorts, although fertility declined for both urban and rural couples between the two cohorts.

Religion

The relationship between fertility and religion in 19th-century Australia is difficult to interpret. The 1911 census data on children ever born to married women by religion show no clear trends for the first three cohorts, possibly due to small numbers in some of the cells (Table 2.6). However, fertility fell steadily for most religious groups from the 1842–46 birth cohort onwards. In the 1842–46 cohort, Methodists and Lutherans had the highest fertility; Catholics (undefined) and Congregationalists had the lowest. By the time the 1862–66 cohort had completed their childbearing, the Lutherans still had the highest fertility, but the fertility of Methodists had fallen markedly. Congregationalists still had the lowest fertility—only very slightly lower than that of Jewish people. In South Australia, where the Lutherans had a strong presence, they maintained large families from the 1842–46 to the 1885–89 marriage cohorts (Anderson 1999).

Table 2.6 Average number of children ever born to married women by religion, selected groups, Australia, 1911

Birth cohort	1832–36	1837–41	1842–46	1847–51	1852–56	1857–61	1862–66
Religion	Mean children ever born						
Church of England	6.92	7.05	7.00	6.72	6.37	5.84	5.15
Roman Catholic	6.75	6.76	6.96	6.86	6.76	6.29	5.57
Methodist	7.92	7.40	7.39	7.11	6.75	6.17	5.42
Presbyterian	6.82	7.12	7.04	6.59	6.17	5.54	4.95
Baptist	6.69	6.68	7.10	6.61	6.05	5.71	5.10
Protestant (undefined)	5.92	7.14	6.90	6.35	6.06	5.61	4.99
Congregational	6.48	6.27	6.68	6.13	5.79	5.20	4.50
Catholic (undefined)	5.98	7.83	6.56	6.64	6.70	6.30	5.67
Lutheran	6.78	6.69	7.17	7.00	7.40	6.97	6.31
Jewish	7.33	6.16	6.72	6.09	5.83	4.99	4.51

Sources: Commonwealth of Australia (1914c: 1144); Jones (1971: 317).

Data from the 1901 NSW census, compiled by Coghlan (1903), show a somewhat different pattern. Lutherans are not included as a separate group in this tabulation because the proportion of Lutherans in New South Wales was very small. These data show that, among all women who had completed their childbearing in 1901 (all cohorts born before 1856), Roman Catholic women had the highest numbers of children at most ages at marriage, Anglican women the lowest of the Protestant groups and Jewish women the lowest of all (Table 2.7). Coghlan (1903: 42) argues that since most of these women had their children before fertility control was generally practised, these differences are 'due to social habits rather than to differences in inherent fertility'.

Table 2.7 Average number of children of married women who completed childbearing by 1901, by age at marriage and religious denomination, NSW 1901 census

Religion	Church of England	Roman Catholic	Methodist	Presbyterian	Jewish	Other
Age at marriage	Mean number of children ever born					
< 20 years	9.54	9.66	9.62	9.43	8.38	9.18
20–24 years	7.69	8.11	7.83	7.80	7.50	7.19

Religion	Church of England	Roman Catholic	Methodist	Presbyterian	Jewish	Other
Age at marriage	Mean number of children ever born					
25–29 years	5.56	5.99	5.83	5.79	4.71	5.46
30–34 years	3.60	3.77	4.10	3.86	3.53	3.53
35–39 years	1.84	1.91	1.96	1.73	1.09	1.61
40–45 years	0.57	0.62	0.49	0.49	0.50	0.51

Source: Coghlan (1903: 42).

Mother's birthplace

Data on fertility by mother's birthplace are only available from the population censuses. According to the 1911 Australian census, there were distinct variations in completed family size by mother's birthplace (Table 2.8). The fertility of married women born in Australia was higher than that of married women born in the United Kingdom for every birth cohort and higher than that of women born in the rest of Europe in all birth cohorts prior to the 1852–56 cohort. Among women born in the United Kingdom, English women had higher fertility than Irish women in the older birth cohorts, but the fertility of English-born women fell so steeply from the 1847–51 cohort onwards that their fertility fell below that of Irish women in the two youngest cohorts.

Table 2.8 Average number of children ever born to married women by birth cohort and birthplace, Australia, 1911

Birth cohort	1832–36	1837–41	1842–46	1847–51	1852–56	1857–61	1862–66
Birthplace	Mean number of children ever born						
Australia	7.72	7.88	7.75	7.28	6.78	6.10	5.33
United Kingdom	6.96	6.90	6.70	6.40	6.01	5.48	4.97
England	7.08	6.98	6.73	6.40	6.01	5.35	4.82
Wales	6.78	7.15	7.33	6.66	6.09	5.89	5.09
Scotland	6.87	7.03	6.87	6.63	6.01	5.49	5.01
Ireland	6.83	6.72	6.55	6.26	5.99	5.72	5.21
Other Europe	6.38	6.68	6.94	6.70	6.97	6.41	5.97

Source: Commonwealth of Australia (1914c: 1160–1).

Summary

As outlined above, the Australian historical fertility decline has been examined previously using data from the population censuses or in small studies that have used vital registration data from specific colonies or regional areas. All the data analyses have been bivariate; there have been no multivariate analyses of Australian historical data.

As far as can be determined, fertility began to fall in Australia in the early 1880s, although the decline may have occurred slightly later in Tasmania and from a higher level. There were marked variations in the fertility decline by husband's occupation, urban/rural location and mother's birthplace. The decline probably started earlier in urban areas, for the upper and middle classes and for women born in the United Kingdom. There were some variations in the fertility decline by religion and mother's birthplace. The differences in fertility across religious groups and birthplace groups were relatively small compared with the urban/rural differences and the differences by husband's occupation. These trends are very similar to findings from research on the fertility decline in Western European and other English-speaking countries discussed in the previous chapter.

3
Tasmania in the 19th and early 20th centuries

To set a context for the analysis presented in this book, this chapter provides a brief history of Tasmania in the 19th and early 20th centuries, examines changes in its population size and structure and looks at some characteristics of Tasmanian society that are relevant to theories of fertility decline: religion, education and literacy, occupation and urbanisation. Detailed population data are presented for the years 1861, 1870, 1881 and 1891 to provide a comparison with data for couples marrying in 1860, 1870, 1880 and 1890 who are the subject of the fertility analysis that follows.

Many of the data in this chapter are derived from the Tasmanian population censuses. Legislation for the first Tasmanian census was introduced by Lieutenant-Governor of Tasmania John Franklin in 1841 (Kippen 2002c). These censuses were conducted in 1842, 1843, 1848, 1851, 1857, 1861, 1870, 1881, 1891 and 1901. This chapter uses the published tables from these censuses, since the original records were destroyed (TAS 1842, 1857, 1861, 1870, 1881, 1891, 1901).

Tasmania's history, 1803–1914

Tasmania is an island of just less than 68,500 square kilometres, situated 240 kilometres off the south-east coast of mainland Australia. The first European to sight it was Dutch explorer Abel Tasman, in 1642, who named it Van Diemen's Land (Boyce 2010; Reynolds 2012). The British established a penal colony on the island in 1803 on the Derwent River near present-day Hobart, 15 years after the establishment of the penal colony in Sydney, NSW. The two major cities, Hobart and Launceston, were established three years later, in 1806. Van Diemen's Land was part of the colony of New South Wales until it became a separate colony in 1825 (Boyce 2010). The British transported convicts to Van Diemen's Land for almost 50 years, until the convict system was disbanded in 1853.

In its early years, the colony was administered by a series of lieutenant-governors under the authority of England. The *Australian Colonies Government Act* of 1850 established 'a partially elected legislature with a limited franchise', which subsequently drafted the Tasmanian Constitution (Boyce 2010: 241). Self-government was introduced on 1 January 1856 and the colony's name was changed to Tasmania. There were two houses of parliament, the upper house (or legislative assembly) and the lower house (house of assembly). The franchise was restricted throughout the second half of the 19th century, since men were eligible to vote only if they had property of a certain value. In 1901, Tasmania became a state of the Commonwealth of Australia, following the federation of the six mainland colonies. With Federation, all males 21 years of age and older became eligible to vote (Reynolds 2012). The right to vote was given to all women aged 21 years and older in 1902 for federal elections and in 1903 for state elections.

The colony grew spectacularly in the first 50 years, partly because of the availability of convict labour and investment from England. The British army was a presence in Tasmania throughout the early years until they left the island in the early 1870s.

The colony's economy was predominantly agricultural in its earliest years, mainly sheep farming but also cattle, wheat, dairy farming and other agricultural produce. The land was very fertile, there was plenty of clean water and the climate was temperate (Boyce 2010). Wool was a major export for much of the 19th century; at the end of the 1860s, for example, wool accounted for about half of Tasmania's export income (Reynolds 2012). Timber-cutting was also an important industry in Tasmania's early years (Robson and Roe 1997).

In the 1820s and 1830s, many of the British immigrants obtained large landholdings in Tasmania's fertile Midlands and in the river valleys south of Launceston through free grants or purchase at cheap prices. These landholders became the Tasmanian 'gentry', who used cheap convict labour to develop and maintain their properties (Reynolds 1969; Appendix D: Story 1, this volume). In the early years of the colony, the government granted small landholdings to pardoned convicts and, while many of these were forfeited or sold, several small farms and commercial gardens remained close to the two major cities.

Shipping was another important area of economic activity in the colony from its earliest years, since Hobart was on the major sea routes between the other colonies of Australia and the rest of the world. Ships sailed frequently from Hobart and Launceston to Melbourne, Sydney, Brisbane and New Zealand, carrying both goods and people. In later years, additional routes were added to Adelaide and Fremantle.

Shipbuilding was an important industry in the colony from the early years and increased in importance during the 1830s (Reynolds 2012). During the late 1820s and early 1830s, many manufacturing ventures were set up in Hobart and Launceston, such as soap and candle-making, small breweries and mills.

From the early days of settlement, Hobart's population was in communication with other colonies and other parts of the world. By 1834, Hobart had 'six newspapers, two advertising papers, one official gazette, one magazine and two pocket almanacks' (Haynes 1976: 13). The Hobart newspapers often contained long articles about events in Britain, Europe and the rest of the world, sourced from the British newspapers, which arrived with the ships. If they had the means, people could subscribe to Hobart's reading rooms, where they were able to access many overseas journals and papers (Reynolds 2012).

When transportation of convicts ceased in 1853, money stopped flowing from England. In 1856, a depression set in and did not lift until the discovery of minerals in the early 1870s (Reynolds 2012). There was a decline in shipbuilding and whaling in the 1860s and early 1870s, but, from the mid-1870s, new agricultural industries of hops, fruit-growing and jam-making began to make a substantial contribution to the colony's economy (Meikle 2010). From the late 1870s, the manufacturing industry began to expand to include products such as furniture, biscuits, shoes and clothing (Reynolds 2012). A large brewing company was set up in Launceston in the early 1880s.

By the middle of the 19th century, most of the largest rural estates were owned by families who had obtained the land before the 1830s (Reynolds 1969). These families often intermarried, concentrating land in the hands of these large landowners. The *Waste Land Act* of 1858, however, changed the pattern of landholding in the colony, since it brought the purchase of land within the reach of working men and women with some savings (Meikle 2011). 'Selectors', as these farmers were known, moved into areas of Crown land all over the colony, but particularly on the north-west (Appendix D: Story 2) and north-east coasts and in the Huon Valley south-west of Hobart. Many small farming communities were established in these areas in the late 19th and early 20th centuries.

The long depression that started in 1856 began to end with the discovery of tin in the north-west of the island in 1871 and the building of a smelter in Launceston by the Mount Bischoff Tin Mining Company in 1874. Over the decade there were also discoveries of gold, silver, bismuth, antimony, coal and copper in other parts of the island. There were, however, even greater discoveries on the west coast of Tasmania in the 1880s and 1890s, which led to the development of silver mines in Zeehan from 1882 and gold and copper mines in Queenstown from the 1890s. There was a large movement of the population to these mining areas and settlements grew around the mines—of both miners and their families (if the family moved with them) and workers to service the populations.

Communication within Tasmania improved in the late 1850s with the completion of an electric telegraph line between Hobart and Launceston in 1857, which was soon extended to George Town on the north coast (Cox 2012). A telegraph line was set up between Tasmania and Victoria in 1859, but this did not work properly, and it was not until 1869 that an effective line was set up between the two colonies. Communication with the rest of the world improved dramatically when the telegraphic cable was permanently established between Tasmania and London in 1872. From this time on, Tasmanian newspapers were able to publish news from around the world, particularly articles and reports from the English newspapers, with very little delay. During the 1870s, telegraph lines were extended throughout Tasmania. Telephone exchanges were opened in Hobart and Launceston in 1883, but telephone connections were uncommon and the use of telephones very limited until the 1920s (Reynolds 2012).

The railways came relatively late to Tasmania. The first railway line, from Launceston to Deloraine, was opened in February 1871 and the first train between Hobart and Launceston ran five years later, in November 1876. In 1883, the government constructed railway lines from Launceston to Scottsdale and from Deloraine to Devonport (Reynolds 2012). In 1892, railways lines were built from Strahan to Queenstown in the far west and from Zeehan to other mining areas (Robson and Roe 1997).

In the late 1870s and early 1880s, tourism became an important industry for Hobart, with visitors from Melbourne and Sydney spending their summer holidays in the town and surrounding areas (Bolger 1978). For almost 20 years, Hobart was a favoured destination of tourists and invalids.

The 1880s was a prosperous decade for Tasmania: the mining industry grew and the economy of the colony expanded. By the beginning of the 1880s, the income obtained from exporting minerals was greater than that obtained from wool exports (Reynolds 2012). When minerals were first discovered, numerous small mining companies were established, but they were quickly absorbed into large mining enterprises, such as the Tasmania Mine in Beaconsfield.

The power and influence of the landed gentry declined markedly from 1875 (Reynolds 1969). Wool ceased to be a dominant commodity and the economic importance of the large landowners declined. In the period 1875–80, wool accounted for 40 per cent of Tasmania's total export income, but this had fallen to 14 per cent in 1895–1900. By the beginning of the 20th century, the agricultural produce of the small farms in north-western Tasmania had become more valuable than the Tasmanian wool clip, while the orchards of the Huon Valley had become famous for their output of apples, pears, berries and other fruit (Reynolds 2012).

As in all other Australian colonies, except Western Australia, an economic depression struck in the early 1890s. In Tasmania, the depression started with the failure of the Van Dieman's Land Bank in August 1891 (Robson and Roe 1997). Unemployment rose and there was an increase in families seeking food, clothing and fuel from charitable organisations. Public works were commenced to provide more employment. Economic conditions improved during the 1890s with the mining discoveries in the far west and the building of a new smelter for production in Mount Lyell

(Queenstown). Exports of minerals, but also of timber, boomed (Robson and Roe 1997). By the end of the 19th century, more than half the value of Tasmanian exports was derived from four minerals: copper, tin, gold and silver.

An analysis of raw wages of 'urban' carpenters, bricklayers, masons and blacksmiths in Tasmania shows they increased steadily through the 1880s, but there was a sharp drop in the early 1890s (Famour and Withers 2014). However, by 1900, raw wages for carpenters and bricklayers were back to the levels of the 1880s, while wages for masons and blacksmiths had improved somewhat. The wages of farm labourers and shepherds also fell sharply between 1892 and 1893; they increased until 1900, but not to their former level.

Launceston was the first city in the Southern Hemisphere to have electric light, in 1895, followed by Hobart in 1898 and Zeehan in 1900 (Robson and Roe 1997). Both Launceston and Hobart had been lit by gas since the late 1850s. In 1893, Hobart became the first city in the Southern Hemisphere to have an electric tram network. Bicycles also became a popular form of transport in the 1890s and 1900s for both men and women. Agriculture became more mechanised in the late 19th and early 20th centuries, with the introduction of steam-driven threshing machines (Pink 1990).

Tasmania was generally prosperous in the early years of the 20th century leading up to World War I (Roe and Robson 1997). Mining prosperity lasted until the beginning of the war and jam-making and fruit production were also very important during the first decade of the 20th century. With Federation in 1901, the federal government embarked on a construction program of federal buildings in the state (Reynolds 2012). Federation also brought in free trade with the mainland, which lowered the cost of imported goods but increased competition with Tasmanian produce and manufactured goods. The states, however, were protected from the impact of free trade in the early years of the 20th century, with the federal government returning three-quarters of the customs and excise revenue to the states for the first 10 years.

Population size and composition

1803–1860

In the first 30 years of European settlement, Tasmania's Indigenous population, which was estimated to be about 7,000 in 1817, decreased dramatically, mainly due to massacre by the European population (Boyce 2010). Fewer than 250 of the original inhabitants remained by 1830 (Kippen 2002c). There is little information on the size of the Tasmanian Indigenous population in the 19th and early 20th centuries, since Aboriginal people were not counted in the Tasmanian population censuses.[1]

From 1803 to 1822, the European population grew to 8,422 inhabitants (Table 3.1), 58.1 per cent of whom were convicts, 16.9 per cent of whom were 'free by servitude of pardon' and 25 per cent of whom were free settlers (Borrie 1994: 40). There was a marked imbalance of the sexes in the very early years of the colony among the adult convict population. Between 1821 and 1825, for example, only 8.6 per cent of the 6,101 convicts who arrived in the colony from Britain were female (Borrie 1994: 28).

The population grew rapidly between 1822 and 1842 (Table 3.1). There were increasing numbers of free settlers coming to the colony, with about 11,000 arriving in the 1830s (Robson and Roe 1997). In 1842, convicts made up a smaller proportion of the population than in 1822, accounting for 36.6 per cent of males and 13.2 per cent of females (TAS 1842). Another 7.9 per cent of men and 2 per cent of women were 'ticket-of-leave'—that is, they were convicts on parole (Alexander 2014: 36). Among the remainder of the population: 15.9 per cent of males and 36.1 per cent of females were born in Tasmania; 19.6 per cent of males and 37.8 per cent of females arrived in the colony as free settlers, either from other colonies or from other countries; and 20 per cent of males and 11 per cent of females were 'other free', presumably ex-convicts. It is important to note, however, that the census underreported the convict population, since there was a strong tendency for convict ticket-of-leave holders to represent themselves as free persons (Kippen 2002c; Alexander 2014).

---

1 There were 19,625 Aboriginal and Torres Strait Islander people in Tasmania in 2011, accounting for 4 per cent of the Tasmanian population (ABS 2011).

Table 3.1 Population of Tasmania: 1822, 1832, 1842 and 1857

Year	1822	1832	1842	1851	1857
Males	n.a.	n.a.	39,604	44,080	45,916
Females	n.a.	n.a.	17,816	25,482	34,886
Military[1]	n.a.	n.a.	n.a.	568	690
Total	8,422	25,318	57,420	70,130	81,492

n.a. not available
[1] Military includes wives and children for whom no details were given.
Sources: Borrie (1994: 40); TAS (1842, 1851, 1857).

There was still a marked imbalance in the sexes in 1842. There were 223 males for every 100 females in the total population of the colony (TAS 1842). The convict population, however, was much more imbalanced, with 617 male convicts for every 100 female convicts.

By 1857, the colony's population had grown to 81,492 (Table 3.1). This census year was the last in which the population was categorised according to its 'free' or 'convict' status. In 1857, convicts or ticket-of-leave holders made up only a very small proportion of the adult population (excluding the military): 4.7 per cent of males and 2.5 per cent of females (TAS 1857). About one-third of adult males (33.7 per cent) and 18 per cent of adult females were ex-convicts. Most of the total population—61.7 per cent of males and 79.5 per cent of females—were either free settlers or born in the colony. Just over one-third of the total population (37.3 per cent) in 1857 was born in Tasmania: 32.5 per cent of men and 43.7 per cent of women. Some of those born in the colony would have been the children of former convicts.

There was a marked imbalance of the sexes in 1857 among unmarried males and females aged 14 and over, with 2.64 males for every female (McDonald 1974); however, the imbalance was far greater in the areas outside Hobart, where the ratio was 3.80, than in Hobart and surrounding districts, where it was 1.18.

While free settlers continued to arrive from Britain in the 1840s and 1850s, the colony also lost population during the period, mainly to the colony of Victoria. The outflow of population began in the late 1840s and increased markedly during the Victorian goldrush in the mid-1850s (Reynolds 2012).

1861–1911

Between 1861 and 1901, Tasmania's population almost doubled, from around 90,000 to 172,500 (Table 3.2). Between 1861 and 1879, net migration to Tasmania was negative—that is, more people left the colony than settled there (Table A3.1). Many Tasmanians went to New Zealand in the early 1860s with the discovery of gold in Otago (Kellaway 1999). However, in the 1880s, more people settled in the colony than left, probably due to the mining boom, while in the 1890s the numbers of those settling in the colony were about the same as those who were leaving. Many Tasmanians went to Western Australia in the late 1890s and early 1900s, attracted by the discovery of gold in that colony.

Table 3.2 Population of Tasmania: 1861, 1870, 1881, 1891, 1901 and 1911

Year	1861	1870	1881	1891	1901	1911
Males	49,593	52,853	61,162	77,560	89,624	97,591
Females	40,384	46,475	54,543	69,107	82,851	93,620
Total	89,977	99,328	115,705	146,667	172,475	191,211

Sources: TAS (1861; 1870; 1881: 02_27; 1891: 01_xxxi; 1901: 02_xx); Commonwealth of Australia (1914b: 10–12).

The population of Tasmania was very young in 1861, with around half the female population and around 40 per cent of the male population under 20 years of age (Tables 3.3 and 3.4). Males had an older age structure than females, with the proportion of males over 40 years of age almost twice that of females.

The age structure of the female population changed little over the three decades, although the proportions of the female population in the age ranges 30–49 years fell slightly and the proportion 50 years and older increased (Table 3.3). While the census data for 1861 and 1870 present the population only by 10-year age groups, estimated population data for females aged 15–49 years by five-year age groups show very similar trends (Appendix A: Table A.5).

Table 3.3 Female population by age, Tasmania, 1861, 1870, 1881 and 1891

Year	1861	1870	1881	1891
Age	Percentage			
0–14 years	42.1	45.3	39.8	41.00
15–19 years	9.7	9.8	12.2	9.90
20–29 years	17.7	14.1	17.9	18.30
30–39 years	14.0	11.8	9.6	12.10
40–49 years	9.3	9.1	8.7	7.40
50+ years	7.2	9.8	11.6	11.30
Not specified	0.0	0.0	0.1	0.03
Total (%)	100.0	100.0	100.0	100.00
Total (no.)	40,384	46,475	54,543	69,107

Sources: TAS (1861; 1870; 1881: 02_27; 1891: 01_xxxi).

The age structure of the male population became younger over the three decades, with the proportion of males aged 20–29 years increasing and the proportion of males aged 30 years and older falling, particularly the age group 40–49 years (Table 3.4). Estimated population data for males aged 15–49 years by five-year age groups show the proportions of males in the age ranges 15–29 years increased between 1861 and 1891 while the proportions of males in the age range 35–49 years fell over the same period (Appendix A: Table A.6).

Table 3.4 Male population by age, Tasmania, 1861, 1870, 1881 and 1891

Year	1861	1870	1881	1891
Age	Percentage			
0–14 years	35.0	40.4	36.6	37.4
15–19 years	6.8	8.1	11.0	9.1
20–29 years	12.0	10.7	16.4	18.6
30–39 years	16.1	9.8	9.2	13.2
40–49 years	14.8	11.9	8.2	7.5
50+ years	15.3	19.0	18.1	13.4
Not specified	0.0	0.0	0.4	0.7
Total (%)	100.0	100.0	100.0	100.0
Total (no.)	49,593	52,853	61,162	77,560

Sources: TAS (1861; 1870; 1881: 02_27; 1891: 01_xxxi).

In 1861, there were more than twice as many unmarried adult men in Tasmania as there were unmarried adult women. The ratio of unmarried males aged 15 and over to unmarried females of the same age was 2.1 for the colony as a whole, but varied markedly by geographic region, being 1.07 in Hobart and 2.72 in the rest of the colony (McDonald 1974: 55). In 1881 in Tasmania as a whole, the balance of the sexes in the 'marriage market'—measured as the number of unmarried males aged 17.5–49 years per 100 unmarried females aged 15–44 years (McDonald 1974)—was still uneven at 110. However, in Hobart, there were many fewer unmarried males than unmarried females, with a ratio of 61 unmarried males aged 17.5–49 years to 100 unmarried females aged 15–44 years (TAS 1881: 02_104). By 1891, the balance of the sexes in the marriage market had risen to 122 for Tasmania as a whole, while in Hobart the ratio of unmarried males to unmarried females had risen to 84 (TAS 1891: 04_61).

The proportion of the population born in the colony continued to increase in the final decades of the 19th century, with a corresponding fall in the proportion born in the British Isles (Table 3.5). In 1881 and 1891, the majority of those born in the British Isles—around 60 per cent—were born in England, while about 25 per cent were born in Ireland, 13 per cent in Scotland and 2 per cent in Wales (TAS 1881, 1891). The proportion of the population born in other Australian colonies was very small, although it increased slightly between 1870 and 1891. More than half of those born in other colonies were born in Victoria (TAS 1891). Only a very small proportion of the Tasmanian population was born in a 'foreign' country. In 1881 and 1891, around one-third of this group was born in Germany and another third was born in China. By 1901, 79.3 per cent of the Tasmanian population was born in Tasmania, another 7.2 per cent was born in the other Australian colonies, while the proportion born in the British Isles had fallen to 11.8 per cent (TAS 1901: 02_xlv).

The increase in the native-born population and decrease in the proportion born in the British Isles are related to the age structure of the population. Younger Tasmanians were more likely to have been born in Tasmania, while a greater proportion of the older population comprised ex-convicts and free settlers from the British Isles. Consequently, the large majority of those marrying between 1870 and 1890 would have been born in Tasmania.

Table 3.5 Birthplace of the Tasmanian population, 1870, 1881 and 1891

Year	1870	1881	1891
Birthplace	Percentage		
Tasmania	59.5	69.1	73.6
Other Australian colonies[1]	1.8	3.4	5.0
British Isles	37.4	24.4	18.4
Other British possessions	0.3	0.8	0.6
Foreign countries	0.9	1.9	2.0
Not specified	0.0	0.3	0.4
Total (%)	100.0	100.0	100.0
Total (no.)	99,328	115,705	146,667

[1] Includes New Zealand
Source: TAS (1891: 04_71).

Characteristics of Tasmanian society

Religion

In the first decades of settlement, several religious denominations established ministries in the colony. The Church of England (or Anglican Church) was the established religion in Tasmania, with Robert Knopwood the first minister (Boyce 2010). The first Catholic priest arrived in the colony in 1821 and a Wesleyan missionary settled permanently in 1822 (Robson 1983). Both the Catholic and the Wesleyan churches were highly committed to working with convicts. The first Presbyterian ministry began in Hobart in 1823; a Congregationalist community was founded in Hobart in 1824, with a minister arriving in 1832, and the first Baptist church was established in Hobart in 1835.

The Nonconformist denominations made an important contribution to the intellectual life of the colony (Breward 1988; Robson and Roe 1997). The Presbyterians, Congregationalists and Baptists were often engaged in business or trade and were very important in founding community organisations such as libraries and the Mechanics Institute, 'where the respectable working man might read newspapers and attend improving lectures' (Robson and Roe 1997: 20). The Methodists were responsible for founding Hobart's first public library (Breward 1988). All religious denominations held Sunday schools where children received a basic education in the three 'Rs' (Breward 1993; Robson and Roe 1997).

Religious affiliation was collected in all 19th-century Tasmanian censuses, except in 1881. It is important to note these data were collected for the total population—that is, both adults and children—so differences in religious affiliation over time may be affected by differential changes in fertility among the various religious groups. The 1842 census did not collect religious affiliation from 17 per cent of the population, mainly convicts, so it is difficult to compare these data with the other census years.

The Church of England was the dominant religion in Tasmania in 1851 but the proportion of the population who were Anglican fell between 1851 and 1901 (Table 3.6). Catholics made up around one-fifth of the population in most census years. The arrival in Tasmania of nearly 10,000 convicts from Ireland between 1840 and 1853 markedly increased the Catholic population of the colony (Boyce 2010), but 'Van Dieman's Land was never as Irish or as Catholic as New South Wales' (Alexander 2014: 23). The proportion of Methodists increased between 1851 and 1901, as in the other Australian colonies (Breward 1988). The proportion of 'Other' religions also increased markedly over the period; the rise between 1870 and 1901 was due to an increase in the numbers of 'Mahommedans, Buddhists and other non-Christian sects' and the commencement of the Salvation Army's work in Australia in the 1880s (TAS 1891: 01_xlvii).

Anglicans had the lowest church attendance of all groups in 19th-century Tasmania, followed by Presbyterians (Breward 1988). The Irish Catholics who came to Tasmania in the 1840s had low levels of attendance at Mass— similar to those in rural Ireland (Boyce 2010). The Congregationalists, Methodists and Baptists were probably more committed to their faith than other Protestants because of the discrimination these religious groups had experienced in Britain (Breward 1988). The Nonconformist denominations became 'evangelical in emphasis and practice' from the 1870s and even the Church of England had a strong evangelical wing (Evans 2005). Towards the end of the 19th century, some sections of the Protestant churches became increasingly more liberal, with efforts to 'adapt the Christian message to the findings of science and philosophy' (Breward 1993: 93).

Table 3.6 Population by religion, Tasmania, 1842, 1851, 1861, 1870 and 1891

Year	1842	1851	1861	1870	1891	1901
Religion						
Church of England	60.70	64.20	54.7	53.4	51.70	48.60
Church of Scotland	6.60	6.40	10.0	9.1	6.90	6.70
Wesleyan Methodists	3.90	5.40	6.9	7.2	12.10	14.50
Other Protestants[1]	3.30	3.40	4.5	4.9	5.50	5.90
Roman Catholics	7.80	17.70	21.6	22.4	18.20	17.60
Jews	0.50	0.60	0.4	0.2	0.06	0.06
Other[2]	0.05	0.03	1.9	2.9	5.50	4.70
Religion not stated[3]	17.00	2.20	0.0	0.0	0.00	2.00
Total (%)	100.00	100.00	100.0	100.0	100.00	100.00
Total (no.)	57,420	70,130	89,977	99,328	141,493	172,475

[1] In 1842 and 1851, 'Other Protestant' includes 'Other Protestant dissenters' and, in 1861, 1870 and 1891, 'Independents' and 'Baptists'.

[2] In 1842 and 1851, 'Other' includes 'Mahommedans and Pagans'; in 1861, 'Other sects'; in 1870, 'Mahommedans and Pagans', 'Society of Friends' and 'Other sects'; and in 1891 and 1901, 'Mahommedans, Buddhists and other non-Christian sects', 'Society of Friends', 'Other Christian sects' and 'Salvation Army'.

[3] In 1842, 'Religion not stated' includes 'Employed in government vessels', 'Convicts on public works', 'Convicts at penal settlements on Tasman's Peninsula' and 'Female convicts in house of corrections Hobart'. In 1851, 'Religion not stated' includes 'Military including women and children' and 'Convicts on public works'.

Sources: TAS (1851; 1861; 1870; 1891: 01_xlvii; 1901: 02_lvii).

Religious affiliation may have been more fluid in a rapidly evolving society such as Tasmania than in 19th-century Britain and Western Europe. In the 1830s and 1840s, before the various denominations were able to establish churches or ministries throughout the colony, people in country areas would attend a church service even though they belonged to another Christian denomination (Breward 1988). This practice may have continued in the later half of the 19th century in the newly opened areas of settlement, such as the mining towns of Zeehan and Queenstown. People also changed their religious denomination during their lifetime—for instance, with Presbyterians becoming Anglicans and Anglicans becoming Methodists (Breward 1993; Critchett 2012a).

Education

In the early years of the colony, children's education was provided in a variety of ways: the gentry sent their sons to England for schooling or their sons and daughters had tutors or governesses; there were a number of private fee-paying schools for young ladies and gentlemen; church schools were publicly funded; and small numbers of government schools were established (Grundy and Yuan 1987; Roe and Robson 1997; Reynolds 2010). All schooling, whether public or private, required some monetary contribution from parents. The Board of Education was set up in 1839 to fund and supervise the government schools (Sprod 1984). In 1840, there were 25 schools under the Board of Education, with 1,046 students enrolled.

In 1868, Tasmania became the first Australian colony to have a compulsory state education system, administered by local school boards. This meant girls as well as boys were required to receive an education. Under the 1868 *Education Act*, children aged seven to 12 years who lived within a mile of the school in 'settled districts' were required to attend school unless they were being educated privately, could read and write, were in poor health or their parents depended on their labour (Sprod 1984). In 1873, the *Public Schools Amendment Act* made it compulsory for all children seven to 14 years of age in all districts living within 2 miles (3 kilometres) of a public school to be sent to a public or private school. The local school board was given the discretion to exempt any child, and children 12 years and older were exempt if they were employed by their parents or others.

The *Tasmanian Education Act* of 1885 set up the Department of Education, which worked to improve the education system. The Act also required children to attend school for three days a week, which was amended to five days in 1898 (Sprod 1984). Several exemptions from compulsory schooling were, however, still in force during this period. The education system and school attendance improved from 1905, when Thomas Neale, the new Director of Education, began to reform the public education system. School fees were abolished in 1908 and state education became free.

Absenteeism was a problem throughout the final three decades of the 19th century. While the number of schools and average enrolments almost tripled between 1870 and 1901, average daily attendance as a proportion of average enrolments remained the same throughout the three decades—

around 70–75 per cent (Table 3.7). Attendance, however, had improved with the introduction of compulsory education in 1868. Kippen (2002c: 210) estimated that school attendance for children aged seven to 13 years probably increased from less than 30 per cent to around 70 per cent between 1860 and 1900, suggesting compulsory education had a major impact on daily attendance in the late 1860s.

Table 3.7 State school students and attendance, Tasmania, 1870, 1881, 1891 and 1901

Year to 31 December	1870	1881	1891	1901
Schools	128	175	244	338
Average enrolments[1]	6,678	9,258	13,491	19,236
Average daily attendance	5,041	6,701	9,680	14,259

[1] Average number of students on the roll. This was an average of the monthly, weekly or quarterly enrolments.
Source: Grundy and Yuan (1987: 337).

Government schools were generally attended by children of the lower middle class, skilled workers, small to medium farmers and the urban and rural working classes. Upper middle-class families tended to send their children to private academies and colleges, while the gentry sent their children to 'grammar' schools (Sprod 1984: 24). Catholic families sent their children to Catholic schools, regardless of social class.

Sprod (1984) concluded that the children of the urban and rural working classes and small farmers were the ones who did not attend government schools regularly during the later decades of the 19th century. Most of these children were working on the family farm, looking after younger children and doing domestic chores or working in paid employment outside the family home to supplement the family's income. Although the Tasmanian *Women's and Children's Employment (Factories) Act* of 1884 forbade the employment of children under the age of 12 years in factories, it specifically excluded seasonal work in the jam factories (Sprod 1984). Children aged 12 years and older were legally allowed to work in factories despite being required by law to attend school until they were 14 years of age. This Act was amended in 1905 so that '[n]o person under the age of Thirteen years shall be employed in any factory' (TAS 1905).

Even though some children's school attendance was irregular, they did attend school for some of the time and received at least a basic education. The literacy status of the population improved markedly during the second half of the 19th century, with the proportion of the total population that could read and write increasing between 1861 and 1901 (Table 3.8). The literacy status of the population was not published prior to 1861 and, for the years 1861 and 1870, it was not disaggregated by age or sex. Between 1881 and 1901, the proportion of the population aged 20 and over that was literate increased from 79 per cent to 92.1 per cent. In 1901, almost all the population aged 15–20 years could both read and write. Children's literacy also improved between 1881 and 1901.

Table 3.8 Proportion of the population who could read and write, Tasmania, 1861, 1870, 1881, 1891 and 1901

Year	1861	1870	1881	1891	1901
Age	Percentage				
All ages	53.7	56.3	64.7	70.3	77.5
5–15 years	n.a.	n.a.	61.6	67.0	76.2
15–20 years	n.a.	n.a.	87.5	95.5	96.6
20+ years	n.a.	n.a.	79.0	87.4	92.1

n.a. not available
Sources: TAS (1881: 02_45, 02_55; 1891: 04_89, 04_90; 1901: 02_li).

In relation to further education, the first technical school was established in Hobart in 1888, the University of Tasmania opened in the Hobart Domain in 1890 and a School of Mines and Metallurgy was set up in Zeehan in 1892 by the miners themselves (Robson and Roe 1997). A teachers' training college was established in Hobart in 1906 with the reform of the public education system.

Occupation

Occupational data from various colonial censuses and the first Australian census of 1911 (Appendix A: Tables A.7–13) reflect the economic changes that occurred in Tasmania in the 19th and early 20th centuries. They also show the marked growth in white-collar and more 'modern' occupations in the final two decades of the 19th century.

The occupational categorisations varied somewhat in each census, so the data are not strictly comparable. However, the broad occupational data show the dominance of agriculture between 1842 and 1870, the growth in the importance of industry and mining in the 1880s and 1890s and the emergence of new occupations—for instance, in transport and communication—in these years. Agriculture clearly declined in importance during the final decades of the 19th century, with the proportion of the population employed in agriculture falling from around 50 per cent in 1851, 1861 and 1870 to around 33 per cent in 1891, 1901 and 1911 (Appendix A: Tables A.7–10). More detailed occupational data (discussed below) show the growth of white-collar occupations in the late 19th and early 20th centuries.

Data for occupation by age and sex were published only from 1881. Data on adult men's occupations for 1881, 1891 and 1901 are difficult to compare, since the classifications changed in each census (Appendix A: Tables A.11–13). People who were not employed were classified as 'Indefinite and non-productive' in the 1881 census, but in the two later censuses, the population was divided into 'Breadwinners' and 'Dependants', with 'Breadwinners' classified by occupation. There were several other changes within the occupational categories. Miners, for instance, were classified as 'industrial' in the 1881 census, but as 'primary producers' in later censuses. In 1901, occupations related to transport and communication, which were previously in the 'commercial' category, were given their own separate category, reflecting the growth of these more 'modern' occupations (Appendix D: Story 3).

It is difficult to obtain precise numbers showing the changes in occupations between 1881 and 1891 because of the changes in occupational classifications at the detailed level (TAS 1881: 20_190–6; 1891: 04_290–318; 1901: 05_394–426). However, there was clearly a rise in the number of men employed in white-collar occupations during this period. 'Accountant', for instance, was not an occupational classification in 1881, but there were 162 males employed as accountants in 1891 and 257 in 1901. This was an increase of 57 per cent, compared with an increase of 17.9 per cent in the number of male breadwinners. The number of men employed as 'Agents'—for example, for commission, insurance and sewing machines—also rose markedly between 1881 and 1901, as did the number of 'Clerks' and 'Messengers'. The number of males who were 'Railway clerks and stationmasters' grew more than threefold, from 53 in 1881 to 117 in 1891 and to 185 in 1901. This compares with an increase of 44 per cent in the population of males aged 15 years and older over the same period. The number of schoolteachers, both men and women, almost doubled between 1881 and 1901, from 602 to 1,109.

There is no information about married women's occupations in any of the colonial censuses. In 1881, of the 26,181 women aged 20 years and older, 82 per cent were classified as 'domestic' (TAS 1881: 02_139). Around three-quarters of this group were 'wives and widows with no occupation specified' (TAS 1881: 02_142). It is not possible to tell whether women classified in specific occupations were married or single. In the 1891 census, of the 33,963 women aged 20 years and older, three-quarters were classified as 'dependants', with the remainder 'breadwinners' (TAS 1891: 04_175). The largest group of breadwinners (41.1 per cent) was classified as 'domestic'. McDonald and Quiggin (1985) note that, for the 1891 colonial censuses, colonial statisticians instructed that a woman should be recorded under 'domestic duties' if there was any doubt about her occupation (McDonald and Quiggin 1985: 80). The 1901 Tasmanian census had a similar occupational classification for women.

It appears that in 19th and early 20th–century Tasmania, most married women did not work outside the home, family business or farm. Working on the family farm or in the family shop or hotel, however, was probably reasonably common, as indicated by newspaper articles of the time. Some women did outwork, taking in washing and sewing. In the later part of the 19th century, some married women also worked as schoolteachers. Many married women also worked locally as midwives (Fahy 2007).

The 1911 census, which provides data on women's occupations by marital status, supports this view (Appendix A: Table A.14). Only a small proportion of married women (4.7 per cent) were classified as 'breadwinners', with the largest group working in the 'domestic category', supplying board and lodging or domestic services. 'Breadwinners' included those who were 'assisting (not receiving wages)', most of whom were married women working in lodging houses and shops and on farms.

Urbanisation

Prior to 1881, the Tasmanian censuses did not provide information on the population of any of the towns/cities except Hobart and Launceston. The censuses gave the population of electoral districts such as Campbell Town, which included both a town and its surrounding areas. It is difficult to tell the proportion of the population living in various districts prior to 1857, because the precise locations of the convicts and the military population were not stated.

In 1857, the population of Hobart was 18,258, accounting for 22.6 per cent of the colony's population (excluding the military), while the population of Launceston was much smaller, at 7,874 or 9.7 per cent (TAS 1857). In Tasmania, unlike the other Australian colonies, and reflecting its dependence on agriculture and mining, the proportion of its population living in its capital city, Hobart, did not grow markedly during the 19th century (McCarty 1974). Instead, there was marked growth in the north of the colony. In the late 1870s and 1880s, new towns were established in the north through the expansion into new areas for agriculture, sawmilling and mining (Meikle 2010). It was possible to export from Launceston and from the smaller northern towns of Devonport and Burnie (Burnley 1980). Launceston grew by 62 per cent between 1857 and 1881 compared with Hobart's growth of 15.7 per cent (TAS 1861; 1881: 02_30). Hobart's population may have been understated in 1881, however, since in that year there were several towns adjoining Hobart that by the 1891 and 1901 censuses were classified as 'suburbs of Hobart' (Appendix A: Table A.15).

Between 1881 and 1901, the population of the 'metropolis' of Hobart grew from 21,118 to 24,654 (16.7 per cent), but an additional 7,764 people resided in the Hobart suburbs in 1901 (Appendix A: Table A.15; TAS 1901: 02_viii). In the far west, mining towns such as Zeehan and Queenstown grew spectacularly in the final two decades of the 19th century (Appendix A: Table A.15). Queenstown, which was not even included in the 1891 census, had a population of 5,051 by 1901, while Zeehan grew from 1,965 to 5,014 over the same period. Towns in the north of the colony such as Burnie, Devonport and Ulverstone also grew markedly, while towns in the Midlands, such as Campbell Town and Oatlands, either declined or stagnated. By 1901, there were 27 towns with populations of 500 or more (excluding Hobart and Launceston), most of them close to one another and to the larger cities of Hobart and Launceston. At the same time, there were small settlements, such as Marrawah on the far north-western coast, which were very remote (Appendix D: Story 2). By 1901, 30.1 per cent of Tasmania's population was living in Hobart and Launceston and their suburbs, 21 per cent lived in other towns of 500 people or more and 48.9 per cent lived in the remainder of the state.

Summary

In its first 50 years, the colony's history was dominated by convict settlement, but after transportation ceased in 1853, the convict society began to die out. By 1857, free settlers or people born in the colony accounted for most of the population. Convicts made up only a very small proportion of the population.

Tasmania was highly dependent on agriculture in its early years, but from the 1870s, mining emerged as a major industry. The colony was prosperous from settlement until the mid-1850s, when a depression set in, but this lifted in the early 1870s with the mining discoveries. Like most other colonies, Tasmania experienced a great depression in the early 1890s, but the economy improved at the end of the 19th century and in the early 20th century. The late 19th and early 20th centuries were a time of great social and economic change for the colony, with improvements in communication and transportation, the introduction of electricity to cities, compulsory primary school education and universal suffrage.

By the final decade of the 19th century, a high proportion of the population was born in Tasmania and was literate. There was a large rise in white-collar and 'modern' occupations, communication was good and news from other colonies and overseas reached Tasmania with very little delay. The population was not strongly religious and there was a relatively high urban orientation.

It is against this backdrop that the historical fertility decline took place.

4

Research design and data sources

This chapter describes the research design for the quantitative analysis, the data sources used to construct the database and the issues encountered in its construction.

Family reconstitution of four Tasmanian marriage cohorts

To obtain the data for the bivariate and multivariate analyses, I reconstituted families in four Tasmanian marriage cohorts using 19th-century Tasmanian registration data plus information from many other sources. The family reconstitution involved tracking couples from marriage through their childbearing years. This allowed me to compare the fertility and birth patterns of couples in these marriage cohorts according to various characteristics.

I used a marriage cohort approach in my study because examining the birth histories of couples provided me with the information needed to answer my research questions—that is, when, how and why fertility fell during this period. The cohort approach also allowed me to look at the impact of temporal change on fertility in broad terms—for instance, the effects of the 1890s depression, which lasted for about 10 years. The task of reconstructing the birth histories of four marriage cohorts, while time-consuming, is at least feasible. A cross-sectional approach is not feasible. Because the birth registration data do not provide information on the age of the mother at the birth, parity of the birth or whether the birth is the last, I would have had to reconstitute the birth histories of all mothers giving birth in any of the years under examination. Additionally, because of the under-registration of births, I would have had to examine the birth histories of every married woman of childbearing age to try to find births that were not registered. This is an impossible task. Cross-sectional data would have allowed me to examine the impact of short-term events on fertility, but to do this thoroughly I would have had to include births in every single year within the period, which would also have been unfeasible. Finally, from a theoretical perspective, it can be expected that the long-term trend towards lower fertility was the result of longer-term social and economic changes over several years rather than of one-off events occurring in single calendar years.

The technique of 'family reconstitution'—that is, the reconstitution of families using parish records on births, deaths and marriages—has been used by demographers to study the decline of fertility in historical populations, but it has several problems (Wrigley 1966; Henry and Blum 1988; Gutmann and Alter 1993; Wrigley et al. 1997). A major problem is the data are only available for events within a parish and families who move out of the parish are excluded from the study, giving rise to issues of the representativeness of the study population (Ruggles 1992; Gutmann and Alter 1993). I used an 'enhanced' form of family reconstitution in my study, in which I first reconstituted families using Tasmanian vital registration data, but then used several other sources to track families who moved out of Tasmania, either temporarily or permanently.

As noted in Chapter 1, I selected the marriage cohorts for 1860, 1870, 1880 and 1890 for my study—that is, the population of couples who were married in Tasmania in these years. Examining the available evidence outlined in Chapter 2, it appeared that the earlier cohorts would have had children before the fertility decline and those in the 1880 and 1890 cohorts would have had children during the fertility transition. I chose the 1860 cohort as my first cohort, rather than an earlier cohort, for several reasons:

- By 1860, the Tasmanian population was more settled: transportation ended in 1853 and the exodus to Victoria as a result of the goldrush was all but over. Most of the population were free settlers or were born in the colony.

- Registration, which started in 1838, had greatly improved by 1860 (Kippen 2002a). Although there was still under-registration of births, registration improved throughout the second half of the 19th century.
- Population data were available from 1860 onwards (Kippen 2002c).

The fertility analysis in this book concentrates on the fall in fertility among those who had children and does not investigate trends in childlessness. It was not possible to obtain an estimate of childlessness among couples in the Tasmanian marriage cohorts, since many couples could not be traced to the end of their childbearing years. It is difficult to tell whether there was an increase in childlessness during the Australian fertility decline, but there was clearly a marked decline in completed family size of couples who had children. According to the 1911 census, the proportion of childless women born in the years 1842–46 to 1862–66 was relatively small and remained unchanged for each birth cohort, at around 8 per cent of all married women (Commonwealth of Australia 1914c: 1136).

I decided to examine completed fertility within marriage and to concentrate on women who had survived their childbearing years and whose childbearing had not been interrupted by widowhood. Consequently, the analysis of marital fertility decline is undertaken for a subpopulation of couples in the marriage cohorts—that is, couples in which the wife was in her first marriage, there was at least one child from the marriage and both partners survived the wife's childbearing years. In the discussion that follows, I refer to this subpopulation as the 'complete' group.

Although the fertility analysis concentrates on the complete group, I reconstituted the birth histories of all couples marrying in the four cohorts for whom the wife was in her first marriage and there were children of that marriage, to provide some descriptive data to set the fertility analysis in context (Moyle 2015: 73–89).

Data sources

I used several databases to reconstitute the families from the four marriage cohorts (Appendix B). The main database used in this study was the Tasmanian Civil Registration Digitised Database—Tasbirths, Tasdeaths and Tasmarriages (Gunn and Kippen 2008; Kippen and Gunn 2011). This database contains digitised records of births, deaths and marriages registered in Tasmania from the beginning of registration in August 1838 until the end of the 19th century. Tasmania was the first British colony to introduce civil registration of vital events, shortly after civil registration was introduced in Britain (Kippen 2002a).

The Tasmanian Civil Registration Digitised Database contains the following information:

- Tasbirths: Data on place of birth; name; sex; name of both parents; maiden name of mother; occupation of father; date and district of registration; name, status and residence of informant; and name of officiating deputy registrar. From 1895, the date and place of the parents' marriage were also listed.
- Tasmarriages: Name; age; occupation of husband and wife (if any); marital status of the husband and wife; date and place of marriage; date and district of registration; religion; names of witnesses; whether the husband and/or wife signed the marriage certificate.
- Tasdeaths: Name; age; sex; occupational status of deceased or spouse (if wife) or father (if a minor); date of death; cause of death; date and district of registration; name, status and residence of informant; and name of officiating deputy registrar.

I was very fortunate to have access to another database that linked the births in the Tasmanian Civil Registration Digitised Database to the marriages (Kippen and Gunn 2011). While this database was not complete, when I reconstituted the families, I found that only about 5 per cent of births in the four marriage cohorts had not been linked to a marriage. Kippen and Gunn (2011) initially linked the births by computer linkage with a 70 per cent success rate, although the rate of linkage was much lower for earlier years than for later years. Once they had completed the computer linkage, they began to link the unlinked births manually, but this process had not been completed by the time I started my study. Of the unlinked births that I was able to attach to a marriage, the majority were births in the 1890s that were a later addition to the original database. Other unlinked births were those to widows, where the birth was registered in the woman's maiden name, not the name in which she married. Widows commonly gave their previously married name at the cohort marriage but used their maiden name when registering the children of the cohort marriage.

Many couples in the 1880 and 1890 marriage cohorts had births in the early decades of the 20th century, and parents in all cohorts, particularly the later cohorts, died during the 20th century. To find births and deaths occurring in Tasmania after 1899, I used the Tasmanian Federation Index, which provides information for births from 1900 to 1919 and for deaths from 1900 to 1930.

The Tasmanian Federation birth index provides information on: date of birth; name; sex; full name of father; full name of mother, including her maiden name; and the place of birth. The Tasmanian Federation death index contains information on name, sex and the date and place of death. I also had access to a sample of digitised Tasmanian death registrations for the period 1900–30 (Kippen 2013). These death registrations contain the following information: name, age and sex of deceased; date and place of death; place of birth; cause of death; occupational status of deceased or spouse (if wife) or father (if a minor); name of medical attendant; name, relationship and place of informant; date and district of registration; and name of deputy registrar.

The Tasmanian vital registration data were not wholly adequate for fully reconstituting families in the four marriage cohorts, partly because many families had births or deaths outside Tasmania and partly because many deaths for the later cohorts occurred after 1930. I therefore used several other sources to reconstitute families (Appendix B). These data sources include digitised newspapers in the National Library of Australia; the *Australian Dictionary of Biography*; the Australian births, deaths and marriages indexes (on the website www.ancestry.com); the Australian and New Zealand electoral rolls; NSW, Victorian, Queensland, South Australian, West Australian and New Zealand historical births, marriages and deaths indexes; UK births, deaths and marriages indexes; English population census forms; the Colonial Tasmanian Family Links Database; Tasmanian divorce records; Tasmanian wills; Tasmanian land records; and service records for the Boer War, World War I and World War II. The Australian digitised newspapers were a very rich source of information. This was because Tasmania had a relatively small population during the 19th and early 20th centuries and, unlike in the other colonies, the newspapers reported mundane events about ordinary people, often in great detail. From 1900, it also became very common for people from all socioeconomic classes to place birth, death and marriage notices in

Tasmanian newspapers. Family trees on the website 'Ancestry.com' were a very useful source of information, but I used these data only if they were confirmed by other sources.

Process of family reconstitution and issues encountered

Using Tasmanian records

To reconstitute a family, I started with a marriage and attached the computer-linked births to the couple's marriage record. I then compared these births with those attributed to the couple on the Colonial Tasmanian Family Links Database to see whether there were any other births listed on that database. If I found additional births, I then searched the unlinked registered births on Tasbirths to confirm that a birth was correctly attributed to a family. I also searched the Tasmanian Federation birth index for births occurring in the 20th century. This index provided me with enough information to be confident that the births I found belonged to the correct family.

Once I had attached all the Tasmanian-registered births to a marriage, I searched for the deaths of infants and children under 15 years and of parents, using a variety of sources. I initially used Tasdeaths and the sample of Tasmanian digitised death registrations for deaths occurring between 1900 and 1930. If I could not find a death on these digitised databases, I searched the Tasmanian Federation death index and then checked with the Australian digitised newspapers and the Australian Cemetery Index to confirm that a death on the index belonged to the correct family. The digitised newspapers and the Australian Cemetery Index were also very useful in finding deaths that occurred after 1930. Death notices in a newspaper almost always provided information on whether that person's spouse was still living—for example, 'death of George Brown, dearly beloved husband of Mary Brown' or 'death of Mary Brown, relict of the late George Brown'. In the case of a child's death, death notices also identified the child's parents.

Family mobility

I did not assume that all couples who married in Tasmania stayed there throughout their lives, so I searched for events that had occurred in other locations. This would not have been possible without the digitised records that have become available on the internet in the past five to 10 years. Larson (1994: 33), writing about family reconstitution in the 1980s and early 1990s, considered one of the problems of family reconstitution was that it was impossible to trace families who moved out of the study area or to learn about events that 'were never recorded, such as a baby born while the family was on a visit to England'. The availability of digitised records accessible through the internet has largely dealt with this problem.

Once I had reconstituted a family using Tasmanian records, I searched for births and deaths that occurred outside Tasmania—that is, in the other colonies, in New Zealand and in other countries. I did not assume that if a couple had births in Tasmania and both parents died in Tasmania all their births had occurred in Tasmania.

The Victorian, NSW, Queensland, South Australian (SA), Western Australian (WA), New Zealand and English births, marriages and deaths indexes, and the English censuses, were useful in providing information on events occurring elsewhere. The Victorian, Queensland and SA indexes all gave births by the wife's maiden name, which gave me a high degree of certainty that the birth belonged to the correct family. The NSW and WA indexes, however, were much less detailed and I attached the birth to the family only if I could find other sources of information that confirmed the relationship. There was very little information on deaths in most of the indexes, although the Victorian, Queensland and NSW indexes gave some information about the parents of the deceased. The digitised newspapers were an important source of information on deaths occurring in other colonies or countries.

I found a wide variety of patterns of mobility among couples in the four marriage cohorts. Some couples had all their births in Tasmania but moved around Tasmania during the wife's childbearing years; some couples had births in Tasmania and in another location, while other couples married in Tasmania but had all their births elsewhere.

Only a small proportion of the couples who married in Tasmania did not have any births in Tasmania. For instance, Ernest Augustus Smith, a solicitor, and Grace Fisher married in Hobart in 1890, but all their children were born in Sydney, NSW, and both Ernest and Grace died there in the 1930s.

Some couples had their first birth outside Tasmania, but the rest of their children were born in the colony. John Blythe, a wealthy landowner, and Caroline Delittle were married in Launceston in 1880 and had a son, Robert, born in Invercargill, New Zealand, in 1881. They returned to Tasmania shortly after and had a daughter, born in Launceston in 1882, and another, born in Beaconsfield in 1887. John died in Tasmania in 1912, but Caroline was still living there in the late 1930s.

Some couples had some of their children in Tasmania and then moved to another place and had other children there. Bowden Carthew, a stonemason, married Mary Anne Carpenter in Swansea in 1860. They had their first child in Glamorgan in 1861, their second in Spring Bay in 1862 and two other children in Hobart, in 1865 and 1866. By 1869, they had moved to Ballarat, Victoria, where they had a child born in that year and another born in 1870. Both Bowden and Mary Anne died in Melbourne.

Other couples had one or more children born in Tasmania, then one or more born elsewhere, then went back to Tasmania and had more children there. Richard Fleming, a farmer, married Eliza Barwick in 1860 in Oatlands (Appendix D: Story 4). They had two children in Oatlands, went to New Zealand, where they had another three children, then returned to Oatlands, where the rest of their 13 children were born. Richard died in Oatlands and Eliza in Launceston.

Some families were extremely mobile and had children in many different locations. Ernest Graham, a labourer, married Sarah Freeman in Hobart in 1890. They had four children born in Hobart between 1892 and 1896 and then moved to New Zealand, where they had another four children, born between 1901 and 1904. In 1908, when their ninth child was born, they were back in Australia, living in Cobar in the far west of New South Wales. At some stage, they moved again, since by 1934 they were living in Darwin, in the Northern Territory, where Ernest was a 'retired civil servant'.

Defining the wife's childbearing years

Although I originally assumed women would have completed their childbearing by age 45, I found that 11 per cent of women in the 1860 and 1870 cohorts had their last birth aged 45–49 years. I thus decided to extend the wife's childbearing years to age 50. However, there was a small number of couples in which one partner died before the wife turned 50, but there were several years between the last birth and the spouse's death, suggesting these couples had completed their childbearing. Within each marriage cohort, I examined the birth patterns of women in couples in which both partners had survived to age 50 to investigate the probability of having another birth. Among those women who gave birth at each age, I looked at the number of women who went on to have another birth and, for those who had another birth, the length of time to the next birth. Based on this analysis, I included couples in the *complete* group where one spouse died before the wife turned 50: if a woman had her last birth in her 20s and there was a 99 per cent probability she had completed her childbearing at the time of the death; if she had her last birth in her 30s and there was a 95 per cent probability of completion; or if her last birth was in her 40s and there was a 90 per cent probability (because of small numbers).

Ascertaining whether both partners lived through the wife's childbearing years

If I could not find any information on the deaths of a husband and wife, I used sources such as the electoral rolls to ascertain whether either or both partners had lived through the wife's childbearing years. The electoral rolls list partners and children living at the same address and give each person's occupation.

However, in every cohort, there was a small proportion of marriages in which the wife was in her first marriage, they had at least one child from that marriage, but they then effectively 'disappeared' from the records. I suspect a relatively high proportion of these marriages ended in separation, particularly in the earlier cohorts. I found separations serendipitously, through sources such as newspaper articles or birth records with the husband or wife having births with another partner. Separations that were initiated by women seem to have been reasonably common in the colony from its earliest years (Boyce 2010). In these situations, the husband often placed a notice in the newspaper disclaiming all responsibility for his wife's debts.

Margaret Clark and John Stacey, for example, were married in 1860, but he subjected her to considerable physical and emotional abuse in the first years of their marriage (*The Mercury*, [Hobart], 15 May 1863, 26 September 1863). When Margaret left him, John put an advertisement in the newspaper, saying:

> CAUTION: My wife, MARGARET STACEY, having left her home without my consent, I hereby caution the public from giving her credit on my account, as I shall not be responsible for any debts she may incur. JOHN STACEY, JUN., Dated this 29th of September, 1863. (*The Mercury*, [Hobart], 1 October 1863)

The digitised divorce records on the Tasmanian Archives website enabled me to find out whether and when a couple divorced. Divorce legislation was first passed into law in Tasmania in September 1860 (Finlay 1999). However, very few of the couples in the study were divorced: in total, only 15 couples in all four cohorts had divorced during the wife's childbearing years. Some couples appear to have separated with one of the partners marrying another partner without being divorced. Some of these men and women went to Victoria and remarried despite having a spouse living in Tasmania. As in earlier times, Victoria was a 'refuge for those seeking … freedom away from social and economic controls' (Boyce 2010: 250). I suspect a small number of men and women also remarried in other parts of Tasmania despite being already legally married at the time.

Where I did not have any information to ascertain whether the couple survived the wife's childbearing years or were separated or divorced, I continued to search the family histories on Ancestry.com to see whether I could find any clues about the family. I also developed my own website, requesting information on the families. I contacted all the state and territory family history societies, asking them to put a short article in their newsletter or magazine about my search. The article briefly summarised the research, gave details of the website and asked for any help in tracing the families. Most of the family history societies very generously agreed to my request, but I obtained little information through this source. Many of the people who contacted me had been unable to trace the relevant individual or couple and had no more information than I did about their fate.

The 1860 cohort proved to be the most difficult to trace (Table 5.1), partly because some of those marrying at this time, mostly men, were ex-convicts. I suspect ex-convicts were more likely to have been mobile and to have changed their names when they moved. I found some instances where a husband or wife was an ex-convict and they had changed their name at marriage or after they married. There were several ex-convict men in the *complete* group in the 1860 marriage cohort and a possible two or three ex-convict women, as far as I can tell, but most of the women were too young to have been convicts. Most ex-convict men marrying in the 1860 cohort married widows, while ex-convict women either were widows or, if marrying for the first time, did not have any children of the marriage. I did not find any ex-convicts in any of the other marriage cohorts.

The 1890 cohort was the easiest to trace (Table 5.1). One of the reasons for this was that names—both first names and last names—became much more diverse throughout the 19th century. In the 1860 cohort, most women were called Margaret, Catherine, Anne, Mary, Jane, Elizabeth or Sarah, while men were mostly called Henry, John, James, George, Thomas, Charles or William. There were also a limited number of last names in the colony. Thus, 'John and Mary Davis' or 'George and Margaret Brown' were almost impossible to identify correctly. From the 1870s, however, children were given a much wider variety of first names, and last names also became more diverse with immigration into the colony, both from other countries and from other colonies.

Unregistered births

Under-registration of births was an issue in Tasmania during the 19th and early 20th centuries (Kippen 2002c). Kippen (2002c) estimated that the proportion of unregistered births was 13 per cent in the 1860s and 1870s, 7 per cent in the 1880s, 5 per cent in the 1890s and fell to 2 per cent by the beginning of the first decade of the 20th century (Kippen 2002c: 55–6; and Personal communication). Kellaway (1999) similarly estimated the proportion of unregistered births in Tasmania at 10.4 per cent for the 1860s and early 1870s. Tasmanian experts writing at the time believed many of the unregistered births were of illegitimate children, although they had no evidence for this (Hall 1872, cited in Kippen 2002c). There is some evidence, however, that in 19th-century Victoria, ex-nuptial births were less likely to be registered than nuptial births (Carmichael 1996).

Searching for unregistered births was a very time-consuming and painstaking task. For this reason, I decided to limit the search for unregistered births to the *complete* group that is the focus of the fertility analysis.

I found unregistered births in Tasmania through several sources:

- Where the family's religion was 'Catholic', I used microfilms of some of the Catholic parish records to search for baptisms of children whose births were not registered. I concentrated on families with very large birth intervals, particularly between marriage and the first birth.
- Some families listed on the Colonial Tasmanian Family Links Database had births attributed to the family (usually sourced from church records) that were not on Tasbirths.
- Some family histories on Ancestry.com had an additional child or children attributed to a family.
- I sometimes found an additional child or children mentioned in a newspaper article or notice about a parent's death.
- I found some infants and/or children whose deaths were registered but for whom there was no birth registration. In most of these cases, the child had lived only a few hours and presumably the family thought it too costly to register the birth. Deaths were more likely to be registered than births, since a family wishing to bury a family member was required to show the death certificate to the clergyman, otherwise he was required to notify the deputy registrar of noncompliance with the registration Act (Kippen 2002a).

When I found the additional child or children, I went through several steps to confirm they belonged to the family in my study. First, I checked to see whether the additional child or children belonged to any other family. If not, I checked the family reconstitution to see whether the child or children fitted into any possible birth gaps. If so, I then used various sources to check on the likelihood of the child belonging to the family. These sources included: the Australian birth index; Victorian, Queensland and NSW death indexes; birth, death and marriage notices in the digitised newspapers; parents' obituaries; the Australian Cemetery Index; names of witnesses at sibling's weddings; and Boer War, World War I and World War II service records:

- The Australian birth index on Ancestry.com listed several births that were not in the Tasmanian digitised database. The birth index gave full date of birth, both parents' first names and surnames, including the mother's maiden name, and place of birth.
- If a person died in Victoria or Queensland, either as a child or as an adult, the death index gave both parents' first names and surnames, including the mother's maiden name. NSW death indexes gave both parents' first names.
- The Australian digitised newspapers were a good source of information. Some births were unregistered but were announced in a newspaper. Marriage notices would often say the person was, for example, the third son of John and Mary Smith. A death notice for the child (as an adult) might also provide evidence that the person belonged to the correct family. Death notices for parents were sometimes very useful, in that they listed all the children in the family by name and in birth order. Newspaper obituaries nearly always listed the number of children by sex and sometimes gave their names.
- The Australian Cemetery Index listed members of the family who were buried with that person.
- The Boer War and World War I and World War II records provided information on age, occupation, geographic location and next of kin.

In using the family trees on the Ancestry.com website, I was very cautious about children attributed to the family who were born before the couple married. Where I did not have a birth registration for the child in the husband's name, I often found a birth registration for the mother, but with another man listed as the father. In these cases, the husband had taken his wife's illegitimate child into the family and given the child his surname. In several instances, I found that a child listed as the youngest in the family was the illegitimate child of one of the older daughters.

Another problem I encountered was that children sometimes changed their names in adulthood. A child who was called 'Charles George' at birth changed his name to 'Claude Carlos George' in adulthood, presumably to distinguish himself from his brother who was called 'Charles Henry'. Children often used their second names, rather than their first, and sometimes had unusual nicknames—for instance, one 'Frederick' was called 'Eric'.

The following examples show the use of various sources in tracking unregistered births:

- William Ritchie and Margaret Fawns married in Morven in 1860. I found five children in the birth registration data: three sons and two daughters. These children were born in 1861, 1863, 1864, 1868 and 1870. William was a solicitor in Launceston throughout his career and, when he died in 1897, his obituary was published in *The Examiner* (Launceston). The obituary stated that he left a widow and six children: three sons and three daughters. It also said one of the daughters had married the previous year William G. Baird, a bank manager. I searched for this marriage and found the daughter referred to was the missing child, Florence Margaret Ritchie. She married William in October 1896 at the age of 29, and her sister Elizabeth Agnes Ritchie was a witness at her wedding. I thus estimated Florence's year of birth as 1867, meaning her birth filled a gap between a birth in October 1864 and the following birth in November 1868.
- Donald McKenzie married Marjorie McDonald in Launceston in 1870. They had six children whose births were registered: John (1872), Jeannie (1875), Margaret (1881), Ann (1883), Mary (1885) and Donald James (1887). All the children were born at roughly two-year intervals, except for a six-year gap between Jeannie and Margaret. Donald McKenzie died in January 1916 and his death certificate was signed by 'his son Lachlan'. I found a notice for Lachlan McKenzie's death in *The Examiner* (Launceston) on 4 April 1951. The notice said Lachlan was the brother of John, Jeannie, Alexander, Margaret, Ann, Mary and James. It also said Lachlan had served in the Australian Imperial Force in World War I. When I looked up the World War I embarkation records, I found Lachlan McKenzie, aged 37, a farmer in Glengarry, along with his brother Donald James, aged 28, a sawmill hand, also of Glengarry, had enlisted on 31 May 1916. Both men gave their next of kin as their brother John McKenzie, also of Glengarry. Lachlan's estimated year of birth was 1879. Since Alexander was listed between Jeannie and Margaret in the newspaper obituary, I estimated his year of birth as 1877, thus filling the six-year gap between two registered births.
- John MacLaine and Emily Salier were married in Hobart in 1870 and went to live on Clarke's Island, 24 kilometres off the north-east coast of Tasmania. They had 11 children, several of whom were unregistered. Several Ancestry.com family trees said the couple had twins, born on

8 July 1877. I could not find any birth registrations, but by searching the Australian digitised newspapers, I found the following birth announcement: 'MACLAINE: On Clarke's Island on the 8th July, the wife of J. Maclaine, of twins (son and daughter)' (The Mercury, [Hobart], 1 October 1877).

I cannot claim to have traced all unregistered births to the *complete* group in the four cohorts, but I have made every effort to find as many as possible. In the process of finding unregistered births in Tasmania, I was also able to find other unregistered births that occurred in other colonies or in New Zealand.

My estimates of unregistered Tasmanian births are consistent with Kippen's findings outlined above in that they show the proportion of Tasmanian births that were not registered fell steadily from the 1860s to the first two decades of the 20th century (Table 4.1). While 6.8 per cent of the 1860s births to the complete group were not registered, this proportion fell to 1.7 per cent for births in the 1890s and to less than 1 per cent for births in the first two decades of the 20th century.

Table 4.1 Unregistered births and total births for children born in Tasmania, complete group: 1860, 1870, 1880 and 1890 marriage cohorts, Tasmania

Year of birth	No. unregistered births	No. total births	Percentage of total births
1860–69	64	939	6.8
1870–79	66	1,667	4.0
1880–89	65	2,563	2.5
1890–99	50	2,955	1.7
1900–09	7	976	0.7
1910–19	1	130	0.8
Total	254	9,231	2.6

The proportion of couples with one or more unregistered births fell markedly, from 24.6 per cent for the 1860 cohort to 4 per cent for the 1890 cohort (Table 4.2). The extent of under-registration was related to the year of the birth, however, and not to the marriage cohort. A slightly higher proportion of couples marrying in 1860, for instance, registered their 1870s births compared with couples marrying in 1870: 3.2 per cent of 1870 births to the 1860 cohort were unregistered compared with

4.4 per cent of 1870 births to the 1870 cohort. Several families had more than one unregistered birth, with 62 families in the 1860 cohort, for instance, having a total of 85 unregistered births. Many of these families were Catholics, who were less likely to register their births than parents from other religions in every marriage cohort. In 1860, for example, Catholic families accounted for 12.5 per cent of complete families, but 19 per cent of those who had unregistered births. In an extreme case, one Catholic family in the 1870 cohort had all their children baptised, but none of the births was registered.

Table 4.2 Couples with unregistered births in Tasmania as a proportion of couples with at least one birth in Tasmania, complete group: 1860, 1870, 1880 and 1890 marriage cohorts, Tasmania

Marriage cohort	No. couples with unregistered births	No. total couples	Percentage of all couples
1860	62	256	24.2
1870	48	286	16.8
1880	44	417	10.6
1890	21	529	4.0
Total	182	1,442	11.8

Date of birth

As noted above, the full date of birth was missing for some of the unregistered births. Similarly, for births in New South Wales, Victoria, Western Australia and New Zealand, birth indexes gave only the year of birth, not the day and month. I found some full birthdates from notices in the digitised newspapers or from the family histories on Ancestry.com. For some births, I had the month of birth, but for the others I imputed a birth month based on the birth spacing in the family. A birthday of 30 was imputed where the birth month was June, and a day of 15 for every other month.

Missing (full) dates of birth were much more of an issue for children born outside Tasmania. In the complete group, day of birth was missing for 626 of the 952 births occurring outside Tasmania, compared with 136 of the 9,235 births occurring in Tasmania. I ran the multivariate analysis on birth spacing for the complete group, excluding families who had no children born in Tasmania, and had identical results to the analysis for the entire group, indicating the imputation of birthdates had little impact on the birth spacing analysis.

Stillbirths

Data on the reconstituted families include only births that were 'live births' and do not include 'stillbirths', since parents were not required to register stillbirths as either births or deaths in 19th-century Tasmania (Kippen 2002c). Although there were 179 stillbirths registered as 'deaths' in the Tasdeaths database, only three of these occurred after 1869 and most occurred before 1860.

The family reconstitution data suggest there was probably a change in the definition of 'live births' some time in the 1860s. Data on infant deaths show that in the 1860 marriage cohort the proportion of deaths occurring on the same day as the birth was much lower than in the three later cohorts. In the 1860 cohort, only three of the 129 infant deaths occurred on the day the infant was born, compared with 28 of the 158 infant deaths in the 1870 cohort, 22 of the 219 infant deaths in the 1880 cohort and 20 of the 191 infant deaths in the 1890 cohort. This strongly suggests that, prior to the late 1860s, when infants died within a few hours of birth, many were classified as stillbirths and neither the birth nor the death was registered (Kippen 2002c). This suggests another source of under-registration for births as well as deaths during this period. From the late 1860s, most infants who were alive at birth but died shortly afterwards were classified as 'live births' and both their birth and their death were registered.

Ex-nuptial births

As noted above, there is some evidence that ex-nuptial births were less likely to be registered than births within marriage. Where Tasmanian ex-nuptial births were registered, it was often difficult to allocate a birth to a woman in my study because of insufficient information on the registration certificate. Thus, ex-nuptial births were mainly allocated to women with unusual names living in small towns or remote areas. For instance, it was relatively easy to allocate a birth to 'Sedina Woodlands' living in Glamorgan, but impossible to know whether the birth to 'Mary Ann Jones' living in Hobart was to the woman in my study unless I found evidence from other sources. It was also very difficult to find ex-nuptial births that occurred outside Tasmania. In cases where a woman had more than one ex-nuptial birth, however, I had enough information to be confident I had allocated the births correctly.

In cases where I could ascertain that the wife had an ex-nuptial birth and there was no father named on the birth certificate, it was impossible to tell whether this was a birth to the couple who later married. Unless I had evidence to the contrary, I assumed the husband was not the child's father.

The number of women I identified as having an ex-nuptial birth prior to marriage to a man other than the husband was relatively small. In 1860, for instance, only eight of 482 women in their first marriage with at least one child of that marriage had one ex-nuptial child with another man prior to marriage. It is highly likely this understates the number having an ex-nuptial birth because of the problems of under-registration and of correctly allocating those ex-nuptial births that were registered. For these reasons, I did not use data on these ex-nuptial children in my analysis of completed fertility.

In relation to all births outside marriage, I excluded from the fertility analysis a small number of couples who had one or more births before their marriage because the timing of their births was different from other couples in the marriage cohort—for instance, their marriage took place between the first and second births or between the second and third births or even later. A few couples had several children some years before they married, suggesting the husband or wife may not have been free to marry. I also excluded a very small number of couples for whom the woman had several ex-nuptial births with another man or men before her marriage, since I reasoned her birth pattern more closely resembled that of widows.

Marital status

Marital status was missing for a relatively large proportion of husbands in the 1860 and 1870 cohorts and a smaller proportion of wives, but the recording of marital status improved in the two later cohorts (Table 5.2). Where a woman's marital status was missing and the woman had children from the cohort marriage, I checked the mother's name in the birth registrations. Because of the naming practices for widows, noted above, if the last name given in the birth registration/s was different from the last name at marriage, the woman was classified as a widow. Where the husband's marital status was missing, I tried to find a previous marriage or children from that marriage to ascertain whether he was a widower or bachelor.

In a small number of cases, men and women stated they were a 'Bachelor' or a 'Spinster' but I found a previous marriage for the person, children of that marriage and the death of the previous spouse. In my analysis, I classified these people as a widow or widower, rather than according to the status they gave at the marriage.

Age of husband and wife

Where an actual age at marriage was provided, I used these data to estimate the year of birth from the year of marriage. In a proportion of marriages, age was given only as 'of age' or 'not of age'—that is, the person was or was not of a legal age to marry without the consent of their parents. If I found the husband's or wife's death, I estimated birth year from age at death—either from the death registration data or from other sources such as the digitised newspapers or the Australian Cemetery Index. For those cases where I did not have the actual age at marriage or at death, I tried to find the husband's or wife's date of birth. It was easier to find the date of birth for those in the two later cohorts since a much higher proportion of spouses were born in Tasmania. However, it was harder to find the age at death for the later cohorts, since many of the husbands and wives died in the 1940s and 1950s.

I concentrated my efforts on finding the birth year of the parents of the *complete* group, since 'age' was a crucial variable for my analysis. For the complete group, I obtained the age (or an estimate of the age) of all mothers in the 1860 and 1870 cohorts and 99 per cent of mothers in the two later cohorts (Table 5.3). I also obtained data on the age of 98–99 per cent of their husbands (Table 5.4).

Occupational status

Data on Tasmanian births from 1900 onwards were derived from the Tasmanian Federation Index, which did not contain details of the husband's occupation. Data indexes for other colonies and for New Zealand also did not provide information on occupation. In some instances, I was able to find information from sources such as digitised newspapers or electoral rolls. Where a child or parent had died in Tasmania in the early 20th century, I was able to obtain information on the husband's occupation from the digitised death record.

In the bivariate analysis, I used occupation at the birth of the first child, since the data were of better quality than occupation at marriage. Where occupation at the birth of the first child was missing and I could not find any information on the husband's occupation at the birth of the next child, I used the husband's occupation at marriage. In the multivariate analysis, where occupation was missing for children other than the first, I used occupation at the birth of the previous child (Vézina et al. 2014).

Although information on a woman's occupation was recorded on the marriage registration certificate, these data were missing for around three-quarters of couples in the earlier three cohorts. Most of the female occupations listed for women in these cohorts were servant, dressmaker, farmer's daughter or free (not a convict). Occupation at marriage was recorded for around half of women in the 1890 cohort, but these occupations were mainly domestic, servant or daughter of a farmer (or labourer or carpenter). Mother's occupation was not recorded on the birth registration certificate. Married women's occupation on the death certificate either related to their husband's occupation—for instance, widow (wife) of farmer—or was listed as 'domestic duties'.

Summary of accuracy

Throughout the family reconstitutions, I was very careful to avoid recording information unless it could be verified. In the end, I have a high degree of confidence about the accuracy and completeness of the family histories in my *complete* group. This gives me a database with complete birth histories of couples in all social strata of Tasmania, including those who left Tasmania either temporarily or permanently at some time after they married. This database is used in the descriptive analysis of the marriage cohorts in Chapter 5, in the bivariate analyses of the fertility of couples in the complete group in Chapter 6 and in the bivariate and multivariate analyses of starting, stopping and spacing behaviours in Chapter 7.

5
Characteristics of the Tasmanian marriage cohorts

This chapter describes the characteristics of the group of interest in the analysis of the Tasmanian historical fertility decline—that is, the *complete* group, in which women were in their first marriage, had at least one child of that marriage and both partners survived the wife's childbearing years. The chapter examines these couples according to their characteristics at marriage: marital status, age at marriage, age difference between husband and wife, religion and whether the husband and/or wife signed the marriage register. The husband's socioeconomic status and the couple's geographic location—two important characteristics relating to theories of fertility decline—are also examined.

In the first section of this chapter, I describe the types of marriages in each of the four marriage cohorts, to look at the complete group in the context of the entire marriage cohort.

Types of marriage

The database consisted of 3,184 couples marrying in Tasmania in the years 1860, 1870, 1880 and 1890 (Table 5.1). The smallest marriage cohort was the 1870 cohort, with 673 couples, while the 1890 cohort was the largest, with 952 couples.

Most couples marrying in Tasmania in these years were couples in which the wife was in her first marriage and there were children of that marriage. There were four types of these couples: the 'complete' group, in which both parents survived the childbearing years (the study population); the 'incomplete' group, in which one or both parents died during the wife's childbearing years; the 'unobserved' group, in which the couple could not be traced to the end of the wife's childbearing years; and couples with prenuptial births or two or more ex-nuptial births. The remainder were couples for whom the wife was in her first marriage and there were no children of the marriage and couples for whom the woman was a widow when marrying.

Table 5.1 Type of marriage: 1860, 1870, 1880 and 1890 marriage cohorts, Tasmania

Marriage cohort	1860	1870	1880	1890
Type of marriage	Number			
Widow at marriage	104	102	93	81
Wife's first marriage, no children	86	79	92	102
Wife's marital status unknown, no children	41	17	5	4
Wife's first marriage with children				
Complete	256	283	417	529
Incomplete	121	122	156	162
Unobserved	75	40	59	50
Premarital births	30	30	29	24
Total	713	673	846	952
	Percentage			
Widow at marriage	14.6	15.2	11.0	8.5
Wife's first marriage, no children	12.1	11.7	10.9	10.7
Wife's marital status unknown, no children	5.8	2.5	0.6	0.4
Wife's first marriage with children	67.6	70.6	78.1	80.4
Complete	53.1	59.6	63.1	69.2
Incomplete	25.1	25.7	23.6	21.2
Unobserved	15.6	8.4	8.9	6.5
Premarital births	6.2	6.3	4.4	3.1
Total	100.0	100.0	100.0	100.0

Women who were in their first marriage and had children of that marriage accounted for two-thirds of women marrying in 1860, but this rose to 80 per cent by 1890 (Table 5.1).

Of this group, the proportion for whom both partners survived the wife's childbearing years—the *complete* group—increased from just over half in 1860 to around two-thirds in 1890. For almost all these couples, both husband and wife survived until the wife turned 50 years of age. However, as noted, there was a small proportion where both partners did not survive until the wife turned 50 but there was a very high probability the couple had completed their childbearing.

The proportion of couples where the husband and/or wife died before the wife turned 50 and who had not completed their childbearing—the *incomplete* group—fell slightly, from 25.1 per cent in 1860 to 21.2 per cent in 1890. In the 1860 and 1880 cohorts, a higher proportion of husbands than wives died, whereas a higher proportion of wives than husbands died in the other two cohorts (Appendix A: Table A.16). A small number of couples in the *incomplete* group were separated or divorced.

The *unobserved* group—that is, couples whom I could not trace to the end of the wife's childbearing years—accounted for 15.6 per cent of couples with children in the 1860 cohort, but that fell to 6.5 per cent in the 1890 cohort (Table 5.1). The relatively high proportion of 'unknown' couples in the 1860 cohort reflects the difficulty of tracing these couples compared with couples in the other cohorts.

Most *couples with premarital births* had one or more births before marriage. Only a small proportion were couples where the wife had two or more ex-nuptial births with a man other than the husband. The proportion of couples with premarital births halved from 6.2 per cent in 1860 to 3.1 per cent in 1890 (Table 5.1). Some of these couples survived the wife's childbearing years; in others, one spouse died, while others had unobserved outcomes. As discussed previously, these couples are excluded from the fertility analysis.

Widows made up a much larger proportion of the women marrying in the early cohorts, accounting for around 15 per cent of women marrying in 1860 and 1870, but only 8.5 per cent in 1890 (Table 5.1).

Women in their first marriage with no children of that marriage accounted for 11–12 per cent of every marriage cohort (Table 5.1).

In every marriage cohort, there was a small proportion of *women without children whose marital status was unknown* (Table 5.1). However, the proportion dropped from 5.8 per cent of women in the 1860 cohort to 0.4 per cent in the 1890 cohort, with the improvement in the recording of marital status over the period. Around half of these women were aged 25 years and older, suggesting they may have been widows.

Characteristics of the complete group

Data on the detailed characteristics of the incomplete and unknown groups can be found in Moyle (2015: Appendix Tables A5.10–A5.26).

Marital status of husband and wife

It is difficult to comment on the marital status of men marrying in the two earlier marriage cohorts, because so many of the data are missing. However, in 1880 and 1890, almost all women married bachelors, with only a very small proportion marrying widowers (Table 5.2).

Table 5.2 Marital status of husband and wife, complete group: 1860, 1870, 1880 and 1890 marriage cohorts, Tasmania

Marriage cohort	1860	1870	1880	1890
Marital status of husband and wife at marriage	Percentage			
Spinster, husband's marital status not given	35.5	25.1	0.4	1.7
Spinster married bachelor	57.0	69.6	92.8	94.1
Spinster married widower	7.4	5.3	6.7	4.2
Total (%)	100.0	100.0	100.0	100.0
Total (no.)	256	283	417	529

Wife's age at marriage

Legally, men and women who were single at marriage could not marry if they were under 21 years of age unless they had obtained their parents' consent to the marriage. Most women were young at marriage, with the mean age of 21.5 years (median 21.5) for the 1860 cohort, increasing to 23.1 years (median 22.3) for the 1890 cohort (Table 5.3).

Just under half of the women in the first three marriage cohorts were aged under 21 years at marriage, but this fell sharply to 31.2 per cent for the 1890 cohort. The proportion of women marrying as teenagers also fell markedly between the 1860 and 1890 cohorts, from 38.3 per cent to 21.4 per cent, while the proportion marrying at ages 25–29 years almost doubled over the four marriage cohorts. These differences are not explained by differences in the age structure of the population (Table 3.3, Appendix A: Table A.5), but may be related to the increase in the ratio of unmarried women to unmarried men in the marriageable age group.

Table 5.3 Wife's age at marriage, complete group: 1860, 1870, 1880 and 1890 marriage cohorts, Tasmania

Marriage cohort	1860	1870	1880	1890
Age at marriage	Percentage			
< 20 years	38.3	35.3	30.5	21.4
< 21 years	49.6	46.6	45.8	31.2
21–24 years	34.4	33.2	37.6	40.3
25–29 years	11.3	14.8	9.6	20.8
30–34 years	3.9	4.2	4.8	5.8
35–39 years	0.8	1.1	1.4	0.8
40–44 years	0.0	0.0	0.0	0.2
Missing	0.0	0.0	0.7	0.9
Total (%)	100.0	100.0	100.0	100.0
Total (no.)	256	283	417	529
Mean/median	Age at marriage			
Mean	21.5	22.0	22.0	23.1
Median	21.0	21.3	21.2	22.3

Note: Means and medians exclude missing data.

The high proportion of women in Tasmania marrying at a young age is consistent with trends in similar 19th-century frontier societies (Bean et al. 1992; Gauvreau 1992, cited in Vézina et al. 2014). The mean age at marriage for those marrying in the Saguenay region of Quebec, for example, was 21–22 years for those marrying in the second half of the 19th century (Vézina et al. 2014).

The somewhat later age of marriage for women in the 1890 Tasmanian cohort is similar to trends in other Australian colonies. Women marrying in Victoria in 1881 and 1891 and in South Australia in 1891 also married at somewhat older ages than in previous years (McDonald 1974). McDonald attributes this partly to the idea of a 'proper time to marry'—that is, the need to maintain living standards for the middle classes and the rising aspirations of the working class.

Husband's age at marriage

On average, men were five or six years older than their wives, with the mean age at marriage for men 26–27 years (Table 5.4). Mean age at marriage fell from 27.6 years (median 26.7) for the 1860 cohort to

26.2 years (median 24.5 years) for the 1870 cohort and then increased to 26.8 years (median 25.4) for the 1890 cohort. Unlike women, in every marriage cohort, only a small proportion of men married under the age of consent. The proportion of men marrying at age 35 and older was higher in 1860 than in the other three marriage cohorts, with 15.3 per cent of men aged 35 years or older in 1860 compared with 9–10 per cent in the other cohorts. This is consistent with changes in the age structure of the male population in Tasmania over this period, with the male population becoming younger between 1861 and 1891 (Table 3.4, Appendix A: Table A.6).

Table 5.4 Husband's age at marriage, complete group: 1860, 1870, 1880 and 1890 marriage cohorts, Tasmania

Marriage cohort	1860	1870	1880	1890
Age at marriage	Percentage			
< 21 years	9.8	11.3	7.7	8.3
21–24 years	31.3	42.8	44.6	36.1
25–29 years	31.6	23.7	29.5	32.5
30–34 years	12.1	12.4	9.1	14.0
35–39 years	9.0	4.9	5.0	4.2
40–44 years	3.5	0.7	1.4	3.0
> 45 years	1.6	2.8	0.7	0.8
Missing	1.2	1.4	1.9	1.1
Total (%)	100.0	100.0	100.0	100.0
Total (no.)	256	283	417	529
Mean/median	Age at marriage			
Mean	27.6	26.2	26.0	26.8
Median	26.7	24.5	24.8	25.4

Note: Means and medians exclude missing data.

Age difference between husband and wife

Although husbands were older than their wives on average, a slightly different picture emerges when looking at the actual age difference between spouses (Table 5.5). The largest proportion of couples was those where the men were the same age as their wives or up to four years older, ranging from 36.7 per cent of the 1860 cohort to 46.1 per cent of the 1890 cohort. Men in the 1860 cohort were more likely to be much older than their wives: just over half of men in the 1860 cohort were five or more years older than their wives compared with around one-third in the other marriage cohorts. One-quarter of all men in the 1860 cohort were 10 or more years older than their spouse. In contrast, women in the 1860 marriage cohort were less likely to be older than their husbands: around 10 per cent of women in the 1860 marriage cohort were older than their husbands, compared with 17–18 per cent of wives in all other cohorts. These differences may be related to changes in the age structure of the male population over the period.

Table 5.5 Age difference between husband and wife at marriage, complete group: 1860, 1870, 1880 and 1890 marriage cohorts, Tasmania

Marriage cohort	1860	1870	1880	1890
Age difference	Percentage			
Wife 5 or more years older	1.2	1.1	3.2	2.3
Wife 1–4 years older	8.6	16.6	13.7	16.1
Same age or husband 1–4 years older	36.7	43.5	44.8	46.1
Husband 5–9 years older	27.3	20.1	24.5	20.8
Husband 10–14 years older	16.8	11.0	8.4	9.2
Husband 15 or more years older	8.2	6.4	3.8	3.6
Husband's and/or wife's age unknown	1.2	1.4	1.9	1.9
Total (%)	100.0	100.0	100.0	100.0
Total (no.)	256	283	417	529

Religion

Almost all couples were married by a minister of religion, in either a church or a minister's house, although some couples were married by a minister in a private residence. Only four couples were married in a civil ceremony in a registry office—one in 1880 and three in 1890.

Couples were married according to several different types of religious rites (Table 5.6). Couples who married according to the rites of the Church of England or the United Church of England and Ireland are classified as *Anglican* and those married according to the rites of the Holy Catholic Church are classified as *Catholics*. *Presbyterians* are couples marrying according to the rites of the (Free) Presbyterian Church and the (Free) Church of Scotland. *Methodists* are couples who married according to the rites of the Wesleyan Methodist Church, the Primitive

Methodist Church and the United Free Methodist Church. *Other Nonconformists* are couples who married according to the rites of the Baptist Church, Congregationalist/Independent Church, the Christian Mission Church and those marrying in a civil ceremony. The composition of Other Nonconformists changed over the marriage cohorts, with Congregationalists/Independents accounting for almost all the group in the 1860 and 1870 cohorts, but Baptists making up half the group in the 1890 cohort (Moyle 2015: Table A5.16). A very small number of couples in all cohorts married in two ceremonies—as Catholics and according to the rites of another religion. I have classified these couples as Catholics for the purposes of the fertility analysis.

Anglicans made up just under half of couples marrying in 1860, but this fell over the four marriage cohorts to just under one-third in 1890 (Table 5.6). Catholics made up 9–12 per cent of couples in every marriage cohort and Presbyterians 13–17 per cent. Methodists and Other Nonconformists accounted for an increasing proportion of couples marrying in each cohort. Between 1860 and 1890, the proportion of Methodists increased from 13.3 per cent to 22.3 per cent, while that of Other Nonconformists increased from 11.3 per cent to 20 per cent.

Table 5.6 Type of religion at marriage, complete group: 1860, 1870, 1880 and 1890 marriage cohorts, Tasmania

Marriage cohort	1860	1870	1880	1890
Type of religion at marriage	Percentage			
Anglican	45.7	37.1	33.3	31.8
Catholic	12.5	8.8	12.5	10.0
Presbyterian	16.8	13.8	12.9	15.8
Methodist	13.3	19.1	23.3	22.3
Other Nonconformist	11.3	21.2	18.0	20.0
Missing	0.4	0.0	0.0	0.0
Total (%)	100.0	100.0	100.0	100.0
Total (no.)	256	283	417	529

It is difficult to compare the distribution of religion at marriage for the complete group with population data, since the census data are not disaggregated by age or sex and include persons under 15 years of age and over 45 years—that is, people who were not in the 'marrying ages' (Table 3.6). In both 1861 and 1870, Catholics accounted for around

22 per cent of the population of Tasmania, but the Catholic population consisted of a large proportion of Irish ex-convicts who would have been over 45 years of age (Alexander 2014).

Signing the marriage register

Both husband and wife signed the marriage register in most marriages, with the proportion increasing from 76.2 per cent in the 1860 cohort to 94.9 per cent in the 1890 cohort (Table 5.7). This increase reflects the introduction of compulsory education in 1868 and the subsequent increase in literacy over the period (Table 3.8). In only a very small proportion of couples, neither the husband nor the wife signed the marriage register, with the proportion falling from 6.6 per cent to 0.8 per cent between the 1860 and 1890 cohorts. These trends are very similar to population trends, with the proportion of the population (of any age) able to read and write increasing from 53.7 per cent to 70.3 per cent between 1861 and 1891 (Table 3.8). The proportion of couples in the 1890 cohort of whom both husband and wife signed the register (94.9 per cent) was very similar to the proportion of the Tasmanian population aged 20–29 years who could read and write (93.3 per cent) (TAS 1891: 04_90).

Table 5.7 Whether husband and/or wife signed the marriage register, complete group: 1860, 1870, 1880 and 1890 marriage cohorts, Tasmania

Marriage cohort	1860	1870	1880	1890
Signing the marriage register	Percentage			
Both husband and wife signed	76.2	80.6	86.8	94.9
Wife did not sign, husband signed	9.8	7.8	4.8	1.3
Husband did not sign, wife signed	7.4	6.4	7.0	3.0
Neither husband nor wife signed	6.6	5.3	1.4	0.8
Total (%)	100.0	100.0	100.0	100.0
Total (no.)	256	283	417	529

Occupation and socioeconomic status

As outlined in Chapter 4, the husband's occupation was obtained from the birth registration data or imputed from other sources. Data on married women's occupations were not available. In 19th-century Tasmania, married women were unlikely to work outside the home, although many women helped in the family business or on the farm and some women took in washing or sewing at home.

As noted in Chapter 4, for the bivariate analysis, I examined the husband's occupation and socioeconomic status according to his occupation at the birth of the first child, and for the multivariate analysis, I used the husband's occupation at the birth of each specific child. This is important since occupation and socioeconomic status could change over the course of the wife's childbearing years. The more births the couple had, the more information is available about changes in the husband's occupation. However, if a couple had a small number of births in a relatively short period, the opportunity to observe occupational change is very limited.

It is also important to note that the composition of various occupational groups may have changed between the marriage cohorts. For example, given the changes in farming that occurred in Tasmania in the second half of the 19th century with the growth of selectors, the waning importance of sheep farming and increasing importance of fruit growing, farmers in the 1860 cohort may have been quite a different group from those in the 1890 cohort.

The occupational data in the Tasmanian Civil Registration Database were classified to the detailed five-digit classification system of the Historical International Classification of Occupations (HISCO) and then to the nine broad HISCO occupational groups (HISCO 2013). Each HISCO code was then classified to one of the 12 occupational Historical International Social Class Scheme (HISCLASS) categories to obtain a measure of socioeconomic status (Van Leeuwen and Maas 2005).

In all four marriage cohorts, the largest proportion of men was engaged in mining, manufacturing and transport (Table 5.8). More than one-third of men in the 1860 and 1870 cohorts were engaged in agriculture, forestry, fishery and hunting, but this dropped to one-quarter in the 1880 and 1890 cohorts, with a corresponding rise in the proportions engaged in mining, manufacturing and transport. The proportion of men who were professional, administrative, clerical, sales or service workers was lowest in 1870, at 16.3 per cent, but had risen to 21 per cent by 1890.

These trends mirror changes in economic conditions in Tasmania over the period and are consistent with trends in the broad occupational data for the Tasmanian population (Appendix A: Tables A.8–10). Examination of the detailed occupational data in the four marriage cohorts (Moyle 2012) shows an increase in the diversity of occupations that occurred in late 19th-century Australia (McDonald 1974). New occupations—such as mining manager, railway porter, coffee house proprietor and pastry cook—appeared from 1880. Specialist shopkeepers, such as florists, tobacconists and wine merchants, also became more common, reflecting improving living standards.

Table 5.8 Husband's occupational group (HISCO) at the birth of the first child, complete group: 1860, 1870, 1880 and 1890 marriage cohorts, Tasmania

Marriage cohort	1860	1870	1880	1890
HISCO occupational group	Percentage			
Professional, technical and related workers	5.1	4.2	5.0	5.3
Administrative and managerial workers	1.2	2.5	2.6	4.5
Clerical and related workers	5.1	2.8	3.6	4.7
Sales workers	3.9	3.9	3.4	4.7
Service workers	2.0	2.8	3.4	1.7
Agriculture, forestry, fishery, hunting	35.2	41.0	27.8	26.3
Mining, manufacturing and transport	46.5	42.0	53.7	52.0
Missing	1.2	0.7	0.5	0.8
Total (%)	100.0	100.0	100.0	100.0
Total (no.)	256	283	417	529

In relation to socioeconomic status, based on HISCLASS, farmers accounted for around one-quarter of all men, except in the 1870 cohort, in which they accounted for more than one-third (Table 5.9). The proportion of men who were unskilled workers was 32.4 per cent in the 1860 cohort but fell to 25.6 per cent in the 1890 cohort, mainly because of the fall in the proportion of unskilled farm workers. The proportions of lower-skilled and of managerial, professional, clerical and sales workers increased between the 1860 and 1890 cohorts, from 7 per cent to 14 per cent for lower-skilled workers and from 16 per cent to 21 per cent for managerial, professional, clerical and sales workers. Skilled workers made up around 16 per cent of workers in all marriage cohorts. These data are not comparable with population census data because the census did not classify occupation by socioeconomic status; however, they appear to be consistent with the census data.

Table 5.9 Husband's socioeconomic status (HISCLASS) at the birth of the first child, complete group: 1860, 1870, 1880 and 1890 marriage cohorts, Tasmania

Marriage cohort	1860	1870	1880	1890
HISCLASS group	Percentage			
Higher managers (1)	0.0	1.1	1.4	1.3
Higher professionals (2)	3.1	2.8	4.6	4.5
Lower managers (3)	1.6	2.5	1.9	4.7
Lower professional and clerical, sales (4)	7.4	6.0	5.3	6.6
Lower clerical and sales (5)	3.9	3.2	4.8	3.8
Foremen (6)	0.4	0.0	0.0	0.0
Skilled workers (7)	16.4	14.5	17.3	16.1
Farmers (8)	27.0	36.4	24.0	23.3
Lower-skilled workers (9)	6.6	6.0	11.5	14.0
Lower-skilled farm workers (10)	0.4	1.1	1.2	0.0
Unskilled workers (11)	24.2	22.3	25.4	22.6
Unskilled farm workers (12)	8.2	3.5	2.6	3.0
Missing	0.8	0.7	0.0	0.0
Total (%)	100.0	100.0	100.0	100.0
Total (no.)	256	283	417	529

Note: Numbers in parentheses are the HISCLASS category numbers.

In Table 5.9, all men who gave their occupation as farmer are classified in the HISCLASS category 'Farmer (8)'. However, the occupation 'farmer' is difficult to classify, since the term can cover a wide range of circumstances (Van Leeuwen and Maas 2005). In 19th-century Tasmania, there was a group of gentlemen farmers, many of whom owned large properties in the Midlands (Reynolds 1969, 2012; Meikle 2011). They called themselves farmers but employed others to manage their landholdings. I reclassified farmers to the HISCLASS category 'Higher manager (1)' if the husband or wife was a member of these large landowning families identified in Boyce (2010) and Reynolds (1969, 2012). I also reclassified other men to this category who identified themselves as 'gentleman farmer' on their children's birth registrations if I could find information supporting their claim—for instance, their marriage was reported in a newspaper and they were named as an 'Esquire' or the 'son of an Esquire'. The number of farmers reclassified as 'Higher manager (1)' was 12 in 1860, 10 in 1870, 11 in 1880 and seven in 1890.

Because of small numbers in some HISCLASS groups, in the analyses that follow, the husband's socioeconomic status has been reclassified into five groups: *white-collar* (HISCLASS 1, 2, 3, 4 and 5); *skilled workers* (6 and 7); *farmers* (8); *lower-skilled workers* (9 and 10); and *unskilled workers* (11 and 12). With the reclassification of gentlemen farmers as higher managers, white-collar workers accounted for around 20 per cent of men in all marriage cohorts, while farmers made up around 22 per cent of every cohort except the 1870 cohort, of which they accounted for one-third (Table 5.10). The 1870 group of farmers probably included a large group of 'selectors', some of whom were unsuccessful at farming in the longer term.

Table 5.10 Husband's socioeconomic status at the birth of the first child, complete group: 1860, 1870, 1880 and 1890 marriage cohorts, Tasmania

Marriage cohort	1860	1870	1880	1890
Occupational status	Percentage			
White-collar	20.7	19.1	20.6	22.5
Skilled workers	16.8	14.5	17.3	16.1
Farmers	22.3	32.9	21.3	21.7
Lower-skilled	7.0	7.1	12.7	14.0
Unskilled	32.4	25.8	28.1	25.7
Missing	0.8	0.7	0.0	0.0
Total (%)	100.0	100.0	100.0	100.0
Total (no.)	256	283	417	529

As noted above, men did not necessarily stay in the same occupation for the duration of their wife's childbearing years. Around 40 per cent of men in the three earlier marriage cohorts who had more than one child changed their socioeconomic status some time between the birth of the first child and the birth of the last child (Table 5.11). Many also changed their occupation but stayed within the same socioeconomic status group. The patterns of change by socioeconomic status were varied: some men had the same socioeconomic status for most of the wife's childbearing years and then changed their occupation and status towards the end of this period; others had one occupation for the first few years, but changed their occupation and status for the remainder of the period; others changed their occupation and status at some time and then changed back to their previous occupation (and status) for the rest of the period; while others changed their occupation (and status) periodically.

Table 5.11 Occupational characteristics of husbands between first and last births for couples with more than one child, complete group: 1860, 1870, 1880 and 1890 marriage cohorts, Tasmania

Marriage cohort	1860	1870	1880	1890
Occupational characteristic	Percentage of total			
Changed occupational status	42.0	43.7	42.9	30.2
Was a farmer for some or all of the period	42.8	49.3	36.0	33.1

Note: Includes only couples with two or more children.

One reason for these changes may be that a large proportion of men were farmers at some time during this period (Table 5.11). Some of these men may have taken up a different occupation because they were unsuccessful at farming, while others may have been selectors, who often worked as labourers, miners or sawyers while they were establishing their farms in the rugged and inaccessible country in the north of Tasmania (Reynolds 2012). The discovery of precious minerals in various parts of Tasmania in the final three decades of the 19th century also encouraged men to leave their jobs and work as miners. The proportion of men who changed their occupational status and/or were ever a farmer was somewhat lower in the 1890 cohort. This is probably because the occupational data for 20th-century births were of much poorer quality and because people tended to have smaller families so opportunities to observe occupational change were more limited.

Geographic location

In examining the geographic area where the family lived, I used the location of the children's births rather than the location of the marriage. Couples were often married in a location different from that of the births of their first and subsequent children. For instance, a couple may have married in the bride's parents' house, but then gone to live in another location.

In 19th and early 20th–century Tasmania, most children were born in the parents' home, although a small number were born in private hospitals (lying-in homes). Births did not take place in public hospitals until well into the 20th century. Only nine of the 2,974 births to the 1890 cohort were in a public hospital. There is a small number of cases where it appears a woman may have come from the country to give birth in a hospital in Hobart or Launceston, but in almost all cases the location of the place of birth was the same as the location of the family's residence.

When I began to develop a classification of geographic location of the family's residence, I wanted to use a measure that discriminated between rural and more remote geographic areas and differentiated the population living in large towns such as Devonport and Beaconsfield from the population living in smaller hamlets. However, prior to 1896, although parents were required to register the 'place of birth', only the registration district was recorded on most birth registrations. Rural registration districts covered both regional towns and more remote areas. Boundaries often changed and the number of registration districts increased markedly between 1859 and 1913, from 30 to 55 (TAHO 2014). From 1896, the name of the place where a child was born was included on all birth registrations, probably because the 1895 *Registration Act* brought in a fine of £10 for parents who 'did not give to the Registrar … information of the particulars required to be registered' (TAS 1895). Even where a placename was given, this often covered a large area—for instance, a mining town and the agricultural areas surrounding that town. This made it impossible to develop a consistent, detailed geographic classification for the four marriage cohorts or even to develop a detailed classification for the last cohort.

For this reason, I assigned the Tasmanian births to an *urban* or *rural* category, with *urban* comprising the Hobart and Launceston registration districts and *rural* all other Tasmanian registration districts. Even this was not perfect, since both the Hobart and the Launceston registration districts contained some outlying rural areas, such as Glenorchy in the Hobart registration district. Births that occurred outside Tasmania were assigned to the category *Outside Tasmania*, as I did not always have the information to classify the location to an urban or rural category and numbers were relatively small.

While the bivariate analysis is based on the type of geographic location at the birth of the couple's first child, as noted, many couples were very mobile and had children born in different geographic locations. A couple could move from an urban area to a rural area, for instance, or from an urban area in Tasmania to another colony. Many couples also moved within rural areas—for instance, from the Tasmanian Midlands to the north-west of the island. It is very difficult to develop data on moves within rural areas of Tasmania because of the constant addition of new registration districts and changes in registration district boundaries. As with data on husband's occupation, the more births the couple had, the more information I have about their geographical mobility. As with socioeconomic status, the actual geographic location at the time of each child's birth is used in the multivariate analysis.

Consistent with the spread of the population in Tasmania, higher proportions of first births to all cohorts were in areas outside Hobart and Launceston (rural) than in the two cities (urban) (Table 5.12). In the last three marriage cohorts, around 60 per cent of first births were in Tasmanian rural districts, while 32–37 per cent were in urban areas. Only a small proportion of first births in all cohorts (4–8 per cent) were outside Tasmania.

Table 5.12 Type of location of first birth, complete group: 1860, 1870, 1880 and 1890 marriage cohorts, Tasmania

Marriage cohort	1860	1870	1880	1890
Type of location	Percentage			
Urban	42.2	32.2	37.2	35.9
Rural	51.2	60.1	58.5	59.0
Outside Tasmania	6.6	7.8	4.3	5.1
Total (%)	100.0	100.0	100.0	100.0
Total (no.)	256	283	417	529

In looking at geographic mobility, as measured by the location of couples' births, I developed a classification that categorised couples according to whether all their children were born in Tasmania, whether they had some births in Tasmania and one or more elsewhere or whether all their children were born elsewhere. The proportion of couples who had all births in Tasmania increased over the marriage cohorts, from 78.9 per cent to 88.7 per cent (Table 5.12). This was because of a decrease in the proportion of couples having some births in Tasmania and some elsewhere, from 15.2 per cent in the 1860 cohort to 7.4 per cent in the 1890 cohort. The proportion of couples who had all births outside Tasmania was very small in all cohorts, from 3–6 per cent.

Table 5.13 Location of all births, complete group: 1860, 1870, 1880 and 1890 marriage cohorts, Tasmania

Marriage cohort	1860	1870	1880	1890
Location of family births	Percentage			
All births in Tasmania	78.9	82.7	87.1	88.7
Births in and outside Tasmania	15.2	11.7	10.1	7.4
All births outside Tasmania	5.9	5.7	2.9	4.0
Total (%)	100.0	100.0	100.0	100.0
Total (no.)	256	283	417	529

Even using such a broad geographic measure, there is evidence that a substantial proportion of couples were mobile, particularly in the earliest cohort. In the 1860 cohort, one-third of all couples with two or more children changed their geographic location between their first and last births—for instance, they moved from an urban location to a rural location or from Tasmania to another colony (Table 5.14)

Table 5.14 Changes in type of geographic location (urban, rural, outside Tasmania) during the period between the first and last births for couples with more than one child, complete group: 1860, 1870, 1880 and 1890 marriage cohorts, Tasmania

Marriage cohort	1860	1870	1880	1890
Geographic mobility	Percentage			
Remained in same type of location	66.7	70.4	71.8	75.0
Changed type of geographic location	33.3	29.6	21.2	25.0
Total (%)	100.0	100.0	100.0	100.0
Total (no.)	243	270	408	504

Note: Includes only couples with two or more children.

Summary

This chapter has examined the characteristics of couples in the four marriage cohorts for whom women were in their first marriage with at least one child of that marriage and both husband and wife survived the wife's childbearing years. An examination of the characteristics of the incomplete and unobserved groups (Moyle 2015: 75–89, 212–18) found the three groups are very similar. This indicates that the complete group is representative of marriages in which the wife was in her first marriage and there were children of that marriage, thus making it appropriate to use this group to analyse the decline in marital fertility over the period.

Alf Gale. *Emma with son "Beau" (1915).*

Alf and Emma Gale (1890 marriage cohort) with their son Athol ('Beau'), Marrawah, Tasmania, 1915

Source: Stanley Discovery Museum, Stanley, Tasmania.

Joseph Harrington, train driver (1890 marriage cohort), Waratah, Tasmania, 1907

Source: Waratah Museum.

Eliza Fleming (1860 marriage cohort), Oatlands, Tasmania, c. 1880
Source: Oatlands History Room.

Childhood home of Joseph Lyons, son of Michael and Ellen Lyons (1870 marriage cohort), Stanley, Tasmania
Source: P. McDonald.

Woolmers House, Woolmers Estate, home of Thomas and Eleanor Archer (1890 marriage cohort), Longford, Tasmania
Source: P. McDonald.

Penghana School, Queenstown, Tasmania, c. 1900
Source: Eric Thomas Galley Museum, Queenstown, Tasmania.

Timber family, near Queenstown, Tasmania, c. 1895
Source: Eric Thomas Galley Museum, Queenstown, Tasmania.

Employees of the Oohan Silver Mine, Zeehan, Tasmania, 1894
Source: West Coast Pioneers' Memorial Museum, Zeehan, Tasmania.

Sheffield Women's Cricket Team playing a Devonport Team at Sheffield, Tasmania, 1906
Source: Kentish History Museum, Sheffield, Tasmania.

Queenstown Tennis Club, Queenstown, Tasmania, 1898
Source: Eric Thomas Galley Museum, Queenstown, Tasmania.

(47)

W. J. RENDELL,
Chemist and Druggist,
26, GREAT BATH STREET,
CLERKENWELL, LONDON, E.C.

PURE DRUGS AND CHEMICALS.
Malthusian Appliances and Surgical Instruments of all kinds.
PATENT MEDICINES, PROPRIETARY ARTICLES, ETC.

HIGGINSON'S SYRINGE,
Best make, with Reverse or Direct Current, 4s. 6d. post free.

"THE WIFE'S FRIEND" SOLUBLE PESSARY,
2s. per dozen, post free.

India Rubber Check Pessary,
2s. 3d. each post free.

Powder for Lotion as Recommended by Dr. Palfrey,
1s. 2d. post free.

Orders, Prescriptions, and Enquiries by Post receive prompt and careful attention.

W. J. RENDELL, from his central position, is exceptionally well placed for quickly obtaining any article not generally kept in stock.

26, GREAT BATH STREET, CLERKENWELL,
LONDON, E.C.

Advertisement by W.J. Rendell for female contraceptives, including Rendell's pessaries, in Annie Besant's book *The Law of Population*
Source: Besant (1887: 47).

(48)

The IMPROVED VERTICAL and Reverse Current SYRINGE.

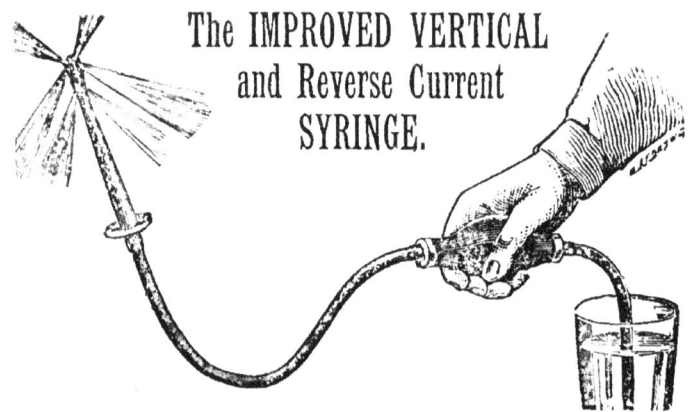

¶ The Improved Appliance is a powerful Enema of Higginson's pattern, fitted with a new Vertical and Reverse Current Vaginal Tube, producing a continual current treble the power of the ordinary tubes used for this purpose, thoroughly cleansing the parts it is applied to. It is to be used with injection of sufficient power to destroy the life properties of the spermatic fluid without injury to the person, and if the instructions are followed it can be used with success and safety.

Complete in Box, with particulars for Injection, and directions for use,
Post free, 3/6 and 4/6 each.

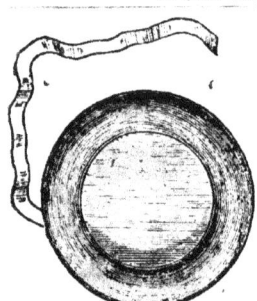

IMPROVED CHECK PESSARY.
RELIABLE, SAFE, AND DURABLE;

Is a simply devised instrument of pure, soft, medicated rubber, to be worn by the female (during coition) as a protection against conception. It is constructed on a common-sense principle, and strictly in accordance with the female organisation; can be worn any length of time with ease and comfort; is easily adjusted and removed, adapts itself perfectly, and no apprehension of it going too far or doing the slightest harm need be felt, and with care will last for years. If used with Quinine Compound, as supplied, is doubly reliable.

Post free with Directions for Use,
2s. 3d. each.

IRRIGATOR AND ENEMA APPARATUS.
VERTICAL AND REVERSE CURRENT.

This preventive apparatus can be used either in or out of bed, according to the needs of the case. The advantages of such instruments over syringes will be obvious to everyone, apart from the facts that the current is constant and its force can be regulated, it prevents the woman from taking a chill when used in bed, and can always be kept ready for use. Complete, with directions for use, 7s. 6d. and 10s. 6d. each, per Parcels Post,

MALTHUSIAN SPECIALITIES, in boxes of one dozen, 3/- post free.

E. LAMBERT & SON, Manufacturers, 38–44, Mayfield Rd., Kingsland, London.
Established 1860.

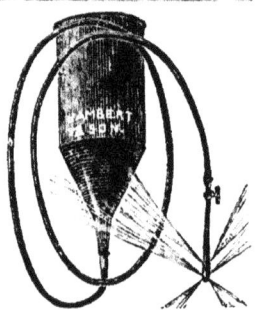

Illustrations of female contraceptives in an advertisement in Annie Besant's book *The Law of Population*
Source: Besant (1887: 48).

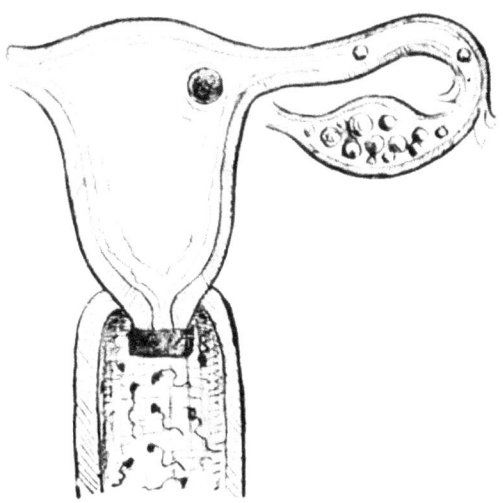

Preventative on Mouth of Womb.

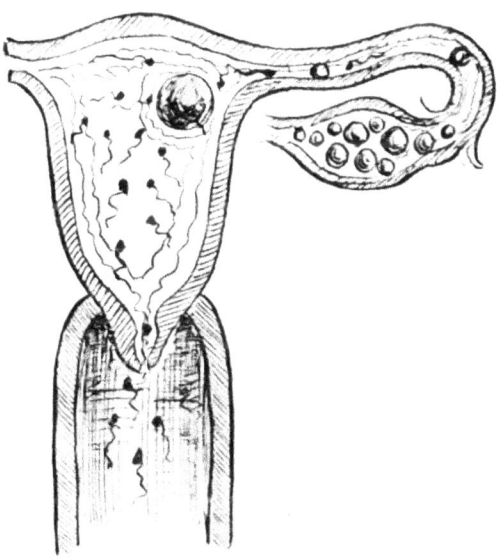

Preventative off, showing the Animalcula entering the Ovum.

Diagram of female reproductive system, with and without a contraceptive device inserted, in Brettena Smyth's book *The Limitation of Offspring*
Source: Smyth (1893: 25).

6

Fertility patterns of the couples in the marriage cohorts

In this chapter, I undertake a bivariate analysis of the fertility of the complete group in the four marriage cohorts. I look at patterns of fertility and infant/young child mortality, mean (median) numbers of children according to family characteristics and parity progression ratios.

Patterns of fertility and infant/young child mortality

Marriage cohort

According to theories of why fertility declined, there would be differences in the fertility behaviour of the various marriage cohorts because couples were having their children in very different periods in Tasmanian society.

There were marked differences between the earlier cohorts and the 1890 cohort in the mean (median) numbers of children ever born (Table 6.1). Families in the 1860 and 1870 cohorts tended to be very large, with a mean of 7.84 children (median 8) for the 1860 cohort and 7.98 (median 8) for the 1870 cohort. The average number of children was somewhat lower for the 1880 cohort, with a mean of 7.06 (median 7), but fell markedly for the 1890 cohort to a mean of 5.62 (median 5).

The 1860–70 levels of completed fertility are very similar to those for the completed fertility of couples in Utah who married about the same time, although fertility declined more slowly in Utah. Completed fertility in Utah declined from a mean of 8.11 for couples married from 1860 to 1874 to a mean of 6.44 for the 1895–1904 marriage cohorts (Mineau et al. 2002).

Table 6.1 Number of children ever born, complete group: 1860, 1870, 1880 and 1890 marriage cohorts, Tasmania

Marriage cohort	1860	1870	1880	1890
No. of children	Percentage			
One	5.1	4.6	2.2	4.7
Two	3.5	3.9	4.3	10.0
Three	5.9	5.7	8.2	12.9
Four	3.9	4.6	8.2	12.9
Five	7.4	5.3	13.2	15.7
Six	9.4	8.1	8.9	9.1
Seven	8.6	10.2	10.8	8.7
Eight	11.7	10.2	9.4	8.1
Nine	9.4	9.9	12.0	6.4
Ten	11.7	11.7	9.8	3.2
Eleven	6.6	9.5	4.8	4.5
Twelve	6.6	7.8	3.8	2.1
Thirteen	6.6	3.9	1.7	0.8
Fourteen	2.0	2.5	1.2	0.4
Fifteen	1.6	1.4	1.4	0.4
Sixteen	0.0	0.7	0.2	0.2
Total (%)	100.0	100.0	100.0	100.0
Total (no.)	256	283	417	529
Mean/median	Number of children ever born			
Mean	7.84	7.98	7.06	5.62
Median	8	8	7	5

A relatively large proportion of couples in the 1860 and 1870 cohorts had very large families, with 35.2 per cent of the 1860 cohort and 37.5 per cent of the 1870 cohort having 10 or more children (Figure 6.1). The proportion of couples with very large families fell markedly in the 1880 cohort, to 23 per cent, and then halved in the 1890 cohort, to

11.5 per cent. Similarly, the proportion of medium-sized families (4–6 children) increased from the 1870 to the 1880 cohorts and then to the 1890 cohort. The proportion of small families (1–3 children) remained about 14 per cent for the three earlier cohorts, but almost doubled to 27.6 per cent in the 1890 cohort. The proportion of large families (7–9 children) was about the same in the three earliest cohorts, but fell from the 1880 to the 1890 cohorts.

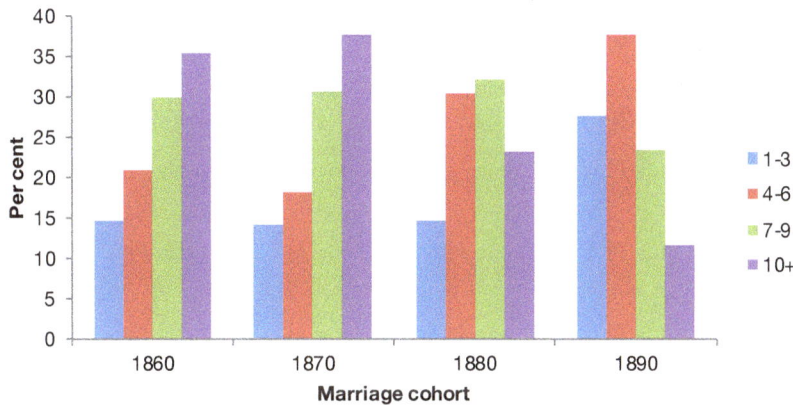

Figure 6.1 Proportions of families by number of children, complete group: 1860, 1870, 1880 and 1890 marriage cohorts, Tasmania
Source: Appendix A: Table A.17 (this volume).

Thus, the fall in the mean number of children from the 1870 to the 1890 cohorts was due to a decline in the proportions of large and very large families and an increase in the proportions of small and medium-sized families. This is consistent with trends in the fertility decline for Australia as a whole (see Figure 2.5). The decline in fertility from the 1870 to the 1880 cohorts was different from the decline from the 1880 to the 1890 cohorts. The decrease in the proportion of very large families and increase in the proportion of medium-sized families began in the 1880 cohort, while the decrease in the proportion of large families and increase in the proportion of small families did not occur until the 1890 cohort. This suggests these two cohorts were stopping their childbearing at different parities. This will be investigated in the analysis of parity progression ratios.

Multiple births

The number of children ever born to a mother is not necessarily the same as her number of pregnancies because of the incidence of multiple births. The proportions of families in the four marriage cohorts having multiple births was small, ranging from 8.6 per cent in the 1860 cohort to 4.3 per cent in the 1890 cohort (Table 6.2). The fall in the proportion of couples with multiple births is related to the fall in the proportion of large families and in the mother's age at last birth (see Table 7.3), since there are higher rates of twins at high parities and/or where mothers are older (Rao 1978). Twins made up only a tiny proportion of all pregnancies, falling from 1.3 per cent in the 1860 cohort to 0.8 per cent in the 1890 cohort.

Most multiple births were of twins, although one couple in the 1880 cohort and one in the 1890 cohort had triplets. Some families had more than one set of twins. One couple in the 1860 cohort, three in the 1870 cohort and two in the 1880 cohort had two sets of twins, while one couple in the 1860 cohort had three sets of twins.

Table 6.2 Couples with multiple births, complete group: 1860, 1870, 1880 and 1890 marriage cohorts, Tasmania

Marriage cohort	1860	1870	1880	1890
Type of family	Percentage			
Multiple birth/s	8.6	8.5	5.0	4.3
Singletons only	91.4	91.5	94.7	95.7
Total (%)	100.0	100.0	100.0	100.0
Total (no.)	256	283	417	529

In all the Tasmanian marriage cohorts, couples with twins tended to have larger families than couples with singleton births only (Table 6.3). The difference between the two types of families was largest for the 1890 cohort, with families with twins having a mean of 8.13 children (median 8) and those without twins a mean of 5.51 (median 5). Fertility fell for both groups from the 1870 to the 1880 cohorts, although the fall in fertility was steeper from the 1880 to the 1890 cohorts.

A study of women born in Utah between 1807 and 1899 found that mothers with twins tended to have larger families than other mothers (Robson and Smith 2011). The authors concluded that mothers of twins had higher fecundity because of their genetic make-up (Robson and Smith 2012).

Table 6.3 Mean and median numbers of children by singleton/multiple births, complete group: 1860, 1870, 1880 and 1890 cohorts, Tasmania

Marriage cohort	1860	1870	1880	1890
Multiple births	Mean			
Twins in family[1]	9.00	9.50	9.19	8.13
Singleton only	7.73	7.84	6.95	5.51
	Median			
Twins in family	8.5	10	10	8
Singleton only	8	8	7	5

[1] Means are illustrative only, because of small numbers in this group—that is, in 1860, n = 22; in 1870, n = 24; in 1880, n = 21; in 1890, n = 2.

Deaths of infants and children under five years

In Tasmania as a whole, there were large fluctuations in infant mortality for the period 1860–99, but the overall trend 'remained fairly flat' (Kippen 2002c: 65). In contrast, mortality of children aged one to 14 years fell over the same period, although there were some large annual fluctuations due to epidemics of measles and scarlet fever.

Consistent with these trends, in every marriage cohort, there were between 64 and 74 infant deaths per 1,000 births (Table 6.4). In every cohort, male infants were more likely to die than female infants—for example, in the 1860 cohort, there were 70 infant deaths per 1,000 male births compared with 56 infant deaths per 1,000 female births. The rates of young children dying aged between one and four years were smaller and fell for each subsequent marriage cohort, from 45 deaths per 1,000 children in the 1860 cohort to 22 deaths per 1,000 in the 1890 cohort.

Table 6.4 Infant and child mortality rates, complete group: 1860, 1870, 1880 and 1890 marriage cohorts, Tasmania

Marriage cohort	1860	1870	1880	1890
Type of death	Per 1,000			
Infant deaths (< 1 year)	64	70	74	64
Child deaths (1–4 years)	45	40	30	22
Total births (no.)	2,008	2,259	2,946	2,974

Note: Rates for infant deaths are calculated per 1,000 live births; for child deaths, per 1,000 children reaching age one.

The proportion of births where children died in infancy was lower for the 1860 cohort than the 1870 and 1880 cohorts: 64 infant deaths per 1,000 births compared with 70 and 74, respectively. This may be due to a change in the practice of defining a birth as either a live birth or a stillbirth, as discussed in Chapter 4.

While the trends in infant mortality for the complete group are consistent with the trends for Tasmania overall, the infant mortality rates are lower. The Tasmanian infant mortality rates 'ranged from 90 to 140 deaths per 1,000 male births, and 70 to 140 deaths per 1,000 female births' for the period 1860–99 (Kippen 2002c: 65). However, it is important to note that births to the complete group accounted for only a proportion of Tasmanian births—that is, total registered births to the complete group made up an estimated 50–60 per cent of all registered births in Tasmania in any year.

It is likely infant mortality rates for couples in which both partners survived the wife's childbearing years were lower than for other groups giving birth in the same period, possibly because these families were healthier. Infant mortality rates for the incomplete group were higher than for the complete group in every marriage cohort and for the unobserved group in the first two marriage cohorts (Appendix A: Tables A.18, A.19). A study of maternal and infant mortality in New York State in the 1930s found infants were 5.5 times as likely to die within the first month of life when their mother died in childbirth (Yerushalmy et al. 1940). In 19th-century New South Wales and Victoria, infant mortality rates for ex-nuptial children were markedly higher than for children born in wedlock over the period (NSW 1904a; Swain and Howe 1995).

Although the proportion of infants and young children who died was relatively small, the proportion of families who experienced the death of an infant and/or young child was much higher. In the 1860 cohort, half of all couples experienced the death of an infant and/or young child, with 34.8 per cent experiencing the death of an infant and 25 per cent the death of a young child (Table 6.5). The proportion of families experiencing the death of an infant and/or young child fell markedly in subsequent marriage cohorts, from 51.6 per cent for the 1860 cohort to 34.4 per cent for the 1890 cohort. This was mainly due to a fall in the proportion of couples experiencing the death of a young child.

Table 6.5 Proportion of families with at least one infant and/or child death, complete group: 1860, 1870, 1880 and 1890 marriage cohorts, Tasmania

Marriage cohort	1860	1870	1880	1890
Infant/child death in family	Percentage			
Infant death/s (< 1 year)	34.8	34.6	33.6	26.7
Child death/s (1–4 years)	25.0	24.7	17.5	11.2
Infant and/or child death/s (< 5 years)	51.6	49.5	45.3	34.4
Total families (no.)	256	283	417	529

Of all families who experienced the death of an infant and/or young child, most experienced only one death, with the proportion about 60 per cent for the 1860 and 1870 cohorts and increasing to 72 per cent for the 1890 cohort (Table 6.6). The proportion experiencing three or more deaths was about 15 per cent in the earliest three cohorts but fell to 7.6 per cent in the 1890 cohort. This is related to the marked fall in the number of very large families, since families with three or more deaths tended to be those with nine or more children. For instance, in the 1870 cohort, 18 of the 20 families who experienced the deaths of three or more infants and/or young children had nine or more children. This is consistent with findings about the relationship between high fertility and high infant mortality discussed in Chapter 1.

Table 6.6 Number of deaths for families experiencing at least one death of an infant and/or young child, complete group: 1860, 1870, 1880 and 1890 marriage cohorts, Tasmania

Marriage cohort	1860	1870	1880	1890
Number of deaths	Percentage			
One	61.4	57.9	66.1	72.0
Two	23.5	27.9	18.5	20.3
Three	9.1	6.4	9.5	5.5
Four	3.8	2.9	3.2	1.6
Five or more	2.3	5.0	2.7	0.5
Total (%)	100.0	100.0	100.0	100.0
Total families (no.)	132	140	189	182

Children ever born

In this section, I look at mean and median numbers of children ever born according to family characteristics that relate to the theories of fertility decline discussed in Chapter 1 or are associated with a woman's fecundity. These characteristics are: wife's age at marriage, the age difference between husbands and wives, socioeconomic status, type of geographic location, religion and literacy.

Wife's age at marriage

In examining the mean (median) number of children by women's age at marriage, because of the small numbers of women marrying at older ages, age at marriage is divided into three categories: under 20 years, 20–24 years and 25 years or older. I have used the category under 20 years for the youngest group because I wanted to look at women who married as teenagers, rather than using the category under 21 years, which refers to the group that required their parents' consent to marry.

Table 6.7 Mean and median numbers of children by mother's age at marriage, complete group: 1860, 1870, 1880 and 1890 marriage cohorts, Tasmania

Marriage cohort	1860	1870	1880	1890
Age at marriage	Mean			
< 20 years	9.38	9.51	8.42	7.33
20 to < 25 years	7.65	7.77	6.87	5.64
25+ years	4.73	5.77	5.11	4.32
	Median			
< 20 years	10	10	8	7
20 to < 25 years	8	8	7	5
25+ years	5	5	5	4

Note: Excludes three women in the 1880 cohort and five in the 1890 cohort for whom age at marriage was missing.

In all marriage cohorts, women who married at younger ages had substantially higher mean (median) numbers of children than other women (Table 6.7). In the 1870 cohort, for example, the mean number of children for women marrying under the age of 20 was 9.51 (median 10), compared with a mean of 7.77 (median 8) for women marrying aged 20–24 years and 5.77 (median 5) for women marrying at age 25 and older. While the mean (median) number of children fell for all women across the cohorts, it fell markedly for woman marrying under 25 years of age.

Age difference between husbands and wives

The relationship between fertility and the age difference between husband and wife is affected by the wife's age at marriage, since women who are older than their husbands are likely to be older at marriage and those with much older husbands are likely to be younger at marriage. For this reason, I examine the relationship between fertility and the age difference between husbands and wives for women who married at ages 20–24 years.

Table 6.8 Mean and median numbers of children by difference in age between husbands and wives for women marrying aged 20–24 years, complete group: 1860, 1870, 1880 and 1890 marriage cohorts, Tasmania

Marriage cohort	1860	1870	1880	1890
Difference in age	Mean			
Wife older[1]	8.62	7.21	6.80	5.88
Same age or husband 1–4 years older	7.91	8.37	7.03	5.49
Husband 5 or more years older	7.23	7.11	6.74	5.83
	Median			
Wife older	8	7	7	6
Same age or husband 1–4 years older	8	9	7	5
Husband 5 or more years older	7	7	7	5

[1] Means for 1860 and 1870 are illustrative only because of small numbers in the group — that is, n = 13 for 1860 and n = 28 for 1870.

Note: There are three women in the 1880 cohort and five in the 1890 cohort for whom age is missing. Also excludes one couple in the 1860 cohort, two in the 1870 cohort, four in the 1880 cohort and two in the 1890 cohort for whom age of husband is missing.

There were no consistent differences in fertility across the marriage cohorts according to the age difference between husband and wife (Table 6.8). In the two earliest cohorts, couples where the husband was much older than the wife had fewer children on average than couples where the husband was the same age or one to four years older. In the 1880 cohort, couples where the wife was older than the husband or the husband was much older than the wife had fewer children on average than couples where the husband was the same age or one to four years older, although the differences were relatively small. In the 1890 cohort, however, couples of the same age or where the husband was one to four years older had slightly fewer children on average than other couples: they had a mean of 5.49 (median 5) children compared with a mean of 5.88 (median 6) for couples where the wife was older than the husband and 5.83 (median 5) for couples where the husband was much older than the wife.

Socioeconomic status

While fertility declined for every socioeconomic group across the four marriage cohorts, there were marked differences in the mean (and median) numbers of children according to the husband's socioeconomic status (Table 6.9). White-collar workers had the lowest mean (median) numbers of children in every marriage cohort, while farmers and unskilled workers had the highest. In the 1860 cohort, the mean number of children for white-collar workers was 6.34 (median 6) compared with a mean of 9.02 (median 9) for farmers and 8.55 (median 9) for unskilled workers. The fertility of white-collar workers in 1860 was considerably lower than fertility overall (Table 6.1). White-collar workers in the 1860 cohort may have had lower fertility because they started to restrict their fertility earlier than other groups or because they married at older ages. This will be investigated in the multivariate analysis.

There were differences in the timing of the fertility decline between the socioeconomic groups, according to falls in the mean numbers of children. Fertility fell steadily for white-collar workers over the cohorts, with the largest fall from the 1880 to the 1890 cohorts. Fertility fell for skilled workers, farmers and unskilled workers from the 1870 to the 1880 cohorts onwards, but the decline was larger for skilled and unskilled workers from the 1880 to the 1890 cohorts and for farmers from the 1870 to the 1880 cohorts. While the means are illustrative only for the two earlier cohorts, lower-skilled workers' fertility declined from the 1860 cohort onwards, with the largest decline from the 1880 to the 1890 cohorts.

Table 6.9 Mean and median numbers of children by husband's socioeconomic status at first birth, complete group: 1860, 1870, 1880 and 1890 marriage cohorts, Tasmania

Marriage cohort	1860	1870	1880	1890
Occupational status	Mean			
White-collar	6.34	6.20	5.76	4.19
Skilled	6.98	7.29	6.69	4.90
Farmers	9.02	8.80	7.48	6.90
Lower-skilled[1]	7.44	7.05	7.09	5.35
Unskilled	8.55	8.86	7.92	6.35
	Median			
White-collar	6	7	5	4
Skilled	7	8	7	4
Farmers	9	9	8	7
Lower-skilled	8	7/8	7	5
Unskilled	9	10	8	6

[1] Means are illustrative only for lower-skilled workers in 1860 and 1870 because of small numbers—that is, in 1860, n = 18 and, in 1870, n = 20.

Note: Excludes three couples in the 1860 cohort, three in the 1870 cohort and two in the 1880 cohort for whom socioeconomic status was missing.

Type of geographic location

Couples living in urban areas had fewer children on average than those living in rural areas in all marriage cohorts (Table 6.10). In the 1860 cohort, couples in urban areas had a mean of 7.24 children (median 7/8) while couples in rural areas had a mean of 8.41 (median 9). Fertility fell steadily for urban couples from the 1860 cohort, while for rural couples it began to fall from the 1870 to the 1880 cohorts. For both urban and rural couples, fertility declined more from the 1880 to the 1890 cohorts than between earlier cohorts. By the 1890 cohort, the mean number of children for couples living in urban areas had fallen to 4.74 (median 4), while the mean for rural couples had fallen to 6.25 (median 6). Although the means (medians) are illustrative only, couples who had their first birth outside Tasmania had fewer children on average than couples who had their first birth in Hobart or Launceston, except in the 1860 cohort.

Table 6.10 Mean and median numbers of children by location at first birth, complete group: 1860, 1870, 1880 and 1890 marriage cohorts, Tasmania

Marriage cohort	1860	1870	1880	1890
Type of location	Mean			
Urban	7.25	6.81	6.25	4.74
Rural	8.41	8.81	7.74	6.25
Outside Tasmania[1]	7.24	6.41	4.89	4.48
	Median			
Urban	7/8	7	6	4
Rural	9	9	8	6
Outside Tasmania	8	6	5	4

[1] Means are illustrative only because of small numbers—that is, in 1860, n = 17; in 1870, n = 22; in 1880, n = 18; and in 1890, n = 27.

As noted previously, even if couples had one birth in Tasmania, they did not necessarily have all their births in Tasmania. In every cohort except the 1880 cohort, couples who had births in Tasmania and elsewhere had more children on average than couples who had all their births in Tasmania (Table 6.11). Fertility fell from the 1870 to the 1880 cohorts onwards for couples who had some or all of their births in Tasmania, although for couples who had births in Tasmania and elsewhere the fall in fertility was larger from the 1870 to the 1880 cohorts than from the 1880 to the 1890 cohorts. Although the means (medians) are illustrative only, couples who had all their births outside Tasmania had fewer children on average than other couples and their fertility fell from the 1860 to the 1870 cohorts onwards.

Table 6.11 Mean and median numbers of children by location of family births, complete group: 1860, 1870, 1880 and 1890 marriage cohorts, Tasmania

Marriage cohort	1860	1870	1880	1890
Type of location of family births	Mean			
All births in Tasmania	7.69	8.03	7.22	5.65
Births in Tasmania and elsewhere	7.92	8.61	6.35	5.95
All births outside Tasmania[1]	7.13	6.00	4.92	4.29
	Median			
All births in Tasmania	8	9	7	5
Births in Tasmania and elsewhere	8	8	6	5
All births outside Tasmania	8	5.5	5	4

[1] Means are illustrative only, because of small numbers in this group—that is, in 1860, n = 15; in 1870, n = 16; in 1880, n = 12; and in 1890, n = 21.

Religion

The relationship between religion and the number of children ever born is not very clear. Catholics had the highest mean (median) numbers of children in most marriage cohorts (Table 6.12). No other religious group consistently had the smallest mean (median) numbers of children, although Presbyterians and Other Nonconformists tended to have lower fertility than Anglicans and Methodists. The fall in fertility occurred later for Catholics than for the other religious groups. The mean (median) numbers of children fell from the 1880 cohort to the 1890 cohort for Catholics, while for Anglicans, Methodists and Other Nonconformists, fertility started to fall from the 1870 to the 1880 cohorts onwards. Fertility fell steadily for Presbyterians from the 1860 cohort to the 1890 cohorts. Methodists tended to have more children than the other Protestant groups and their fertility fell more slowly.

Table 6.12 Mean and median numbers of children by religion at marriage, complete group: 1860, 1870, 1880 and 1890 marriage cohorts, Tasmania

Marriage cohort	1860	1870	1880	1890
Type of religion	Mean			
Anglican	7.74	8.50	6.87	5.51
Catholic[1]	8.28	7.44	8.00	6.36
Presbyterian	7.95	6.97	6.22	5.27
Methodist	7.97	8.37	7.57	6.21
Other Nonconformist	7.51	7.62	6.73	5.12
	Median			
Anglican	8.0	9	7.0	5
Catholic	8.5	8	8.5	6
Presbyterian/Church of Scotland	8.0	7	6.0	5
Methodist	8.0	8/9	7.0	6
Other Nonconformist	8.0	7	7.0	5

[1] Means are illustrative only for 1870 because of the small number: n = 25.
Note: Religion missing for one couple in the 1860 cohort.

Literacy

In the analysis of literacy and fertility, I use data on whether the husband and/or wife signed the marriage certificate as an indicator of the husband and wife's literacy (Alter 1988). In examining mean (median) numbers of children by couples' literacy levels, I collapsed the categorisation used in Chapter 5 from four to two groups: both partners literate and husband and/or wife illiterate. This is because of small numbers in the illiterate groups, particularly in the two later cohorts.

In all marriage cohorts, the mean (median) numbers of children were considerably higher for couples where the husband and/or wife was illiterate compared with couples where both were literate, but the differences were much smaller for the 1890 cohort than for the earlier cohorts (Table 6.13). In the 1860 cohort, couples where the husband and/or wife was illiterate had a mean of 9 children (median 10), while the mean for couples where both were literate was 7.48 (median 8). By the 1890 cohort, the comparable means were 6 (median 6) for the illiterate group and 5.6 (median 5) for the literate group. Fertility fell for illiterate couples from the 1860 to the 1870 cohorts onwards and for literate couples from the 1870 to the 1880 cohorts onwards. For both literate and illiterate couples, the largest fall in fertility was from the 1880 to the 1890 cohorts.

Table 6.13 Mean and median numbers of children by parents' literacy, complete group: 1860, 1870, 1880 and 1890 marriage cohorts, Tasmania

Marriage cohort	1860	1870	1880	1890
Literacy type	Mean			
Husband and/or wife illiterate[1]	9.00	8.47	8.05	6.00
Both husband and wife literate	7.48	7.86	6.91	5.60
Literacy type	Median			
Husband and/or wife illiterate	10	9	8	6
Both husband and wife literate	8	8	7	5

[1] Means are illustrative only for 1890 because of the small number in this group: n = 27.

Parity progression ratios

In this final section, I examine parity progression ratios by marriage cohort and by three family characteristics that are important in relation to theories of fertility decline: socioeconomic status, type of geographic location and religion.

Marriage cohorts

Parity progression ratios—that is, the proportion of mothers at a given parity who went on to have another child—were fairly similar for mothers in the 1860 and 1870 cohorts (Table 6.14). However, parity progression ratios began to fall from the third to the fourth child onwards in the 1880 cohort and from the second to the third child onwards in the 1890 cohort. The largest percentage falls in progression between the 1870 and the 1880 cohorts were at parities five, nine and ten. For example, in the 1870 cohort, 93.5 per cent of those who had five children went on to have another child, whereas in the 1880 cohort, the corresponding proportion was 82.9 per cent. The differences in the percentage falls in parity progression ratios at low parities were larger between the 1880 and 1890 cohorts than between the 1870 and 1880 cohorts. For instance, 94.7 per cent of women in the 1870 cohort who had four children went on to have a fifth child, compared with 90.5 per cent of women in the 1880 cohort and 82.3 per cent in the 1890 cohort.

Table 6.14 Parity progression ratios, complete group: 1860, 1870, 1880 and 1890 marriage cohorts, Tasmania

Marriage cohort	1860	1870	1880	1890
Parity i	Parity progression ratios (i, i + 1)			
One	0.9531	0.9541	0.9784	0.9528
Two	0.9590	0.9593	0.9559	0.8950
Three	0.9359	0.9382	0.9128	0.8496
Four	0.9543	0.9465	0.9045	0.8229
Five	0.9091	0.9348	0.8292	0.7373
Six	0.8737	0.8930	0.8614	0.7940
Seven	0.8675	0.8490	0.8043	0.7514
Eight	0.7917	0.8221	0.7892	0.6906
Nine	0.7895	0.7910	0.6575	0.6458

Marriage cohort	1860	1870	1880	1890
Parity i	Parity progression ratios (i, i + 1)			
Ten	0.6667	0.6887	0.5729	0.7258
Eleven	0.7167	0.6301	0.6364	0.4667
Twelve	0.6047	0.5217	0.5429	0.4762
Thirteen	0.3462	0.5417	0.6316	0.6000
Fourteen	0.4444	0.4615	0.5833	0.6667
Fifteen	0.0000	0.3333	0.1429	0.0000
Sixteen	..	0.0000	0.0000	..
Total families (no.)	256	283	417	529

.. not applicable

Parity progression ratios can be used to calculate the percentage of mothers reaching each parity—that is, *proportion of mothers having 'i' children = proportion of mothers having 'i – 1' children * parity progression ratio 'i'*. This is a useful way of measuring the fertility and changes in fertility of different groups.

The fertility levels of the 1860 and the 1870 cohorts were very similar, with very small differences in the proportions of women reaching each parity (Figure 6.2). For example, 85.6 per cent of women in the 1860 cohort had four or more children compared with 85.9 per cent in the 1870 cohort, while 56.3 per cent of the 1860 cohort had eight or more children compared with 57.6 per cent of the 1870 cohort.

Fertility fell from the 1870 cohort to the 1880 cohort and then to the 1890 cohort. From the 1870 to the 1880 cohorts, the proportions of women reaching each parity began to fall steadily after parity four. In the 1870 cohort, for instance, 76 per cent of mothers had six or more children, compared with 64 per cent of mothers in the 1880 cohort, while for those with 11 or more children, the proportions were 25.8 per cent and 13.2 per cent, respectively.

There was a much larger fall in fertility from the 1880 to the 1890 cohorts, with the proportion of women reaching each parity dropping sharply after parity two. In the 1880 cohort, 85.4 per cent of mothers had four or more children compared with 72.5 per cent in the 1890 cohort, while 35 per cent of mothers in the 1880 cohort had nine or more children compared with 18.1 per cent in the 1890 cohort.

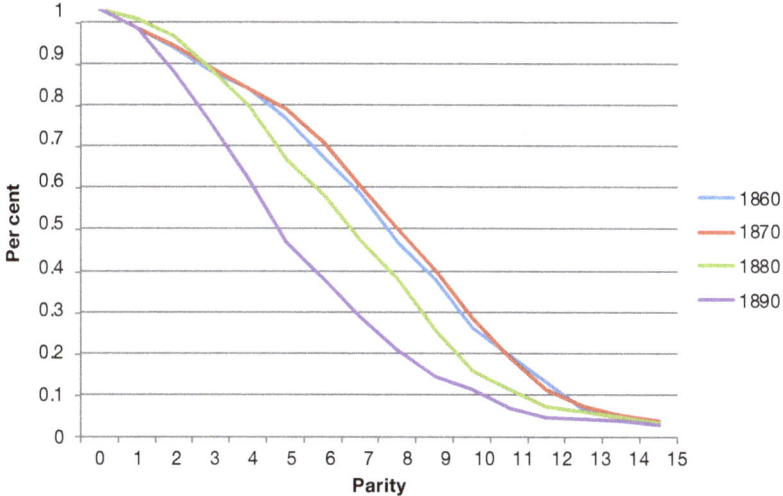

Figure 6.2 Proportions of women reaching each parity, complete group: 1860, 1870, 1880 and 1890 marriage cohorts, Tasmania
Source: Author's calculations.

Since the proportions of mothers reaching each parity were very similar in the 1860 and 1870 cohorts and the numbers in each cohort are considerably smaller than in the other two cohorts, these cohorts are combined in the fertility analysis that follows.

For each characteristic—socioeconomic status, geographic location and religion—the following analysis compares the proportion of mothers reaching each parity by the various groups for each marriage cohort, then looks at trends for each group across the marriage cohorts.

Socioeconomic status

Examining the proportion of mothers reaching each parity by husband's socioeconomic status shows differences in fertility among the various socioeconomic groups within each marriage cohort (Figure 6.3). In the 1860/70 cohorts, white-collar workers had the lowest fertility while farmers and unskilled workers had the highest. The largest differences in the proportions of women reaching each parity were between the white-collar, skilled and lower-skilled workers, on the one hand, and farmers and unskilled workers on the other. For instance, 69.2 per cent of white-collar workers had five or more children, compared with 76.2 per cent of skilled workers, 76.9 per cent of lower-skilled workers, 86.9 per cent of unskilled workers and 88.7 per cent of farmers.

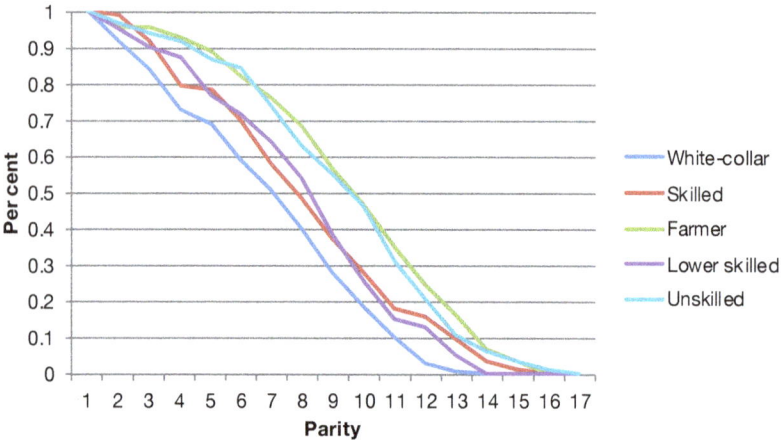

Figure 6.3 Proportions of women reaching each parity by socioeconomic status, complete group: 1860/70 marriage cohorts, Tasmania
Source: Author's calculations.

White-collar workers again had the lowest fertility in the 1880 cohort, but their fertility was substantially lower than the other four groups of workers (Figure 6.4). The fertility levels of farmers and unskilled workers were closer to those of the skilled and lower-skilled workers than in the earlier cohorts. The proportion of women in white-collar couples reaching parities higher than five was much smaller than for other groups. Only 45.4 per cent of white-collar couples had six or more children, compared with 57.7 per cent of skilled workers, 77.4 per cent of lower-skilled workers, 79.3 per cent of unskilled workers and 83.2 per cent of farmers.

White-collar workers still had the lowest fertility in the 1890 cohort, but the largest differences were between the white-collar, skilled and lower-skilled workers, on the one hand, and the farmers and unskilled workers on the other, particularly at higher parities (Figure 6.5). The proportions of farmers and unskilled workers with eight or more children, for instance, were more than double those of white-collar, skilled and unskilled workers: 43.5 per cent of farmers and 38.2 per cent of unskilled workers had eight or more children, compared with 9.3 per cent of white-collar workers, 14.1 per cent of skilled workers and 17.6 per cent of lower-skilled workers.

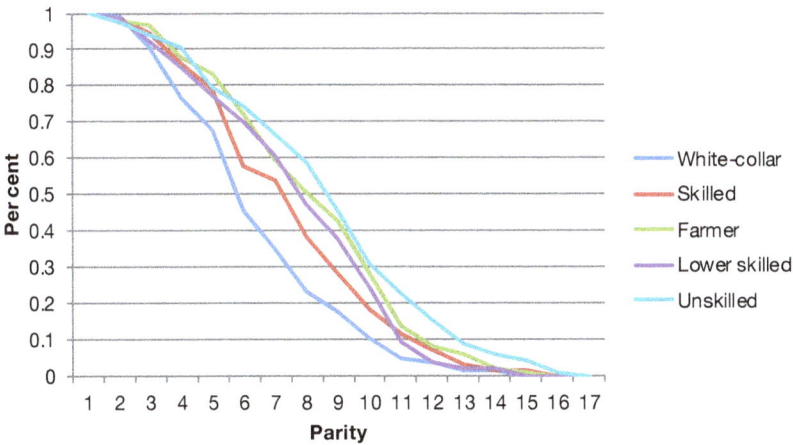

Figure 6.4 Proportions of women reaching each parity by socioeconomic status, complete group: 1880 marriage cohort, Tasmania

Source: Author's calculations.

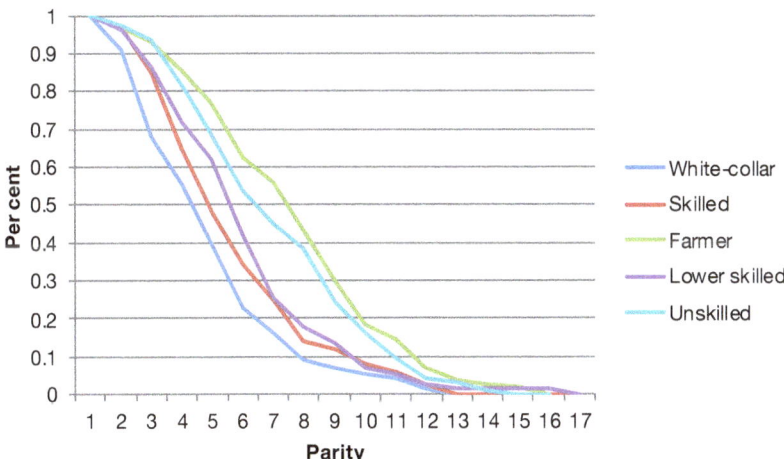

Figure 6.5 Proportions of women reaching each parity by socioeconomic status, complete group: 1890 marriage cohort, Tasmania

Source: Author's calculations.

Fertility fell for white-collar workers from the 1860/70 cohorts to the 1880 cohort (Figure 6.6). While the 1880 cohort had a somewhat higher proportion of women reaching the lower parities than the 1860/70 cohorts, the proportion of women at each parity fell steadily after the fifth. Fertility also fell between the 1880 and 1890 cohorts, with the proportions of mothers reaching each parity falling after parity one and falling sharply after parity two.

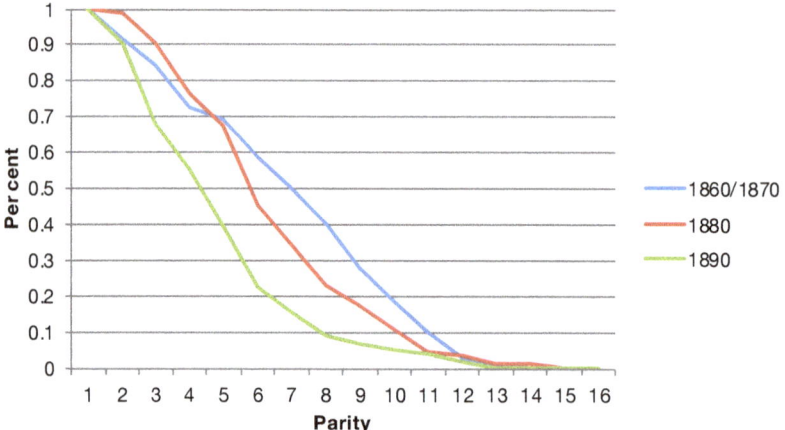

Figure 6.6 White-collar workers, proportions of women reaching each parity, complete group: 1860/70, 1880 and 1890 marriage cohorts, Tasmania
Source: Author's calculations.

Fertility fell somewhat for skilled workers from the 1860/70 cohorts to the 1880 cohort (Figure 6.7), with the proportion of women reaching each parity falling after parity five. The fall in fertility was much more substantial between the 1880 and the 1890 cohorts, with the proportions of women at each parity falling sharply after parity two.

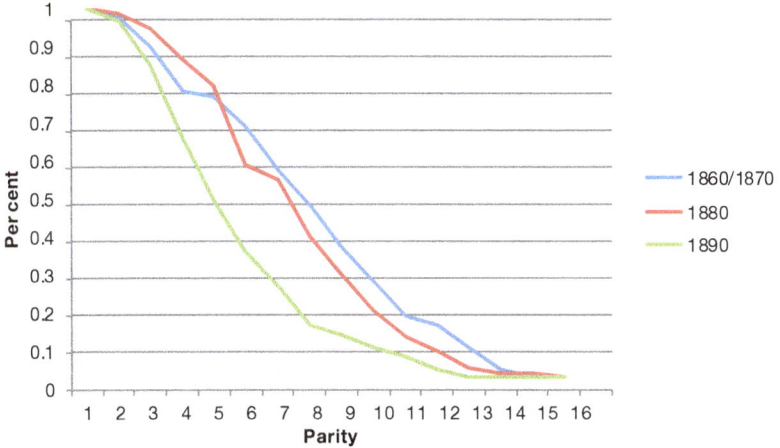

Figure 6.7 Skilled workers, proportions of women reaching each parity, complete group: 1860/70, 1880 and 1890 marriage cohorts, Tasmania
Source: Author's calculations.

In contrast, there was a substantial fall in the fertility of farmers' wives between the 1860/70 cohorts and the 1880 cohort (Figure 6.8). The proportion of women reaching each parity began to fall after parity three, but the differences were not large until after the sixth parity. Fertility also fell from the 1880 to the 1890 cohorts after parity four, but the differences in the proportions reaching each parity were not as large as between the earlier cohorts.

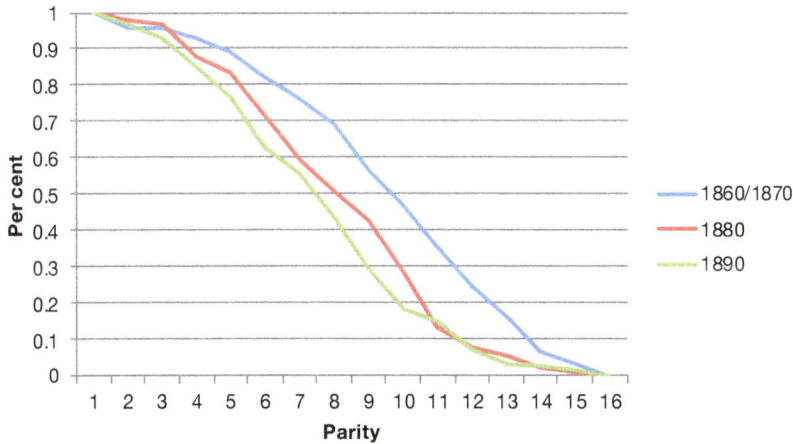

Figure 6.8 Farmers, proportions of women reaching each parity, complete group: 1860/70, 1880 and 1890 marriage cohorts, Tasmania
Source: Author's calculations.

The fertility levels of lower-skilled workers were very similar in the 1860/70 and 1880 cohorts, except for a fall in the proportions of women reaching very high parities in the 1880 cohort—that is, after parity 10 (Figure 6.9). Fertility fell markedly between the 1880 and 1890 cohorts, with the proportions of lower-skilled workers' wives reaching each parity dropping sharply after parity two.

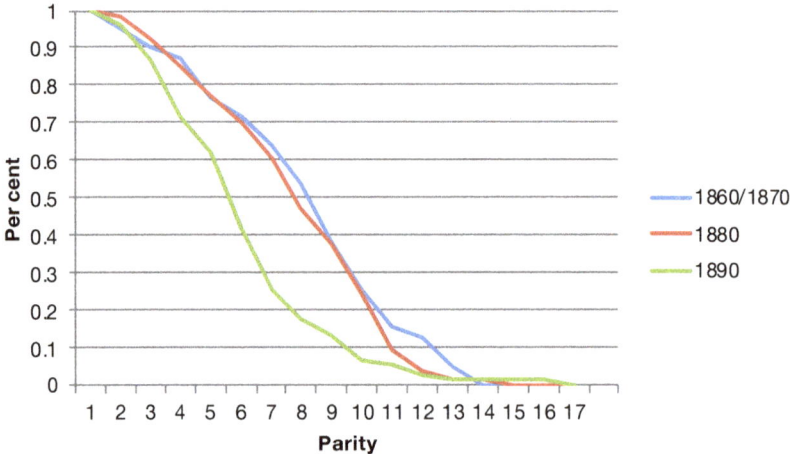

Figure 6.9 Lower-skilled workers, proportions of women reaching each parity, complete group: 1860/70, 1880 and 1890 marriage cohorts, Tasmania
Source: Author's calculations.

The large fall between the 1880 and 1890 cohorts may be related to changes in the composition of the lower-skilled group, with the 1890 cohort including men in the more 'modern' occupations of 'engine driver' and 'fireman–gas works'.

Fertility fell for unskilled workers between the 1860/70 and 1880 cohorts, with the proportion reaching each parity falling after parity four (Figure 6.10). The fall in fertility was much larger between the 1880 and the 1890 cohorts and occurred after parity three.

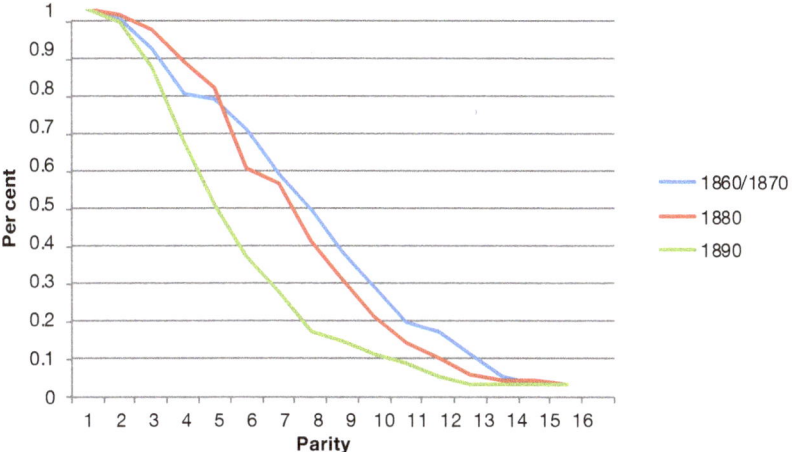

Figure 6.10 Unskilled workers, proportions of women reaching each parity, complete group: 1860/70, 1880 and 1890 marriage cohorts, Tasmania
Source: Author's calculations.

Type of geographic location

Women having their first birth outside Tasmania are excluded from this analysis because of the small numbers in the group.

In the 1860/70 cohorts, the proportions of women reaching each parity were lower for those living in urban areas than for those in rural areas at every parity after parity one, with the differences being greater at higher parities (Figure 6.11). The proportion of women in rural areas with four or more children was 90.7 per cent compared with 79.4 per cent for women in urban areas, while the proportions with nine or more were 56.2 per cent and 33.7 per cent, respectively. Urban women had a maximum of 15 children compared with 16 for rural women.

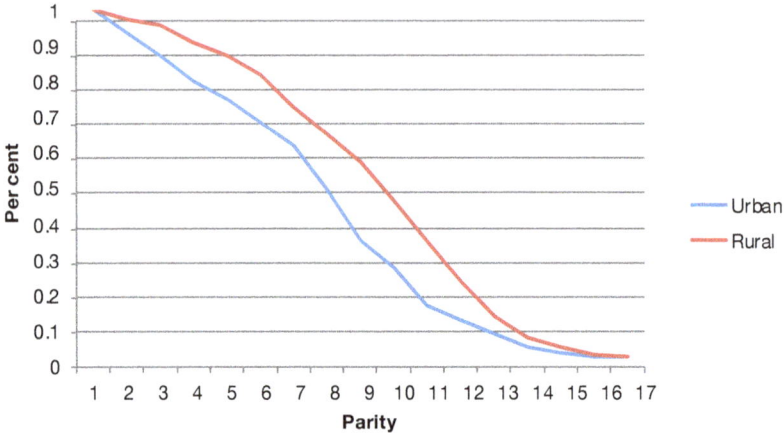

Figure 6.11 Proportions of women reaching each parity by urban/rural location, complete group: 1860/70 marriage cohorts, Tasmania
Source: Author's calculations.

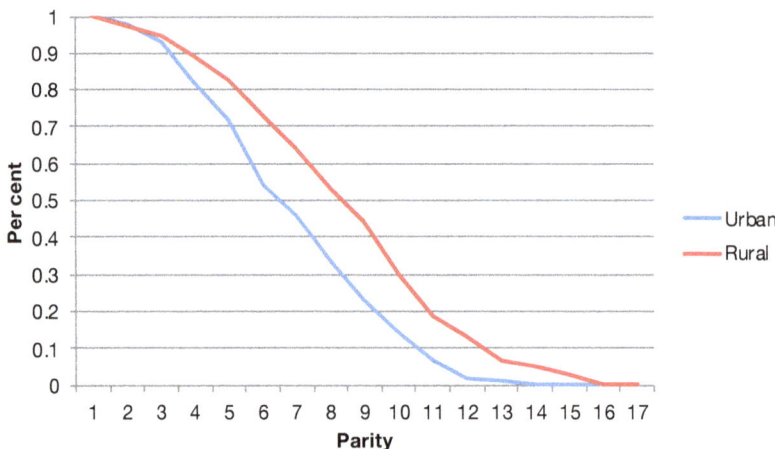

Figure 6.12 Proportions of women reaching each parity by urban/rural location, complete group: 1880 marriage cohort, Tasmania
Source: Author's calculations.

The fertility of urban women was also substantially lower than that of rural women in the 1880 cohort, although the proportions reaching each parity were similar up to parity three (Figure 6.12). As with the 1860/70 cohorts, the differences between urban and rural women's fertility were larger at higher parities. The proportion of rural women with four or more children was 88.9 per cent compared with 81.9 per cent for urban women, but the corresponding proportions for women with eight or more children were 53.3 per cent and 33.5 per cent, respectively. The maximum number of children fell to 13 for urban women but remained at 16 for rural women.

These trends continued in the 1890 cohort, with the proportions reaching each parity being lower for urban women than for rural women at every parity after parity one (Figure 6.13). In this cohort, however, the differences between the two groups were substantial at both low and high parities. For example, 90.6 per cent of rural women had three or more children compared with 79.4 per cent of urban women, while 24.4 per cent of rural women had nine or more compared with 10 per cent of urban women. The maximum number of children for rural woman remained at 16, while the maximum for urban women fell to 12.

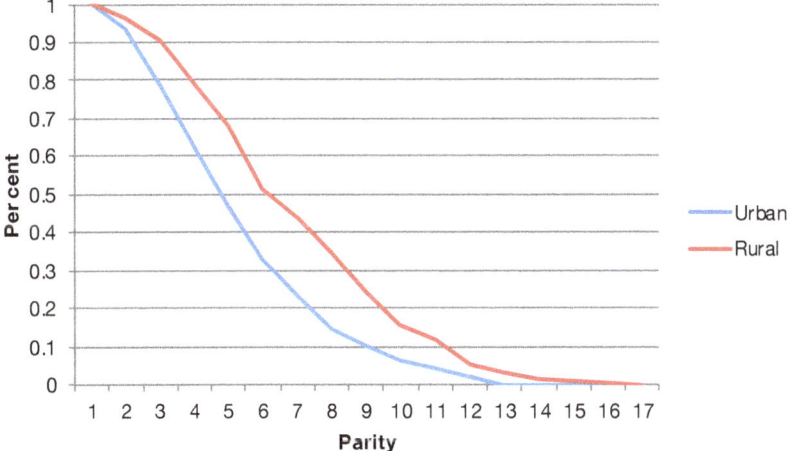

Figure 6.13 Proportions of women reaching each parity by urban/rural location, complete group: 1890 marriage cohort, Tasmania
Source: Author's calculations.

Fertility fell for urban women between the 1860/70 cohorts and the 1880 cohort (Figure 6.14). The proportions of women reaching each parity were slightly higher at low parities for the 1880 cohort compared with the 1860/70 cohorts, but they began to fall steadily after parity four.

There was a larger fall in fertility for urban women from the 1880 to the 1890 cohorts. Falls in the proportions of women reaching each parity were much larger between these two cohorts than the previous cohorts and occurred after parity one, with a sharp fall after parity two.

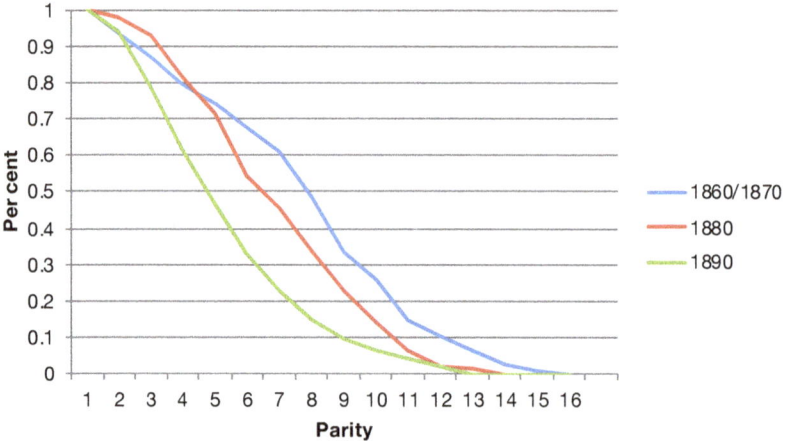

Figure 6.14 Proportions of women reaching each parity for couples living in an urban area, complete group: 1860/70, 1880 and 1890 marriage cohorts, Tasmania

Source: Author's calculations.

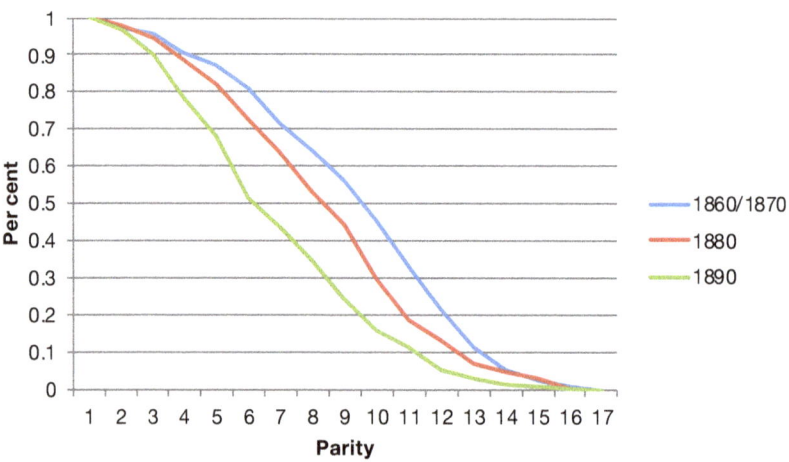

Figure 6.15 Proportions of women reaching each parity for couples living in a rural area, complete group: 1860/70, 1880 and 1890 marriage cohorts, Tasmania

Fertility also fell for women in rural areas from the 1860/70 cohorts to the 1880 cohort, with the proportions of women reaching each parity falling steadily after parity four (Figure 6.15). There was a more substantial fall in fertility between the 1880 and 1890 cohorts, with the proportion of rural women reaching each parity falling steadily after parity two.

Religion

There were no clear differences in the fertility of the various religious groups in the 1860/70 cohorts, although Other Nonconformists and Presbyterians tended to have lower proportions of women reaching each parity than other groups (Figure 6.16). Among Other Nonconformists, for instance, 69.7 per cent had five or more children, compared with 71.9 per cent of Presbyterians, 76.1 per cent of Methodists, 77 per cent of Anglicans and 80.4 per cent of Catholics.

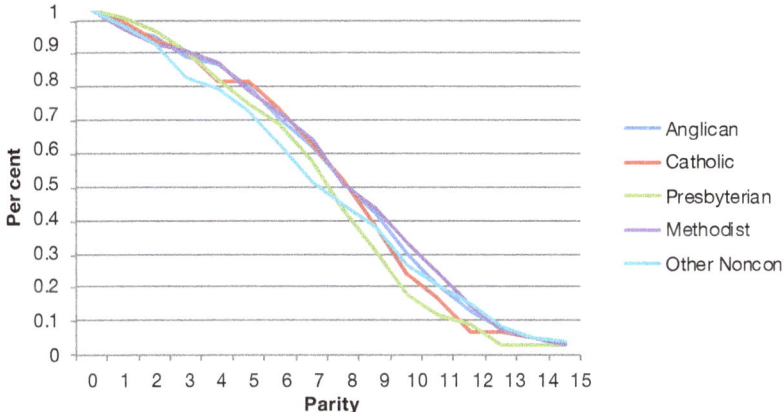

Figure 6.16 Proportions of women reaching each parity by religion, complete group: 1860/70 marriage cohorts, Tasmania
Source: Author's calculations.

Catholic fertility was substantially higher than that of other religious groups in the 1880 cohort, while Methodist fertility tended to be higher than that of other Protestant groups (Figure 6.17). Presbyterians tended to have the lowest fertility, although the proportions of women reaching higher parities were similar to those of Other Nonconformists. At lower parities, for instance, 78.4 per cent of Catholics had five or more children compared with 71.1 per cent of Methodists, 65.8 per cent of Other Nonconformists, 56.8 per cent of Anglicans and 53.7 per cent of Presbyterians. At higher parities, 25.5 per cent of Catholics had 10 or more children, compared with 18.6 per cent of Methodists, 12.2 per cent of Anglicans, 6.6 per cent of Other Nonconformists and 3.7 per cent of Presbyterians.

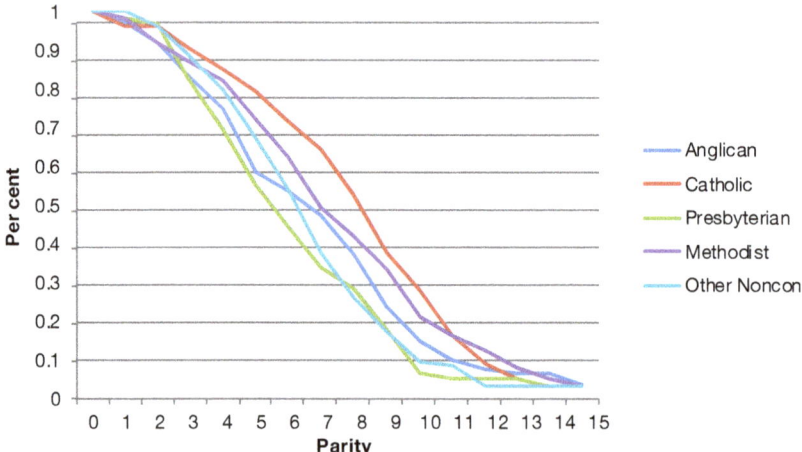

Figure 6.17 Proportions of women reaching each parity by religion, complete group: 1880 marriage cohort, Tasmania
Source: Author's calculations.

In the 1890 cohort, Catholics again had the highest fertility and Presbyterians and Other Nonconformists the lowest, with the proportions of Presbyterians and Other Nonconformists reaching each parity virtually identical at most parities (Figure 6.18). The proportions of Methodists reaching each parity were very similar to those of Catholics between parities five and seven. For instance, 70.1 per cent of Methodists and 69.8 per cent of Catholics had five or more children compared with 57.1 per cent of Anglicans, 52.4 per cent of Presbyterians and 52.3 per cent of Other Nonconformists. However, the proportion of Catholics with 10 or more children was higher than for other groups, at 18.9 per cent, compared with 13.7 per cent of Methodists, 10.1 per cent of Anglicans, 9.5 per cent of Presbyterians and 9.3 per cent of Other Nonconformists.

6. FERTILITY PATTERNS OF THE COUPLES IN THE MARRIAGE COHORTS

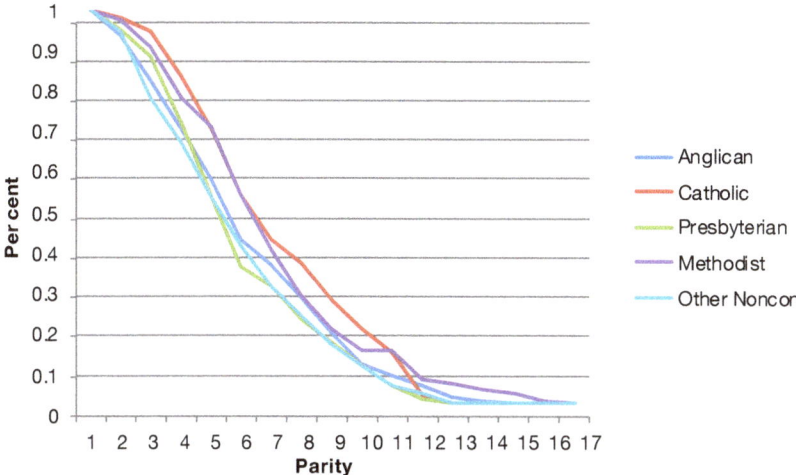

Figure 6.18 Proportions of women reaching each parity by religion, complete group: 1890 marriage cohort, Tasmania
Source: Author's calculations.

Fertility fell markedly for Anglicans from the 1860/70 cohorts to the 1880 cohort, with the proportion of women reaching each parity falling after parity three (Figure 6.19). Fertility also fell substantially in the 1890 cohort after parity one. The percentage differences between the 1880 and 1890 cohorts were higher at lower parities and lower at higher parities, compared with the differences between the 1860/70 cohorts and the 1880 cohort.

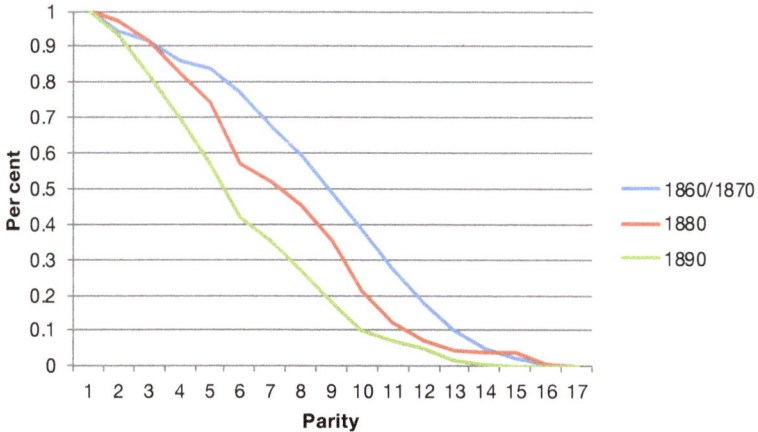

Figure 6.19 Anglicans, proportions of women reaching each parity, complete group: 1860/70, 1880 and 1890 marriage cohorts, Tasmania
Source: Author's calculations.

The fertility levels of Catholic women in the 1860/70 and 1880 cohorts were very similar, although the proportions of women reaching each parity were slightly higher in the 1880 cohort at some lower and some higher parities (Figure 6.20). Fertility fell substantially from the 1880 to the 1890 cohorts, with the proportion of Catholic women reaching each parity falling sharply after parity three.

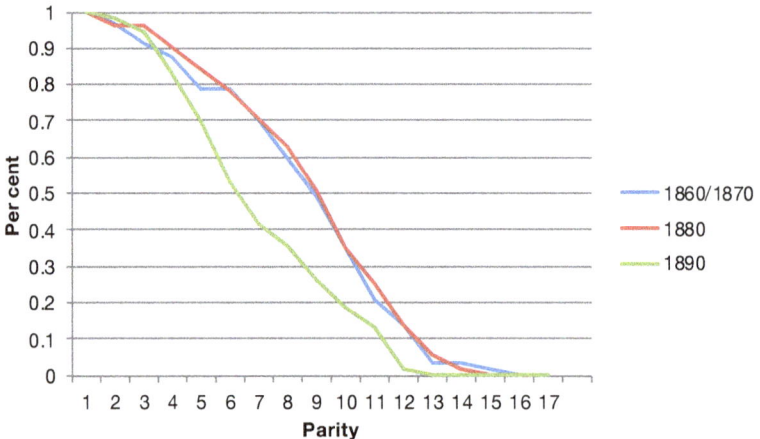

Figure 6.20 Catholics, proportions of women reaching each parity, complete group: 1860/70, 1880 and 1890 marriage cohorts, Tasmania
Source: Author's calculations.

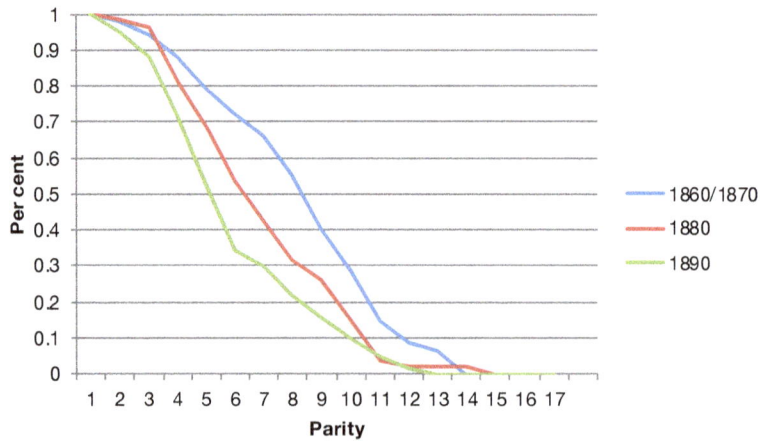

Figure 6.21 Presbyterians, proportions of women reaching each parity, complete group: 1860/70, 1880 and 1890 marriage cohorts, Tasmania
Source: Author's calculations.

Fertility fell for Presbyterians from the 1860/70 cohorts to the 1880 cohort, with the proportion of Presbyterian women reaching each parity falling sharply after parity three (Figure 6.21). The fall in fertility from the 1880 to the 1890 cohorts was not as large, but occurred after parity one, with steep falls between parities three and seven.

The fertility of Methodist women also fell from the 1860/70 cohorts to the 1880 cohort, although the falls were not as large as for Presbyterian or Anglican women (Figure 6.22). There was a steady fall in the proportion of women reaching each parity after parity four. The fall in fertility from the 1880 to the 1890 cohorts was much larger and occurred after parity three. In the 1860/70 cohorts, there were slightly higher proportions of Methodist women reaching the lowest parities—parities two and three—than in the two later cohorts.

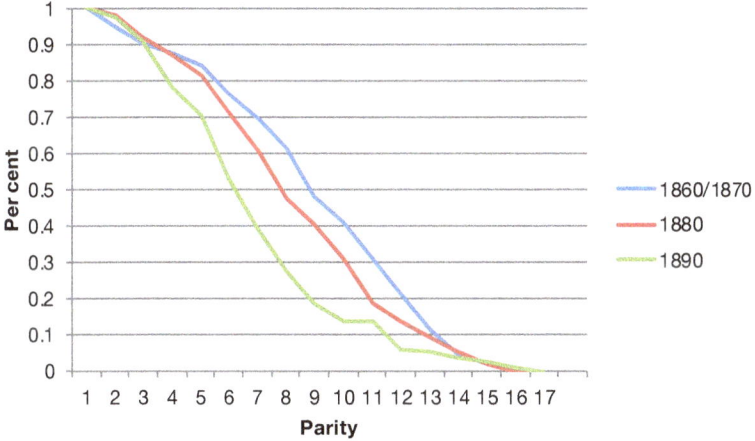

Figure 6.22 Methodists, proportions of women reaching each parity, complete group: 1860/70, 1880 and 1890 marriage cohorts, Tasmania
Source: Author's calculations.

Other Nonconformists' fertility also fell from the 1860/70 cohorts to the 1880 cohort, with the proportion of women reaching each parity falling sharply after parity five (Figure 6.23). The proportions of women reaching lower parities, however, were higher in the 1880 cohort than the 1860/70 cohorts. There was a large fall in fertility from the 1880 to the 1890 cohorts from parity two onwards. For women at higher parities, the falls were smaller between the 1880 and 1890 cohorts than between the two earlier cohorts.

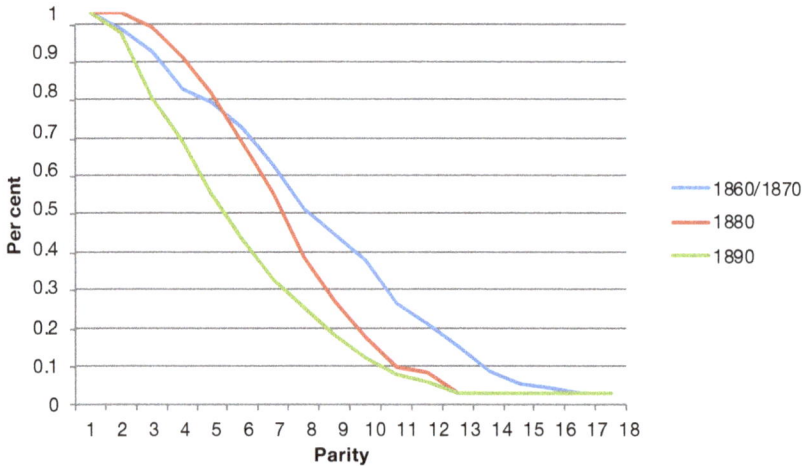

Figure 6.23 Other Nonconformists, proportions of women reaching each parity, complete group: 1860/70, 1880 and 1890 marriage cohorts, Tasmania

Source: Author's calculations.

Discussion

Bivariate analyses of the mean (median) numbers of children ever born and of parity progression ratios for the complete group in the four Tasmanian marriage cohorts provide support for some of the theories of why fertility declined in the late 19th century.

Fertility declined in Tasmania from the second half of the 1880s. Fertility began to fall from the 1860/70 cohorts to the 1880 cohort but there was a much larger fall from the 1880 to the 1890 cohorts. In the 1880 cohort, fertility fell steadily after parity four, while in the 1890 cohort it dropped sharply after parity two. This supports demographic transition theory, since the 1880s and 1890s were a period of social and economic change and modernisation in Tasmania. This will be expanded on in the qualitative analysis chapter.

There were marked differences in the fertility decline by socioeconomic status, supporting theories of diffusion and economic theories. White-collar workers had lower fertility than all other workers in the 1860/70 cohorts, well before fertility declined in general, indicating that they were the earliest group to control their fertility. The timing of the fertility decline also varied among socioeconomic groups. For white-collar workers, fertility fell across all marriage cohorts, while for skilled, lower-skilled and unskilled workers, fertility fell from the 1880 to the 1890 cohorts. The timing of the fertility decline for farmers was different, with a large fall in fertility between the 1860/70 and 1880 cohorts and a much lower fall between the 1880 and 1890 cohorts. One reason for the large difference in fertility of farmers in the 1860/70 and 1880 cohorts may be related to differences in the composition of the two groups, with farmers in the 1860/70 cohorts more likely to be 'selectors', many of whom failed at farming, while those in the 1880 cohort may have been more successful farmers.

As noted, the bivariate analysis of trends in fertility for different socioeconomic status groups uses husband's occupation at the birth of the first child as the measure of socioeconomic status. Since a relatively high proportion of men changed their socioeconomic status at some time during their wife's childbearing years (Table 5.11), the multivariate analysis, which measures socioeconomic status at the birth of each specific child, will provide a clearer picture of the relationship between socioeconomic status and fertility decline.

There were also marked differences in the fertility decline by urban/rural location, supporting theories of diffusion. Fertility was lower for urban women than for rural women in the 1860/70 cohorts, indicating that they were already controlling their fertility. Fertility fell for both urban and rural women from the 1860/70 cohorts to the 1880 cohort and then to the 1890 cohort. The fall between the 1880 and 1890 cohorts was more substantial than the fall between the 1860/70 and 1880 cohorts. This mirrors the trend in the fertility decline for the complete group as a whole.

Differences in fertility between the religious groups were not very clear and do not provide strong support for secularisation theory. Catholics tended to have higher fertility than other groups, while Presbyterians and Other Nonconformists tended to have lower fertility. Methodists tended to have higher fertility than all other Protestant groups. Fertility fell later for Catholics than the other religious groups, falling from the 1880 to the 1890 cohorts for Catholics and from the 1860/70 cohorts for all other groups.

7

How, when and why did fertility decline?

This chapter uses both bivariate and multivariate methods of analysis to examine whether the historical fertility decline in Tasmania was due to changes in starting, stopping and/or spacing behaviours. These analyses also provide answers to the questions of when fertility fell and why it fell at this time; specifically, how the findings support theories of the historical fertility decline outlined in Chapter 1. In the analysis that follows, measures of starting, stopping and spacing behaviours are based on pregnancies that resulted in a live birth rather than live births, because of the occurrence of twin births in the population.

Bivariate analysis

Starting

As discussed in Chapter 1, scholars have argued that couples did not deliberately control their fertility through marrying earlier or later—that is, starting behaviour was not an individual form of fertility control. Instead, the timing of marriage related to economic, social and psychological factors, not to fertility preferences (McDonald 1981). This argument is supported by findings from studies of marriage in pre-transitional and transitional societies in Western Europe and Asia (Lundh and Kurosu 2014).

Age at marriage for women rose from the 1860/70 cohorts to the 1890 cohort, from a mean of 21.8 years (median 21.2) in the 1860/70 cohorts to a mean of 23.1 years (median 22.3) in the 1890 cohort (Table 7.1). The proportion of women who married as teenagers fell steadily, from 36.7 per cent in the 1860/70 cohorts to 21.4 per cent in the 1890 cohort. By 1890, just over one-quarter of women were aged 25 years or older when they married. As noted previously, the increase in the age at marriage for women may be partly due to the increase in the ratio of females to males of marriageable age that occurred over the period.

Table 7.1 Age at marriage for women with children in their first marriage, complete group: 1860/70, 1880 and 1890 marriage cohorts, Tasmania

Marriage cohort	1860/70	1880	1890
Age at marriage	Percentage		
< 20 years	36.7	30.5	21.4
20 to < 25 years	45.1	53.0	50.1
25+ years	18.2	15.8	27.6
Missing	0.0	0.7	0.9
Total (%)	100.0	100.0	100.0
Total (no.)	539	417	529
Mean/median	Age at marriage		
Mean	21.8	22.0	23.1
Median	21.2	21.2	22.3

Note: Means and medians exclude missing data.

Consistent with trends in age at marriage, age at first birth also increased over the marriage cohorts, from a mean age of 23.2 years (median 22.3) in the 1860/70 cohorts to a mean of 24.3 years (median 23.4) in the 1890 cohort (Table 7.2). The proportion of women having their first birth as a teenager fell markedly, from 23.8 per cent in the 1860/70 cohorts to 14.6 per cent in the 1890 cohort. In all four marriage cohorts, only a small proportion of women had their first birth at 30 years or older.

Table 7.2 Age at first birth, complete group: 1860/70, 1880 and 1890 marriage cohorts, Tasmania

Marriage cohort	1860/70	1880	1890
Age at marriage	Percentage		
< 20 years	23.8	18.0	14.6
20–24 years	48.4	57.1	48.0
25–29 years	19.5	17.0	25.5
30+ years	8.3	7.2	11.0
Missing	0.0	0.7	0.9
Total (%)	100.0	100.0	100.0
Total (no.)	539	417	529
Mean/median	Age at first birth		
Mean	23.2	23.1	24.3
Median	22.3	22.2	23.4

Note: Means and medians exclude missing data.

Measures of stopping and spacing

As discussed in Chapter 1, there are differing views among scholars as to the extent to which couples reduced their fertility through practising stopping and/or spacing behaviours. Part of this controversy involves the methods that have been used to identify stopping and spacing behaviours. A critical review of these methods can be found in Van Bavel (2004b).

I did not construct age-specific marital fertility rates for the complete group in the four marriage cohorts, since these women were not representative of all married women in Tasmania at that time and their age-specific fertility rates would not be comparable with the age-specific marital fertility rates of any other population. Thus, methods used to identify stopping and/or spacing using fertility rates by age, such as Coale and Trussell's (1974, 1978) indices M and m and Ewbank's (1989) indices of marital fertility, are not discussed here.

The mean age of mother at last birth is one of the simplest indicators of stopping behaviour (Knodel 1987; Gutmann and Alter 1993). If the mean age of the mother at the birth of the last child falls, families are assumed to be practising stopping behaviour.

For women in the Tasmanian marriage cohorts, mean age at last birth fell steadily from the 1860/70 cohorts to the 1890 cohort, from 38.8 years (median 40) to 36.1 years (median 37) (Table 7.3). The proportion who had their last birth when they were under 30 years of age increased from 8.7 per cent to 19.7 per cent for the 1860/70 cohorts to the 1890 cohort, while the proportion who were 40 years or older fell from 51.2 per cent to 29.7 per cent.

Table 7.3 Age at last birth, complete group: 1860/70, 1880 and 1890 marriage cohorts, Tasmania

Marriage cohort	1860/70	1880	1890
Age at last birth	Per cent		
< 30 years	8.7	13.9	19.7
30–34 years	11.3	13.4	16.3
35–39 years	28.8	32.1	33.5
40+ years	51.2	39.8	29.7
Missing	0.0	0.7	0.9
Total (%)	100.0	100.0	100.0
Total (no.)	539	417	529
Mean/median	Age at last birth		
Mean	38.8	37.5	36.1
Median	40.0	38.5	37.0

Note: Means and medians exclude missing data.

Some scholars consider mean age at last birth a problematic indicator, since it can be affected by spacing behaviour as well as stopping behaviour (Anderton 1989). Anderton (1989) argues that if families space their births and the onset of sterility does not change, mean age at last birth will fall, because with longer birth spacing the onset of sterility will occur before families can have the next 'spaced' birth. Thus, spacing behaviour also increases the open interval—that is, the period between the last birth and the onset of sterility. Knodel and McDonald (Knodel 1987; McDonald and Knodel 1989) acknowledge that spacing behaviour can affect the mean age at last birth in the way described but argue that spacing has only a modest impact on this indicator. They estimated that a period of, at most, half the increase in the last closed birth interval can be attributed to spacing behaviour when analysing the fall in the mean age at last birth. Thus, if the last closed interval increases by four months, only two months of the decrease in the mean age at last birth can be attributed to spacing behaviour, with the rest attributed to stopping behaviour (Knodel 1987; Okun 1995).

Okun (1995) used Barrett's Monte Carlo microsimulation model of the reproductive process to investigate the extent to which mean age at last birth was affected by stopping and spacing behaviours. She simulated the birth histories of women with various levels of fecundability, who either adopted no fertility control or practised stopping or spacing behaviours with different degrees of success. In her simulation, she found that small reductions in mean age at last birth could not necessarily be attributed to stopping behaviour, since spacing behaviour that was practised continuously through marriage had a greater impact on mean age at last birth than McDonald and Knodel (1989) claimed.

Based on her simulation results, Okun concludes that examining changes in the mean age at last birth according to age at marriage is a more useful way of distinguishing 'stopping' from 'spacing' behaviour than looking at changes in mean age at last birth overall. This is because when couples do not control their fertility, age at marriage does not have any relationship with age at last birth. However, when couples practise stopping behaviour, women who marry at younger ages stop their childbearing earlier (McDonald 1984).

Examining mean age at last birth by age at marriage for the Tasmanian marriage cohorts shows the fall in mean age at last birth was somewhat higher for women marrying under 25 years of age than for women marrying at 25 years or older (Table 7.4). For women marrying under 20 years of age, mean age at last birth was 38.3 years (median 40.4) in the 1860/70 cohorts and fell to 35.5 years (median 37) in the 1890 cohort. The fall in the mean age at last birth, however, was not as large for those marrying at 25 years or older, with mean age at last birth falling from 39.3 years (median 39.9) to 37.7 years (median 38) from the 1860/70 to the 1890 cohorts. The proportion of women completing their childbearing before age 35 years increased markedly for those marrying under 25 years of age, from around 20 per cent of women in the 1860/70 cohorts to around 40 per cent in the 1890 cohorts (Appendix A: Table A.20). Corresponding proportions for those marrying at age 25 years or older were 17.4 per cent and 24 per cent. Therefore, in the Tasmanian marriage cohorts, age at marriage was related to age at last birth, which is consistent with the practice of stopping behaviour.

Table 7.4 Mean (median) age at last birth by age at marriage, complete group: 1860/70, 1880 and 1890 marriage cohorts, Tasmania

Marriage cohort	1860/70	1880	1890
Age at marriage	Mean age at last birth		
< 20 years			
Mean	38.3	36.6	35.5
Median	40.4	37.2	37.0
20–24 years			
Mean	38.7	37.5	35.4
Median	39.8	38.4	36.2
25+ years			
Mean	39.3	36.6	37.7
Median	39.9	39.4	38.0

Note: Excludes three women in the 1880 cohort and five in the 1890 cohort for whom age was missing.

Measures to detect deliberate spacing behaviour are difficult to find (Knodel 1987). In populations with natural fertility, birth intervals can vary markedly because of differences in breastfeeding practices, periodic separation of spouses or factors beyond the couple's control, such as levels of fecundity and intrauterine mortality. Birth intervals that increase with parity do not necessarily mean that couples are practising parity-dependent birth spacing, since birth intervals may increase as women age because of decreasing fecundity or decreased sexual activity. Last birth intervals are thus longer than other birth intervals. Also, very long last birth intervals do not necessarily imply that couples are deliberately spacing their births, as they may reflect failed attempts to stop childbearing. Couples who decide to stop having children, for instance, may have another birth accidently or may have stopped childbearing but decide to have another birth after one of their children dies.

In the Tasmanian marriage cohorts, the mean (median) interval between marriage and first birth was longer for women in the 1860/70 cohorts than for women in the other two cohorts, with a mean of 17 months (median 11.2) for the 1860/70 cohorts compared with 12.9 months (median 10.3) for the 1880 cohort and 15 months (median 10.9) for the 1890 cohort (Table 7.5). This may partly reflect the higher proportion of premarital conceptions in the 1880 and 1890 cohorts: 22.8 per cent of women in the 1880 cohort and 22.1 per cent in the 1890 cohort conceived their first child prior to their marriage compared with 14.8 per cent of women in the 1860/70 cohorts. The increase in the proportion of couples with premarital conceptions may be related to the increase in the age at marriage—in particular, the fall in the proportion of women who were teenagers when they married. As Carmichael (1996) has noted, when the age at marriage increases, the period of exposure to the risk of premarital pregnancy increases and thus the likelihood of couples marrying to legitimise their first child.

Table 7.5 Interval between marriage and first birth, complete group: 1860/70, 1880 and 1890 marriage cohorts, Tasmania

Marriage cohort	1860/70	1880	1890
Age at marriage	Percentage		
Premarital conception	14.8	22.8	22.1
8 to < 12 months	43.2	42.2	38.4
12 to < 24 months	28.6	26.6	29.3
24 to < 36 months	6.5	4.6	5.3
36+ months	6.9	3.8	4.9
Total (%)	100.0	100.0	100.0
Total (no.)	539	417	529
Mean/median	Months		
Mean	17.0	12.9	15.0
Median	11.2	10.3	10.9

As outlined in Chapter 1, those who argue that couples controlled their fertility by deliberate spacing behaviour consider these couples spaced their births from the earliest birth intervals. In the Tasmanian marriage cohorts, first interbirth intervals were much longer on average than the interval between marriage and the first birth but increased only slightly between the 1860/70 and 1890 cohorts, from a mean of 23 months (median 21.4) to a mean of 24.4 months (median 22) (Table 7.6). The proportion of couples with a first interbirth interval of 36 months or more also increased slightly, from 7.1 per cent to 10.7 per cent.

Table 7.6 First interbirth interval, complete group: 1860/70, 1880 and 1890 marriage cohorts, Tasmania

Marriage cohort	1860/70	1880	1890
Age at marriage	Percentage		
< 18 months	29.0	32.5	29.2
18 to < 24 months	34.1	35.1	33.0
24 to < 30 months	21.9	16.5	21.4
30 to < 36 months	7.9	7.2	5.8
36+ months	7.1	8.8	10.7
Total (%)	100.0	100.0	100.0
Total (no.)	493	388	449
Mean/median	Months		
Mean	23.0	23.3	24.4
Median	21.4	20.9	22.0

Note: Excludes couples for whom the second birth is the last.

There was little change in the length of the second interbirth interval from the 1860/70 to the 1890 cohorts, with the mean birth interval remaining about 26 months (median 23.4–23.7 months) (Table 7.7). As with the first interbirth interval, the proportion of couples with a second interbirth interval of 36 months or more increased slightly, from 11 per cent to 14.4 per cent.

Table 7.7 Second interbirth interval, complete group: 1860/70, 1880 and 1890 marriage cohorts, Tasmania

Marriage cohort	1860/70	1880	1890
Age at marriage	Percentage		
< 18 months	15.2	21.3	21.9
18 to < 24 months	36.6	34.0	29.5
24 to < 30 months	28.1	23.0	25.1
30 to < 36 months	9.1	11.8	9.1
36+ months	11.0	9.8	14.4
Total (%)	100.0	100.0	100.0
Total (no.)	462	356	383
Mean/median	Months		
Mean	26.0	25.4	26.1
Median	23.7	23.4	23.6

Note: Excludes couples for whom the third birth is the last.

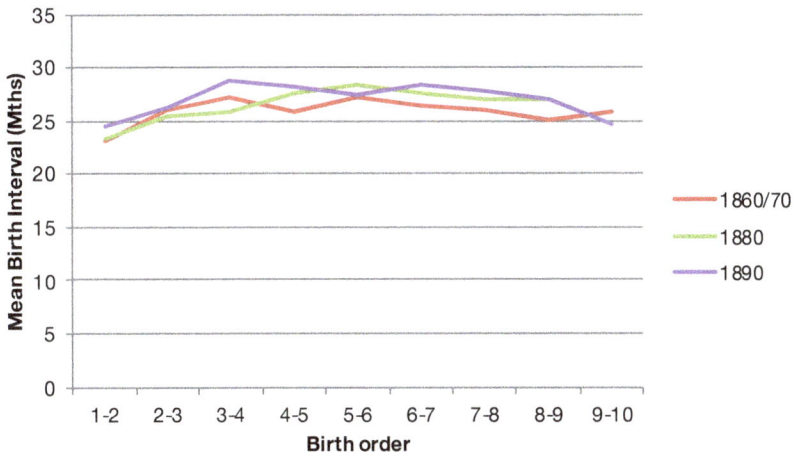

Figure 7.1 Mean birth intervals by birth order (excluding last), complete group: 1860/70, 1880 and 1890 marriage cohorts, Tasmania
Source: Appendix A: Table A.21 (this volume).

For all interbirth intervals up to parity 10, mean birth intervals were generally longest for the 1890 cohort, but they were longer for the 1860/70 cohorts than the 1880 cohort at lower parities and shorter at higher parities (Figure 7.1). These differences were not large, mainly in the order of one to two months. In the 1860/70 cohorts, mean birth intervals were about two years at every parity, indicating the effect of breastfeeding practices on amenorrhoea (Tsuya et al. 2010). While there are no data on the extent of breastfeeding in the Australian colonies, a review of infant feeding in 19th-century Australia indicates that experts advocated breastfeeding for between nine and 18 months and concludes that 'mothers expected to breastfeed their infants, and most probably did so' (Hitchcock 1990: 21).

Last birth intervals were considerably longer than other birth intervals and increased across the cohorts, from a mean of 38.4 months (median 32.1) for the 1860/70 cohorts to a mean of 46.2 months (median 36) for the 1890 cohort (Table 7.8). This was due to the increase in very long last birth intervals, with the proportion of last birth intervals that were 72 months or longer increasing from 7 per cent in the 1860/70 cohorts to 16.5 per cent in the 1890 cohort.

Table 7.8 Last interbirth intervals, complete group: 1860/70, 1880 and 1890 marriage cohorts, Tasmania

Marriage cohort	1860/70	1880	1890
Birth interval	Percentage		
< 18 months	8.2	7.6	6.8
18 to < 24 months	15.6	14.2	13.7
24 to < 30 months	20.6	16.4	17.3
30 to < 36 months	13.2	14.2	11.7
36 months to < 72 months	35.4	36.0	34.1
72+ months	7.0	11.5	16.5
Total (%)	100.0	100.0	100.0
Total (no.)	514	408	504
Mean/median	Months		
Mean	38.4	42.3	46.2
Median	32.1	34.5	36.0

Note: Includes couples with two or more births.

Some authors argue that examining birth intervals by final parity provides a better indication of whether families are practising stopping or spacing behaviour. It is generally agreed that in populations of natural fertility and those that control their fertility, the length of mean birth intervals is inversely related to final parity, with families with large numbers of children having the shortest mean birth intervals (Anderton and Bean 1985; Knodel 1987). With the practice of stopping, birth intervals may reduce for couples with moderate numbers of children, because they behave like those who have large families under conditions of natural fertility (shorter birth intervals) but decide to stop at much lower parities.

During the fertility transition in late 19th-century Utah, mean birth intervals by completed family size remained relatively unchanged (Anderton and Bean 1985). Anderton and Bean (1985) argue this is because families were practising both stopping and spacing behaviours to control their fertility. They claim that under conditions of natural fertility, having a small completed family size (with relatively long birth intervals) was due not to problems with fecundity, but reflected the fact that a small proportion of couples were deliberately both stopping and spacing their births. They consider the fall in fertility over the 19th century reflects an increasing proportion of couples both spacing and stopping their births to achieve these same birth patterns.

Okun (1995) used her simulation model to investigate whether an analysis of birth intervals stratified by birth order and final parity could distinguish between stopping and spacing behaviours. In her model, she examined the last birth interval separately from the preceding intervals, because of the effects of failed stopping in increasing this interval. Okun's simulation showed that mean birth intervals prior to the last decreased with stopping behaviour and increased with spacing behaviour. She concludes that examining changes in mean birth intervals stratified by final parity, excluding the last, is a good method for identifying whether couples are stopping or spacing their births. However, she argues it is not possible to distinguish stopping from spacing behaviour by examining changes in the last birth interval, since the last birth interval increases with both stopping and spacing behaviours. It is worth noting that Okun's analysis involves modelling stopping or spacing behaviour, but not a combination of both, as argued by Anderton and Bean (1985).

Hionidou (1998) termed the interval between the first birth and the penultimate birth the 'overall' interval. In the Tasmanian marriage cohorts, the mean overall birth interval was inversely related to parity in every marriage cohort—for example, decreasing from 30.4 months for couples with three to four children to 22.9 months for couples with 11–16 children in the 1880 cohort (Table 7.9). There was, however, no consistent pattern in the change in the mean overall birth interval from the 1860/70 to the 1890 cohorts for families of different parities. The mean overall birth interval decreased for couples with three or four children, from 33.7 to 29.6 months; it fell only slightly for couples with seven or more children and increased slightly for couples with five or six children. Overall, changes in the mean overall birth intervals were small, providing little evidence of increased spacing.

Table 7.9 Mean overall birth interval by number of children, complete group: 1860/70, 1880 and 1890 marriage cohorts, Tasmania

Marriage cohort	1860/70	1880	1890
Number of children	Mean overall birth interval (months)		
3–4	33.7	30.4	29.6
5–6	27.6	28.2	29.2
7–8	26.8	26.5	25.8
9–10	25.1	24.1	24.5
11–16[1]	23.7	22.9	22.3

[1] Mean in 1890 is illustrative only because of small numbers.

Some scholars have put forward the view that age at marriage may affect birth spacing (Bumpass et al. 1978), since it is generally agreed that birth intervals are shorter when women marry very young (Finnas and Hoem 1980). Anderton and Bean (1985), however, were surprised to find that birth intervals were shorter in the Utah population for those marrying after age 25 years compared with those marrying between the ages of 21 and 25 years. They argue that women who marry at older ages have shorter birth intervals because they aim to have a specific number of children but have less time in which to achieve this than those who marry younger.

Some demographers who consider that both spacing and stopping played a role in the fertility transition argue that there are other questions about the fertility decline that need to be addressed—for instance, what proportion of couples in a marriage cohort were effective in controlling their fertility and how many children did they have on average (David and Sanderson 1988; David et al. 1988)? They developed a method called Cohort Parity Analysis (CPA) to enable such questions to be answered in historical populations that practise both stopping and spacing. CPA derives lower and upper bound estimates for the proportion of a population adopting fertility control by comparing the parity progression ratios of women in the population of interest (the 'target' population) by age at marriage and duration of marriage, with the parity progression ratios of women in a population that is similar, but where there is no fertility control (the 'model' population) (David and Sanderson 1988). The average final parity of women controlling their fertility can also be calculated within the CPA framework. Women in both the target and the model populations are in their first marriage.

Okun (1994) evaluated this method using her simulation model and concluded that CPA is not a useful method of identifying fertility control practices in the early stages of a fertility transition. This was mainly because of her concerns about the large biases in CPA bounds introduced by even small differences between the target and the model populations in relation to 'length of the post-partum non-susceptible period, fecundability and pre-marital exposure to pregnancy' (Okun 1994: 222).

Failed stopping

There is clearly considerable disagreement among demographers about the extent to which long last birth intervals are due to failed stopping, spacing or decreasing fecundity. An analysis of long last birth intervals in the Tasmanian marriage cohorts—that is, intervals of six years or more—may inform this debate. While six years is taken as the minimum length of a long birth interval, some last birth intervals were considerably longer. In the 1890 cohort, for instance, 18 per cent of long last birth intervals were 10 years or more.

Where last birth intervals were long, there was variation between the marriage cohorts in the parity of the last birth (Table 7.10). In the 1860/70 cohorts, long last birth intervals were spread fairly evenly among the parities, with the highest proportion of intervals, 16.7 per cent, between parities seven and eight. Long last birth intervals were more concentrated at specific parities in the other two cohorts. In the 1880 cohort, 21.3 per cent of long last birth intervals were between parities four and five, while in the 1890 cohort, 27.7 per cent were between parities three and four and 19.3 per cent were between four and five. This shows a substantial proportion of couples in the 1880 cohort were trying to stop after parity four and those in the 1890 cohort after parities three and four.

Table 7.10 Parity of last birth, where last birth interval is six years or more, complete group: 1860/70, 1880 and 1890 marriage cohorts, Tasmania

Marriage cohort	1860/70	1880	1890
Parity	Percentage		
Two	8.3	6.4	10.8
Three	2.8	10.6	8.4
Four	8.3	10.6	27.7
Five	8.3	21.3	19.3
Six	8.3	14.9	9.6
Seven	13.9	8.5	8.4
Eight	16.7	10.6	4.8
Nine	8.3	8.5	3.6
Ten	13.9	6.4	2.4
Eleven	8.3	2.1	4.8
Twelve	2.8	0.0	0.0
Total (%)	100.0	100.0	100.0
Total (no.)	36	47	83

Note: Includes couples with two or more births.

It is interesting to examine the length of the interval preceding the long last birth interval, since if long last birth intervals are due to spacing behaviour, the penultimate birth interval should also be relatively long. Most couples with a long last birth interval, however, had a relatively short penultimate birth interval (Table 7.11). More than half of couples in the 1880 cohort and three-quarters of couples in the 1860/70 and 1890 cohorts had penultimate birth intervals of less than three years. It seems highly unlikely this pattern of birth intervals represents spacing behaviour.

Table 7.11 Length of the penultimate interval, where last birth interval is six years or more, complete group: 1860/70, 1880 and 1890 marriage cohorts, Tasmania

Marriage cohort	1860/70	1880	1890
Birth interval	Percentage		
< 24 months	36.4	36.4	37.8
24 to < 36 months	39.4	22.7	39.2
36 to < 54 months	15.2	29.5	12.2
54 to < 72 months	3.0	9.1	9.5
72+ months	6.1	2.3	1.4
Total (%)	100.0	100.0	100.0
Total (no.)	33	44	74

Note: Includes couples with three or more births.

As noted above, last birth intervals tend to be longer than other birth intervals because of the decline in fecundity that women experience as they age. It has been shown, however, that in populations where families practise little or no fertility control, women's fecundity does not decline to any great extent until after age 35 years, and only declines sharply after age 39 years (Menken et al. 1986). Half of the women in the 1890 cohort with long last birth intervals and 42 per cent in the 1880 cohort were under 30 years of age at the penultimate birth (Table 7.12). It seems very unlikely these long birth intervals were due to declining fecundity and more likely they were due to failed stopping. Given that 'fertility, compared with that of women [aged] 20 to 24, is reduced on average by ... 14 per cent for those aged 30 to 34' (Menken et al. 1986: 1389), it is also unlikely that women who were aged 30 to 34 at their penultimate birth had such long birth intervals due to reduced fecundity.

Table 7.12 Age of mother at the penultimate birth, where last birth interval is six years or more, complete group: 1860/70, 1880 and 1890 marriage cohorts, Tasmania

Marriage cohort	1860/70	1880	1890
Age of mother	Percentage		
< 25 years	8.3	2.1	14.5
25–29 years	8.3	40.4	34.9
30–34 years	41.7	27.7	30.1
35–39 years	41.7	29.8	18.1
40+ years	0.0	0.0	1.2
Missing	0.0	0.0	1.2
Total (%)	100.0	100.0	100.0
Total (no.)	36	47	83

Note: Includes couples with two or more births.

As noted above, long last birth intervals have also been attributed to couples having stopped childbearing but changing their minds because one of their children died (Knodel 1987). Only a small proportion of families with long last birth intervals had a child die during the interval: seven in the 1860/70 cohorts, four in the 1880 cohort and 12 in the 1890 cohort. For 16 of these couples, the interval between the death of a child and the birth of the last child was six years or longer. Of the seven families where the time between the child's death and the last birth was shorter than six years, only three couples had a gap of less than four years (Table 7.13). This indicates that most of the couples who experienced a child's death during the long last birth interval did not have their last birth in response to this death.

Table 7.13 Families with long last birth intervals where the gap between death of a child and last birth was less than six years (seven families), complete group: 1860/70, 1880 and 1890 marriage cohorts, Tasmania

Marriage cohort	1860/70	1860/70	1860/70	1880	1880	1890	1890
Last birth interval (months)	73.4	115.7	87.1	73.7	80.4	120.2	115.7
Time between death and last birth interval (months)	53.0	36.0	38.6	10.9	67.3	50.0	49.0
Age at death (years)	1.7	10.9	6.9	5.3	2.6	5.8	11.6

Stopping, starting and spacing: McDonald's formula

McDonald (1984) developed a decomposition technique to identify the extent to which changes in final parity can be attributed to stopping, starting or spacing behaviours. A modified version of McDonald's formula was used by Knodel (1987) in his analysis of the marital fertility of German village populations in the 18th and 19th centuries. The McDonald method has been used in many analyses of the fertility decline in countries of Western Europe (for example, Van Bavel and Kok 2005; Derosas 2006; Reher and Sanz-Gimeno 2007; van Poppel et al. 2012).

As modified by Knodel, the formula is $CEB = 1 + (L-F)/I$, where CEB is the mean number of children ever born, F is the mean age at first birth, L is the mean age at last birth and I is the mean birth interval. Using decomposition analysis, the contribution of mean age at first birth, mean age at last birth and interbirth intervals to changes in the number of children ever born can be assessed by substituting the relevant indicator into the equation for the base year and estimating its impact on the number of children ever born. Although McDonald (1984) originally advocated using a stepwise standardisation approach, Knodel (1987) presented the changes attributable to each factor separately. Because the different factors interact with one another, the sum of the changes attributed to each component (F, L, I) does not necessarily add to the difference in the number of children ever born (CEB) (Knodel 1987). The difference between the two, however, is generally small and the interaction effects can be ignored.

The components used in the formula are presented in Table 7.14. Note that the data for the 1880 and 1890 cohorts on mean numbers of children ever born and mean birth interval are slightly different from those presented elsewhere, because these data exclude couples for whom the mother's age is missing.

Table 7.14 Mean children ever born, mean age of mother at first birth, mean age of mother at last birth and mean birth interval, complete group: 1860/70, 1880 and 1890 marriage cohorts, Tasmania

Marriage cohort	1860/70	1880	1890
Component of change			
Mean children ever born	7.91	7.07	5.64
Mean age of mother at first birth (years)	23.20	23.10	24.30
Mean age of mother at last birth (years)	38.80	37.50	36.10
Mean birth interval (years)	2.27	2.37	2.54
Total (no.)	539	414	524

Note: Excludes couples for whom mother's age is missing.

Using the McDonald formula, comparing the 1860/70 and 1880 cohorts, the drop in the mean number of children ever born (–0.84) was due mainly to the fall in the mean age at last birth (–0.59) and an increase in the length of the mean birth interval (–0.3) (Table 7.15). The very small decrease in the mean age at first birth had a negligible effect (+0.01). Comparing the 1860/70 and 1890 cohorts, the fall in the mean number of children ever born (–2.27) was primarily due to the fall in the mean age at last birth (–1.22), while the increase in the length of the mean birth interval and in the mean age of the mother at the first birth also made substantial contributions (–0.74 and –0.51, respectively).

Table 7.15 Impact of age at first birth, age at last birth and birth intervals for children ever born, McDonald method, complete group: 1860/70, 1880 and 1890 marriage cohorts, Tasmania

Marriage cohort	1860/70 compared with 1880	1860/70 compared with 1890
Component of change		
Mean age of mother at first birth	+0.01	–0.51
Mean age of mother at last birth	–0.59	–1.22
Mean birth interval	–0.30	–0.74
Children ever born	–0.84	–2.27

Note: Excludes couples for whom mother's age is missing.

Both Knodel and McDonald (Knodel 1987; McDonald and Knodel 1989: 472) agree that the formula cannot 'capture all of the subtleties and complexities involved in changes in stopping and spacing behaviour'. For instance, they acknowledge that a fall in the mean age at last birth (L), which the formula attributes to stopping, can in some part be attributed to spacing, but argue that the effect is very small. Knodel (1987) also acknowledges that while increases in the mean birth interval (I) are attributed to spacing, this measure includes the last birth interval, changes in which may be due to 'failed' stopping. Both authors argue that, despite these limitations, the formula can be used with confidence to distinguish the broad effects of the different practices. When McDonald originally developed the formula, he advocated its use as a tool for 'first-stage analysis' and saw it as being followed by a 'second-stage analysis', in which findings would be examined at the individual level (McDonald 1984: 27).

Okun (1995) used her simulation model to look at the accuracy of McDonald's formula in distinguishing between stopping and spacing practices. She concluded that, since the effects of stopping behaviour are primarily shown through changes in the mean age at last birth and spacing behaviour through increases in the mean birth intervals, the McDonald formula 'provides a convenient device for roughly apportioning changes in CEB into its components' (Okun 1995: 92).

Van Bavel (2004b), however, argues that McDonald's technique can differentiate between stopping and spacing only when the population practising fertility control adopts either stopping or spacing behaviour, but not both. He claims that when one section of the population is practising stopping and another practising spacing behaviour, the McDonald method will disguise the effects of stopping behaviour on both the mean age at last birth and the mean birth intervals.

Multivariate analysis

Bivariate analysis, while an important first step in any analysis of the fertility transition, is limited in its explanatory power. In the past 20 or so years, multivariate methods have become commonly used by historical demographers to examine the fertility decline (Gutmann and Alter 1993; Van Bavel 2004b). Van Bavel (2004b) proposes two multivariate analysis methods for investigating stopping and spacing behaviours: logistic regression and event history analysis (or survival analysis). Survival analysis is useful in analysing datasets for which we do not have complete birth histories (Gutmann and Alter 1993). However, survival analysis does not allow us to distinguish spacing from stopping behaviour, since it models the risk of having the next birth, which can reflect either the length of the next birth interval or whether the woman stops having children (Berger et al. 2009; Gray et al. 2010). Since my dataset includes only couples who have completed their childbearing, I use logistic regression to examine stopping behaviour and survival analysis on closed birth intervals to examine spacing behaviour. I was unable to fit a logistic regression model to examine parity progression, so I used survival analysis to examine the risks of a woman at a specific parity proceeding to the next parity.

Stopping behaviour

Logistic regression

In this section, I investigate stopping behaviour using logistic regression to examine the determinants of any given birth being the last (Van Bavel 2004b; Berger et al. 2009). All families with one or more children are included in the analysis.

The dependent variable is whether a birth is the last birth (with '1' = last birth and '0' = not last birth).

Many of the following covariates included in the logistic regression model have been examined in the bivariate analysis in Chapter 6. The covariates used in the model relate to the theories of fertility decline discussed in Chapter 1 or are associated with a woman's fecundity:

- Age of wife at marriage.
- Difference in age between husband and wife.
- Husband's socioeconomic status.
- Type of geographic location.
- Religion.
- Literacy status of husband and wife.
- Whether a pregnancy resulted in the birth of twins.
- Whether the child died in infancy when the wife was not pregnant with another child.
- The number of children alive at the beginning of the birth interval—that is, the number of children born to the couple less the number of children who died under the age of 15 years.

- The number of children who had died (under the age of 15 years) at the beginning of the birth interval.
- The sex composition of the surviving children at the beginning of the birth interval.

In this analysis of Tasmanian marriage cohorts, the sex composition of the family is divided into three categories: more surviving girls than boys, more surviving boys than girls and equal numbers of surviving boys and girls. I chose this categorisation, rather than a categorisation based on whether there were any boys or any girls in the family, because of the very small number of families in the Tasmanian marriage cohorts above parity four who had surviving children of one sex only.

Testing for multicollinearity of the covariates (using 'collin' in STATA) showed the covariates in the model are not highly correlated. Descriptive statistics of the covariates used in the logistic regression model are shown in Appendix A: Table A.22.

The model shows there are many covariates that are significantly associated with stopping behaviour (Table 7.16).

The mother's age at the birth of a child and her age at marriage were important determinants of whether a mother stopped childbearing. The older a mother was at the birth of a child, the more likely she was to stop childbearing. The odds of stopping for a mother who had a birth at age 30 years or older were 4.22 times the odds for women who had a birth aged under 20 years (p = 0.000). Similarly, the older a woman was at marriage, the more likely it was the birth would be her last. The odds of stopping childbearing for a woman who married at 25 years or older were 2.22 times (p = 0.000) the odds for a woman who married under 20 years of age.

Controlling for all other factors, the marriage cohort was a significant determinant of stopping childbearing. The odds of stopping childbearing for a woman in the 1880 cohort were 1.42 times, and the odds for a woman in the 1890 cohort 2.22 times, the odds for a woman in the 1860/70 cohorts (p = 0.000).

In relation to occupational status, farmers and unskilled workers were significantly less likely to stop childbearing than white-collar workers (odds = 0.63 and 0.65, respectively; p = 0.000) as were skilled workers (odds = 0.81, p < 0.05). Couples living in rural areas were significantly less likely to stop childbearing than those in urban areas (odds = 0.69, p = 0.000). No significant differences were found between couples according to their religion or literacy status.

Having a twin birth was not a significant determinant of stopping. Having a child die as an infant while the mother was not pregnant with another was also not significant, but the more infant and/or child deaths the family had experienced at the birth of a child, the more likely they were to stop childbearing (odds = 1.28, p = 0.000). The number of surviving children affected the likelihood of stopping, with the odds of stopping increasing by 24 per cent for each additional surviving child (p = 0.000). However, the sex composition of the surviving children was not significantly associated with stopping.

Table 7.16 Logistic regression of the probability that a birth is the last, complete group: 1860/70, 1880 and 1890 marriage cohorts, Tasmania

Covariate	Odds ratio	Standard error	Significance (p)	
Intercept	0.01	0.003	0.000	**
Mother's age at birth				
< 30 years (ref.)	1.00	—	—	
30 to < 35 years	1.44	0.237	0.027	*
35+ years	4.22	0.700	0.000	**
Mother's age at marriage				
< 20 years (ref.)	1.00	—	—	
20 to < 25 years	1.51	0.120	0.000	**
25+ years	2.22	0.259	0.000	**
Age difference between couple				
Same age or husband up to 5 years older (ref.)	1.00	—	—	
Wife older	0.94	0.088	0.544	
Husband 5+ years older	1.07	0.074	0.352	
Marriage cohort				
1860/70 cohorts (ref.)	1.00	—	—	
1880 cohort	1.42	0.111	0.000	**
1890 cohort	2.20	0.172	0.000	**

Covariate	Odds ratio	Standard error	Significance (p)	
Socioeconomic status				
White-collar (ref.)	1.00	—	—	
Skilled	0.81	0.085	0.041	*
Farmers	0.62	0.059	0.000	**
Lower-skilled	0.86	0.098	0.201	
Unskilled	0.65	0.062	0.000	**
Type of geographic location				
Urban area in Tasmania (ref.)	1.00	—	—	
Rural area in Tasmania	0.69	0.053	0.000	**
Another colony	1.06	0.116	0.567	
Religion				
Anglican (ref.)	1.00	—	—	
Catholic	0.85	0.089	0.119	
Presbyterian	1.05	0.104	0.601	
Methodist	0.88	0.077	0.157	
Other Nonconformist	1.01	0.093	0.901	
Literacy status of husband and wife				
Both literate (ref.)	1.00	—	—	
Husband and/or wife illiterate	0.96	0.092	0.667	
Twin birth	1.60	0.407	0.063	
Child dies as infant before conception of another	0.88	0.115	0.324	
Number of child deaths	1.28	0.045	0.000	**
Number of surviving children	1.24	0.019	0.000	**
Sex composition of surviving children				
More surviving girls than boys (ref.)	1.00	—	—	
More surviving boys than girls	0.96	0.065	0.586	
Equal numbers of surviving boys and girls	0.98	0.090	0.798	
No. of births = 9,923				
Hosmer–Lemeshow chi2(8) = 4.91 Prob > chi2 = 0.7673				

* $p < 0.05$
** $p < 0.01$
— not applicable for the reference category

Van Poppel et al. (2012) argue that actual family size is the most important variable for understanding the fertility decline, not the number of children born to the family. I was unable to include all three covariates—the number of children born to the family, the number of surviving children and the number of infant and child deaths—in my model because of multicollinearity. However, when I ran the model substituting the covariate 'number of children' for the covariate 'number of infant and child deaths', I found the number of surviving children was no longer significantly associated with stopping (odds ratio = 0.97, $p = 0.452$), but the 'number of children' was a significant determinant of stopping (odds ratio = 1.28, $p = 0.000$).

Szreter's (1996) analysis of fertility in 19th-century England and Wales shows that mining families had very high fertility. As noted, mining was a very important industry in late 19th-century Tasmania. In the logistic regression model presented above, 'miners' were classified as 'lower-skilled' workers. No significant differences were found between lower-skilled workers and white-collar workers in the likelihood of stopping childbearing (odds ratio = 0.86, $p = 0.201$). I ran the same model for the 1890 marriage cohort only, classifying 'miners' separately and including the other lower-skilled workers in the skilled category. Using this classification, there were no significant differences between miners and white-collar workers in stopping childbearing or between skilled workers and white-collar workers. For miners, the odds ratio was 1.18 ($p = 0.554$) and for skilled workers it was 0.83 ($p = 0.264$).

In summary, the logistic regression shows that the older a woman was at the birth of her child, the more likely she was to stop childbearing. Similarly, the older a woman was at marriage, the more likely she was to stop childbearing. Women in the 1880 cohort were more likely to stop childbearing than those in the 1860/70 cohorts, while women in the 1890 cohort were even more likely to stop. Farmers, unskilled workers and skilled workers were less likely to stop than white-collar workers, and people living in rural areas of Tasmania were less likely to stop than those living in urban areas. The age difference between husband and wife, religion, literacy and giving birth to twins had no significant association with stopping. However, the more surviving children the couple had, the more likely they were to stop, but the sex of these children had no significant association with stopping. Having an infant die while the mother was not pregnant had no significant association with stopping, but the more infant and child deaths the couple experienced, the more likely they were to stop.

To ascertain whether these findings were affected by couples who had all their births outside the colony, I ran the same model only for couples who had at least one birth in Tasmania. The results were almost identical, except that for those with at least one birth in Tasmania, skilled workers were not significantly less likely to stop childbearing than white-collar workers (odds ratio = 0.83, p = 0.076).

I also ran the model with interaction effects to see whether the relationships within the socioeconomic groups, religious groups and groups living in different geographic areas were consistent across cohorts. I found the interaction effects were not significant, so there was no evidence of any differences in the relationships within the groups in the different marriage cohorts.

Predicted probability

The predicted probability of a birth being the last (calculated from the logistic regression model) also showed the same patterns across cohorts. While the predicted probability of stopping increased over the marriage cohorts, it was highest for white-collar workers in every cohort and lowest for farmers and unskilled workers (Figure 7.2). The predicted probability of stopping for white-collar workers was 0.14 in the 1860/70 cohorts, compared with 0.10 for farmers. By the 1890 cohort, the predicted probability of stopping had increased to 0.24 for white-collar workers and 0.18 for farmers.

Women who married at age 20–24 years, gave birth at 30 years or older and had a husband who was the same age or one to four years older were the most common group in every cohort. The predicted probability of stopping was higher for this group of women than for all women (Figure 7.3). However, the pattern according to socioeconomic status was the same. For white-collar workers, the predicted probability of stopping was 0.19 in the 1860/70 cohorts and rose to 0.32 in the 1890 cohort. The comparable probabilities for farmers were 0.13 and 0.24, respectively.

7. HOW, WHEN AND WHY DID FERTILITY DECLINE?

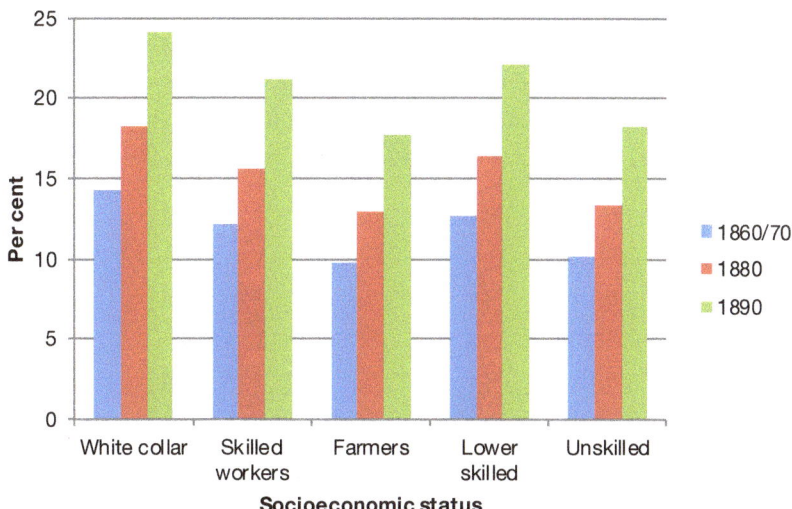

Figure 7.2 Predicted probability that a birth is the last by socioeconomic status, complete group: 1860/70, 1880 and 1890 marriage cohorts, Tasmania

Source: Appendix A: Table A.21 (this volume).

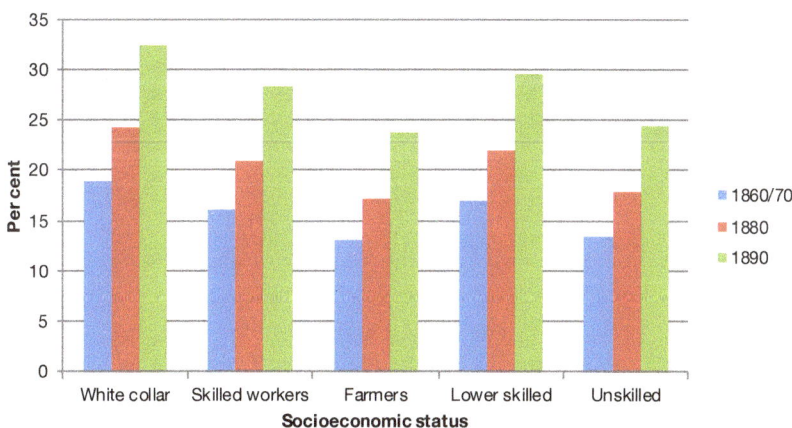

Figure 7.3 Predicted probability that a birth is the last by socioeconomic status for women married at age 20–24 years, giving birth at 30+ years and with a husband the same age or 1–4 years older, complete group: 1860/70, 1880 and 1890 marriage cohorts, Tasmania

Source: Appendix A: Table A.24 (this volume).

169

The predicted probability that a birth was the last increased over the cohorts both for couples living in urban areas and for couples in rural areas and was higher for couples in urban areas in every marriage cohort (Figure 7.4). It increased from 0.13 to 0.23 across the marriage cohorts for those living in urban areas and from 0.10 to 0.18 for those living in rural areas.

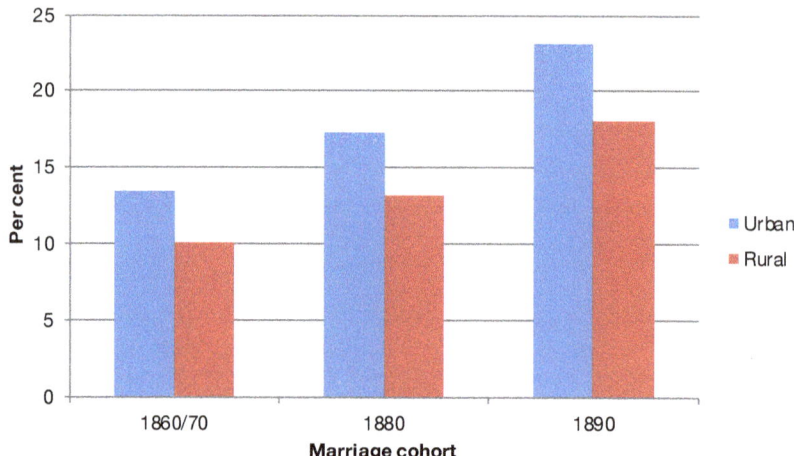

Figure 7.4 Predicted probability that a birth is the last by urban/rural location, complete group: 1860/70, 1880 and 1890 marriage cohorts, Tasmania
Source: Appendix A: Table A.25 (this volume).

As with socioeconomic status, although predicted probabilities of stopping were higher for women married at age 20–24 years, giving birth at 30 years or older with a husband the same age or one to four years older than for all women, the pattern by urban/rural location was the same (Appendix A: Table A.26). For women living in urban areas, the predicted probability of stopping having children increased from 0.18 to 0.31 from the 1860/70 to the 1890 cohorts and for those living in rural areas from 0.13 to 0.24, respectively. The predicted probability increased from 0.22 to 0.37 across the cohorts for this group of women who lived in urban areas and whose husband was a white-collar worker.

The predicted probabilities of stopping with each surviving child can be used in the same way as parity progression ratios to calculate the proportion of women in each cohort predicted to have at least a specific number of surviving children (Figure 7.5). This shows that the predicted probability of women in each marriage cohort having a specific number of surviving children dropped steadily across the marriage cohorts. For instance, the predicted probability of women having four or more surviving children dropped from 0.84 in the 1860/70 cohorts to 0.78 in the 1880 cohort and then to 0.69 in the 1890 cohort. Similarly, the predicted probability of women having 10 or more surviving children dropped from 0.34 in the 1860/70 cohorts to 0.24 in the 1880 cohort and to 0.13 in the 1890 cohort. This indicates that couples in the 1880 and 1890 cohorts had different preferences regarding stopping childbearing.

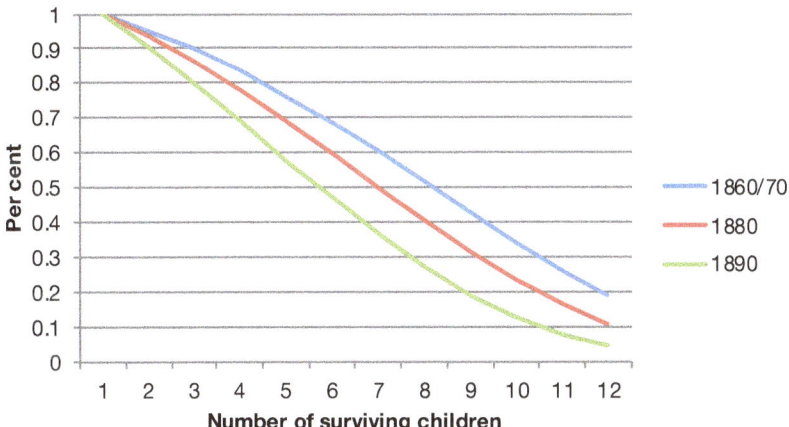

Figure 7.5 Predicted probability of women having at least a specific number of surviving children, complete group: 1860/70, 1880 and 1890 marriage cohorts, Tasmania

Source: Appendix A: Table A.27 (this volume).

Birth spacing

I originally intended to use the Cox regression to analyse the determinants of the length of birth intervals. However, when I undertook the 'ph test' and examined the survival curves, I found my data violated the proportional hazards assumption (Cleves et al. 2010: 208–9). I therefore used a piecewise exponential regression model for my analysis of birth spacing (Cleves et al. 2010: 329).

I did not include the interval between marriage and the first birth in the model, since the marriage cohorts varied markedly in the proportion of first births that were conceived before marriage (see Table 7.2). Many other studies of spacing behaviour have concentrated on interbirth intervals for this reason (for example, Van Bavel and Kok 2004; Tsuya et al. 2010). Thus, the spacing analysis includes only couples with two or more children.

The dependent variable is the length of a birth interval in months (rounded to one decimal place).

I used the same covariates as in the logistic regression with the following exceptions:

- I used the crude parity at the beginning of the birth interval to control for fecundity, since women with higher parities tend to have shorter birth intervals (Van Bavel and Kok 2004, 2010).
- I excluded the number of deaths of infants and young children because of multicollinearity, as discussed above.
- I included a dummy variable that indicates whether the birth interval was the last, to account for the fact that last birth intervals are generally longer than other birth intervals even in circumstances where there is no fertility control (Van Bavel and Kok 2004).

Descriptive statistics of the covariates used in this model are shown in Appendix A: Table A.28.

The model shows there are many covariates that are significantly associated with the length of birth intervals (Table 7.17).

Birth spacing was associated with the mother's age at birth, with birth intervals significantly longer for women who gave birth when they were older. When women gave birth at age 30 years or older, for instance, their birth intervals were longer than when they gave birth under 25 years of age (relative risk = 0.65, $p = 0.000$). In contrast, birth intervals were significantly shorter for women who married at older ages, with women marrying at 25 years or older having much shorter birth intervals than women who married under 20 years of age (relative risk = 1.55, $p = 0.000$). The age difference between the husband and wife had no significant association with the length of the birth interval.

Table 7.17 Estimated effects (relative risks) of various characteristics on the time to the next birth (closed birth intervals), complete group: 1860/70, 1880 and 1890 marriage cohorts, Tasmania

Covariate	Relative risk	Standard error	Significance (p)	
Constant	0.07	0.005	0.000	**
Mother's age at birth of a child				
< 25 years (ref.)	1.00	—	—	
25–29 years	0.75	0.025	0.000	**
30+ years	0.65	0.029	0.000	**
Mother's age at marriage				
< 20 years (ref.)	1.00	—	—	
20–24 years	1.13	0.031	0.000	**
25+ years	1.55	0.073	0.000	**
Age difference between couple				
Same age/husband up to 5 years older (ref.)	1.00	—	—	
Wife older	1.05	0.037	0.214	
Husband 5+ years older	1.01	0.025	0.645	
Marriage cohort				
1860/70 cohorts (ref.)	1.00	—	—	
1880 cohort	0.95	0.026	0.070	
1890 cohort	0.86	0.024	0.000	**
Socioeconomic status				
White-collar (ref.)	1.00	—	—	
Skilled	1.00	0.040	0.859	
Farmers	1.06	0.037	0.071	
Lower-skilled	0.99	0.044	0.917	
Unskilled	1.04	0.037	0.186	
Type of geographic location				
Urban area in Tasmania (ref.)	1.00	—	—	
Rural area in Tasmania	1.07	0.030	0.014	*
Another colony	1.05	0.046	0.309	
Religion				
Anglican (ref.)	1.00	—	—	
Catholic	1.04	0.038	0.288	
Presbyterian	1.00	0.036	0.992	

Covariate	Relative risk	Standard error	Significance (p)	
Methodist	1.05	0.032	0.093	
Other Nonconformist	0.93	0.031	0.036	*
Literacy status of husband and wife				
Both literate (ref.)	1.00	—	—	
Husband and/or wife illiterate	0.96	0.031	0.224	
Twin birth	1.05	0.127	0.669	
Number of children (crude parity)	1.05	0.018	0.008	**
Number of surviving children	0.99	0.018	0.766	
Child dies as infant before conception of another	1.45	0.067	0.000	**
Ultimate birth interval	0.42	0.014	0.000	**
Sex composition of surviving children				
More surviving girls than boys (ref.)	1.00	—	—	
More surviving boys than girls	1.01	0.024	0.640	
Equal numbers of surviving boys and girls	0.96	0.030	0.237	
No. of birth intervals = 8,466				

* $p < 0.05$
** $p < 0.01$
— not applicable for the reference category

The marriage cohort was significantly associated with the length of the birth interval, with intervals significantly longer for women in the 1890 marriage cohort compared with the 1860/70 cohorts (relative risk = 0.86, p = 0.000). Women in rural areas of Tasmania had significantly shorter birth intervals than those in urban areas (relative risk = 1.07, $p < 0.05$), while Other Nonconformists had significantly longer birth intervals than Anglicans (relative risk = 0.93, $p < 0.05$). The socioeconomic status and literacy status of the husband and wife had no significant association with the length of the birth interval.

The higher the parity, the shorter was the birth interval (relative risk = 1.05, $p < 0.01$). Having a child die in infancy while the woman was not pregnant with another significantly reduced the time to the next birth (relative risk = 1.45, p = 0.000). The last birth interval was significantly longer than the other birth intervals (relative risk = 0.42, $p < 0.01$).

However, the number of surviving children was not significantly related to the length of the birth interval, nor was their sex composition. Giving birth to twins also had no significant association with the length of the next birth interval.

To ascertain whether these findings were affected by couples who had all their births outside the colony, I ran the same model for couples who had at least one birth in Tasmania, with similar results, except the parity of the birth was only significant at the $p < 0.05$ level.

I ran the model with interaction effects to see whether there were differences in spacing within socioeconomic status, geographic location and religious groups across the cohorts. I found farmers (relative risk = 1.26, $p < 0.05$) and unskilled workers (relative risk = 1.19, $p < 0.05$) had significantly shorter birth intervals than white-collars workers in the 1890 cohort compared with the 1860/70 cohorts (Appendix A: Table A.29). This indicates that white-collar workers were spacing their births in the 1890 cohort compared with other cohorts. Methodists (relative risk = 1.32, $p < 0.05$) also had significantly shorter birth intervals than Anglicans in the 1880 cohort compared with the 1860/70 cohorts. This finding is not explained by any differences in the composition of the Methodist group in the three cohorts, since the proportions of Wesleyan Methodists, Primitive Methodists and United Free Methodists in the 'Methodist' group did not change between the cohorts.

In summary, birth intervals were significantly longer for mothers who gave birth at older ages, but significantly shorter for mothers who married at older ages. Birth intervals were significantly longer for mothers in the 1890 cohort compared with the 1860/70 cohorts and significantly longer for Other Nonconformists compared with Anglicans. Rural women had significantly shorter birth intervals than urban women. The higher the parity of any birth, the shorter was the birth interval, while having an infant die while the woman was not pregnant with another led to significantly shorter birth intervals. The last birth interval was significantly longer than the other birth intervals.

The covariates of age difference between husband and wife, literacy of the husband and wife, number of surviving children, sex composition of those children and whether the preceding birth was a twin birth were not significantly associated with birth spacing. Socioeconomic status was not significantly associated with birth spacing in the overall model;

however, when interaction effects were examined, in the 1890 cohort, farmers and unskilled workers had significantly shorter birth intervals than white-collar workers compared with the 1860/70 cohorts. In relation to religion, in the 1880 cohort, Methodists had significantly shorter birth intervals than Anglicans, compared with the 1860/70 cohorts.

Parity progression

To investigate the timing of the fertility decline, I used multivariate analysis to look at the determinants of parity progression. I wanted to see whether there were specific parities at which the 1880 and 1890 cohorts were likely to stop childbearing compared with the 1860/70 cohorts. As with the spacing analysis, I used a piecewise exponential regression model since my initial analysis showed the data violated the proportional hazards assumption. I did not estimate the effects of various characteristics on parity progression from parities 10 and over, because of the smaller numbers at these higher parities.

In interpreting the results, it is important to note that differences in the relative risk of having another birth can indicate differences either in spacing or in stopping behaviour.

I used the same covariates as in the logistic regression with some exceptions:

- I excluded the covariate 'number of children dead' at the parity since this was the obverse of the 'number of surviving children' at any parity.
- I excluded the covariate 'twin birth' because of the small number of twin births at each parity.
- I used a different categorisation for 'mother's age at the birth' at low and high parities because of the different numbers in the various categories as women aged. 'Mother's age at birth' was divided into three categories: < 25 years, 25 to < 30 years and 30+ years for parities one to four; and < 30 years, 30 to < 35 years and 35+ years for parities five and over.

The survival analysis models show that the covariates that consistently had significant effects on the risk of progressing from one parity to another were: mother's age at the birth of a child, mother's age at marriage, marriage cohort and whether the child died as an infant while the mother was not pregnant with another child (Tables 7.18a and 7.18b). Detailed information regarding each parity progression can be found in Moyle (2015: Tables A7.11–A7.19).

At every parity except parity nine, the oldest mothers had a significantly lower risk of having another birth than the youngest mothers. For instance, among those with four children, mothers who were 30 years or older had a significantly lower risk of having another birth than those who were under 25 years of age (relative risk = 0.41, p = 0.000).

Women's age at marriage, however, had the opposite effect, with mothers marrying at older ages having a significantly higher risk of having another birth at parities one, three, five and six. Among women with five children, for instance, women who married aged 20–24 years and those who married aged 25 years and over had a significantly higher risk of having another birth than those who married under 20 years of age (relative risks = 1.28 and 2.60, respectively; p < 0.01).

Women in the 1890 marriage cohort had a significantly lower risk of having another birth than women in the 1860/70 cohorts at all parities except parities one and nine, and even at parity one, the risk was almost significant (relative risk = 0.88, p = 0.051). For those in the 1890 cohort, the relative risks of having another birth compared with those in the 1860/70 cohorts ranged from 0.77 at parity two to 0.58 at parity four (p < 0.01). Women in the 1880 cohort also had a significantly lower risk of having another birth compared with those in the 1860/70 marriage cohorts at parities four and five (relative risks = 0.72 and 0.73, respectively; p = 0.000).

Women with a child dying as an infant while they were not pregnant had a significantly higher risk of having another birth than other mothers at all parities except four and eight, with the relative risks ranging from 1.4 at parity one to 1.65 at parity nine (p < 0.01, except at parity seven, where p < 0.05).

Wives of farmers and unskilled workers had a significantly higher risk of having the next birth than white-collar workers at parities two and three (p < 0.01). For farmers' wives, the relative risks were 1.31 at parity two and 1.43 at parity three, while for the wives of unskilled workers, they were 1.3 and 1.32, respectively. Farmers also had a significantly higher risk of having the next birth than white-collar workers at parities one and six (p < 0.05).

Women living in a rural area of Tasmania had a significantly higher risk of having another birth compared with women living in an urban area of Tasmania at parities two, four and seven, with a relative risk at parity four, for instance, of 1.23 ($p < 0.01$).

Some of the other covariates were significantly associated with the risk of having another child at a few parities: the age difference between couples, religion, number of surviving children and sex composition of the surviving children.

Table 7.18a Estimated (significant) effects (relative risks) of various characteristics on parity progression from a piecewise exponential hazard model, complete group: 1860/70, 1880 and 1890 marriage cohorts, Tasmania

	Parity progression			
	1 to 2 Rel. risks	2 to 3 Rel. risks	3 to 4 Rel. risks	4 to 5 Rel. risks
Mother's age at the birth				
< 25 years (ref.)	1.00	1.00	1.00	1.00
25 to < 30 years	0.78 *	0.82 *	0.67 **	
30+ years	0.41 **	0.50 **	0.37 **	0.41 **
Mother's age at marriage				
< 20 years (ref.)	1.00		1.00	
20 to < 25 years			1.25 *	
25+ years	1.32 *		1.63 **	
Age difference between couple				
Same age/husband up to 4 years older (ref.)		1.00		
Wife older		1.25 **		
Husband 5+ years older			0.87 *	
Marriage cohort				
1860/70 cohorts (ref.)		1.00	1.00	
1880 cohort				0.72 **
1890 cohort		0.77 **	0.67 **	0.58 **
Socioeconomic status				
White-collar (ref.)	1.00	1.00		
Farmers	1.24 *	1.31 **	1.43 **	
Unskilled		1.30 **	1.32 **	

7. HOW, WHEN AND WHY DID FERTILITY DECLINE?

	Parity progression			
	1 to 2 Rel. risks	2 to 3 Rel. risks	3 to 4 Rel. risks	4 to 5 Rel. risks
Type of geographic location				
Urban area in Tasmania (ref.)				
Rural area in Tasmania		1.21 **		1.23 *
Child dies as infant before conception of another	1.40 **	1.54 **	1.62 **	
Sex composition of surviving children	n.a.			
More surviving girls than boys (ref.)				1.00
Equal numbers of surviving boys and girls				0.82 *

* $p < 0.05$
** $p < 0.01$
n.a. not available
Source: Moyle (2015: Tables A7.11–7.19).

Table 7.18b Estimated (significant) effects (relative risks) of various characteristics on parity progression from a piecewise exponential hazard model, complete group: 1860/70, 1880 and 1890 marriage cohorts, Tasmania

	Parity progression				
	5 to 6 Rel. risks	6 to 7 Rel. risks	7 to 8 Rel. risks	8 to 9 Rel. risks	9 to 10 Rel. risks
Mother's age at the birth					
< 30 years (ref.)	1.00	1.00	1.00	1.00	
30 to < 35 years	0.61 **	0.81 *	0.53 **		
35+ years	0.15 **	0.29 **	0.20 **	0.32 **	
Mother's age at marriage					
< 20 years (ref.)	1.00	1.00			
20 to < 25 years	1.28 **				
25+ years	2.60 **	1.42 *			
Age difference between couple					
Same age/husband up to 4 years older (ref.)		1.00			
Husband 5+ years older		0.83 *			
Marriage cohort					
1860/70 cohorts (ref.)	1.00	1.00	1.00	1.00	
1880 cohort	0.73 **				
1890 cohort	0.68 **	0.73 **	0.72 **	0.68 **	

	Parity progression				
	5 to 6 Rel. risks	6 to 7 Rel. risks	7 to 8 Rel. risks	8 to 9 Rel. risks	9 to 10 Rel. risks
Socioeconomic status					
White-collar (ref.)		1.00			
Farmers		1.34 *			
Type of geographic location					
Urban area in Tasmania (ref.)			1.00		
Rural area in Tasmania			1.24 *		
Religion					
Anglican (ref.)			1.00		1.00
Methodist			0.76 *		1.39 *
Child dies as infant before conception of another	1.50 *	1.60 **	1.43 *		1.65 *
Number of surviving children	1.13 *		1.11 *		

* $p < 0.05$
** $p < 0.01$
n.a. not available
Source: Moyle (2015: Tables A7.11–7.19).

In summary, women giving birth at older ages had a significantly lower risk of having another birth at most parities. In contrast, women marrying at older ages had a significantly higher risk of having another birth at some low parities. Women in the 1890 cohort had a significantly lower risk of having another birth than women in the 1860/70 cohorts at most parities, while women in the 1890 cohort had a significantly lower risk at parities four and five. Women with a child dying as an infant while they were not pregnant had a significantly higher risk of having another birth at most parities. Wives of farmers and unskilled workers had a significantly higher risk of having another birth than wives of white-collar workers at some low parities. Women living in a rural area of Tasmania had a significantly higher risk of having another birth than women in urban areas at some low to medium parities.

7. HOW, WHEN AND WHY DID FERTILITY DECLINE?

Summary

Bivariate and multivariate analyses of the fertility decline for the complete group in the four Tasmanian marriage cohorts indicate when fertility started to decline and provide support for some of the theories of how and why fertility declined in the late 19th and early 20th centuries.

Fertility declined in Tasmania from the second half of the 1880s and the fall was well established during the 1890s. Fertility began to fall from the 1860/70 cohorts to the 1880 cohort but there was a much larger fall from the 1880 to the 1890 cohorts. Compared with women in the 1860/70 cohorts, women in the 1880 cohort had a significantly lower risk of having another birth at parities four and five while women in the 1890 cohort had a significantly lower risk of having another birth at almost all parities from parity two onwards. The timing of the fertility decline supports demographic transition theory, since this was a period of social and economic change and modernisation in Tasmania.

Analyses of stopping and spacing behaviours provide support for both demographic transition theory (adjustment) and diffusion theory (innovation). The fall in fertility in late 19th-century Tasmania was due primarily to the practice of stopping behaviour in the 1880 and 1890 cohorts, while the practice of spacing behaviour in the 1890 cohort also contributed to the fertility decline. In all marriage cohorts, some groups had longer birth intervals than others, suggesting these groups were deliberately spacing their births before the fertility decline. However, the extent of the spacing was small and this may have been counterbalanced by shorter birth intervals of couples marrying at later ages or those with large families, having little effect on overall fertility levels in the earliest cohorts. Changes in starting behaviour made a small contribution to the fertility decline, due to an increase in the age at marriage, but it is unlikely a change in the age at marriage was related to fertility preferences.

The practice of stopping and spacing behaviours varied by different family characteristics, lending support to some of the theories of why fertility declined at this time.

Socioeconomic status was significantly associated with both stopping and spacing, supporting both diffusion and economic theories of fertility decline. In every marriage cohort, white-collar workers were significantly more likely to stop childbearing than skilled workers, farmers and unskilled workers. This indicates that white-collar workers were controlling their fertility before the fertility decline. In the 1890 cohort, white-collar workers were also spacing their births, compared with farmers and unskilled workers, possibly for economic reasons.

Geographic location was also significantly associated with stopping and spacing behaviours, supporting theories of diffusion. In every marriage cohort, people living in urban areas were more likely to stop having children and more likely to space their births than people living in rural areas. This indicates that people in urban areas were controlling their fertility before the fertility decline.

The findings relating to religion provide mixed support for theories of secularisation. Although there were no significant differences between religious groups in stopping behaviour, there were some differences in spacing behaviour. Other Nonconformists were more likely to space their births than Anglicans in every marriage cohort, indicating they were deliberately spacing their births before the fertility decline. This may also support theories of diffusion, since Other Nonconformists—Congregationalists/Independents and Baptists—may have had higher literacy than Anglicans because of their emphasis on reading the scriptures. Methodists had significantly shorter birth intervals than Anglicans in the 1880 marriage cohort, but this is difficult to explain. It is important to note that the measure of religion used here is a measure of religious affiliation, not of religiosity. It also measures religion at marriage only and some couples may have changed their religious affiliation during their childbearing years.

In Tasmania, the literacy levels of the husband and wife were not significantly associated with fertility control practices, providing no support for theories of diffusion or gender equity. However, the measure of literacy—whether the husband and wife signed the marriage register—is fairly weak.

The analyses of stopping and spacing behaviours do not support the 'replacement' or 'insurance' effects of infant and child mortality on fertility. Having a child die in infancy while a mother was not pregnant was not a significant determinant of stopping. However, the more infant and child deaths the family experienced, the more likely they were to stop childbearing. The number of surviving children also had no significant association with the time to the next birth, indicating that couples were not adjusting their birth spacing in relation to deaths of infants or children.

The analysis of spacing behaviour supports the 'physiological' relationship between infant mortality and fertility. Having a child die as an infant when the woman was not pregnant significantly reduced the time to the next birth. This was because, with the death of an infant, the woman stopped breastfeeding and started to ovulate. The survival analysis of parity progression shows that women who had a child die as an infant had a significantly higher risk of having another birth than other women at most parities, but this may reflect the length of time to the next birth rather than having another birth.

8

Why did fertility fall in Tasmania during this period? Qualitative insights

Some scholars have used contemporary literature to

> shed light on the extent of knowledge of birth control and attitudes toward reproduction and children in the past and help place the newly emerging quantitative results in their social, psychological and cultural context. (Knodel and van de Walle 1979: 219)

This chapter examines how the historical context of Australia, and of Tasmania specifically, and the historical sources of the period provide support for theories of the historical fertility decline discussed in Chapter 1: demographic transition theory, infant and child mortality, the greater accessibility of artificial methods of birth control, diffusion theory, economic theories, secularisation and changes in women's roles and status in society and in the family.

The qualitative analysis in this chapter was undertaken after the quantitative analysis was completed and its purpose is to further inform the quantitative findings and answer questions the quantitative analysis could not answer. As noted, there are three main areas of the historical fertility decline that cannot be examined using the quantitative data: how ideas and values about fertility control and knowledge of methods were diffused, what methods of contraception were used during the fertility decline and the role of women in the decline. The quantitative findings in relation to secularisation were also not definitive. The qualitative findings presented in this chapter address these questions and complement the quantitative findings presented in the previous chapters.

Much of the information in this chapter comes from witness statements and other published material from the 1903 Royal Commission on the Decline of the Birth-Rate and on the Mortality of Infants in New South Wales (NSW 1904a, 1904b). The royal commission was set up in 1903 to

> make a diligent and full Inquiry into the Causes which have contributed to the Decline in the Birth-rate of NSW and the Effects of the Restriction of Child-bearing upon the well-being of the community. (NSW 1904a: 1)

The commissioners quickly concluded that the decline in the birth rate was due to deliberate efforts by parents to restrict their fertility. While the commissioners were vehemently opposed to fertility control and asked very leading questions of the witnesses (Hicks 1978), the published accounts provide valuable information about the historical fertility decline from people living at the time.

The Tasmanian birth rate fell about the same time as the NSW birth rate and, given the similarities between the two states, there is no doubt the qualitative evidence regarding fertility control presented to the commission for New South Wales applied also to Tasmania. The commissioners confirm this in their report, stating:

> We have spoken thus far in this chapter in reference solely to the State whose population is the immediate subject of our inquiry; but what applies to NSW is obviously no less applicable to the whole of Australasia. (NSW 1904a: 172)

During this period, Tasmanian society was very similar to that of New South Wales. The states had the same culture and similar socioeconomic, education and legal systems. They were similar in terms of religion, although New South Wales was more Catholic than Tasmania. New South Wales and Tasmania were the earliest settled colonies of Australia and their settlers had similar British cultural origins. Communication between Tasmania and the other states, including New South Wales, was very good. News from the mainland states was reported daily in the Tasmanian newspapers. Ships carrying goods and people travelled several times a week between Sydney and Tasmanian ports. People moved between New South Wales and Tasmania both temporarily and permanently. Several of the couples in the marriage cohorts had births in Sydney or in other parts of New South Wales, with some remaining in New South Wales and others returning to Tasmania.

Some information about life in 19th and early 20th–century Tasmania comes from the diaries of two women: Amy Walker (1851–1940), who was in the 1870 marriage cohort, and Ida McAulay (1858–1949), who was a prominent feminist in late 19th and early 20th–century Hobart (McAulay 1889–90, 1890, 1897, 1898, 1899, 1900, 1903, 1904, 1905; Walker 1869, 1879, 1880, 1881, 1882, 1888, 1898; Appendix D: Stories 5 and 6, this volume). While these women did not write about family limitation or the fall in the birth rate, their diaries provide an insight into the lives of upper-class women in Tasmania in the final two decades of the 19th century and the first decade of the 20th century and into the social and economic conditions of the time. Pregnancy was not a subject that was discussed by these women in their diaries. On 22 April 1888, Amy Walker said she 'drove to Parsonage to see Fanny who is ill', but it was not until 3 December 1888, when she 'heard that Fanny's little daughter was born last night', that it appears this illness was related to pregnancy (Fanny was Amy's sister) (Walker 1888). Similarly, Ida McAulay wrote in her diary daily during 1898, but it is not until 8 September that we learn that her 'twins born. Ida: 5 lb 3 oz. Mollie 5 lbs 10 ozs' (McAulay 1898).

Other historical sources used in this chapter include articles or items from late 19th and early 20th–century newspapers of Tasmania and other colonies, and stories about people in the Tasmanian marriage cohorts.

Demographic transition theory

The social and economic conditions of Tasmania at the time of the historical fertility decline provide some support for demographic transition theory. Tasmania became more urbanised in the late 19th century and there was marked social and economic development.

The colony became more industrialised in the final two decades of the 19th century with the growth of the mining industry, which overtook agriculture in terms of its importance to Tasmania's economy. The proportion of the population employed in agriculture fell steadily from 1871. By the beginning of the 1880s, the income from mining exports was greater than that from wool and, by the end of the century, more than half the value of Tasmanian exports was derived from minerals. The colony also became more urbanised; by 1901, half the population was living in an urban setting—that is, in Hobart, Launceston and their suburbs, or in towns with populations of 500 or more that were close to one another and to the larger cities of Hobart and Launceston.

The 1870s, 1880s and 1890s were a time of 'modernisation' and economic and social development in Tasmania. The railways came to Tasmania from the early 1870s and spread throughout the colony in the 1880s and 1890s; the electric telegraph link between Tasmania and Europe was established in 1872 and Hobart and Launceston were connected with electric lighting in the 1890s. Agriculture became more mechanised in the 1890s and early 1900s. The *Education Act* of 1868 introduced compulsory education for children aged seven to 12 years and the 1873 *Public Schools Amendment Act* extended this to 14 years. The proportion of the population who could both read and write improved markedly between 1861 and 1901. There was rapid growth in 'modern' occupations, particularly white-collar occupations such as 'accountant', 'bank clerk', 'insurance agent', 'schoolteacher' and 'railway porter'. Some of the new occupations were within the growing transport and communications sectors.

Amy Walker's diaries mention many of the innovations of the time, as do Ida McAulay's diaries, which were written at a later date (Walker 1869, 1879, 1880, 1881, 1882, 1888, 1898; McAulay 1889–90, 1890, 1897, 1898, 1899, 1900, 1903, 1904, 1905).

Both women's diary entries illustrate changes in methods of transportation that occurred in the final two decades of the 19th century. To get from their estate, 'Clarendon', near Gretna, to Hobart, in 1879, the Walkers had to drive in a horse and carriage to Bridgewater to catch the train to Hobart; in 1888, they drove to New Norfolk (closer to Gretna) to take the train to Hobart; while in 1898, 'Captain H. came to dinner also Edgar and Marie David, riding their bicycles from the train' (Walker 1879, 1888, 1898). Both Amy and Ida took the train from Hobart to Launceston on several occasions (Walker 1879, 1880, 1882, 1888; McAulay 1899). Ida McAulay also regularly took the electric tram from Hobart to Sandy Bay (McAulay 1904). Ida bought a bicycle in May 1897 and learned to ride it, going on bicycling expeditions in later years (McAulay 1897, 1904).

Although Amy Walker and Ida McAulay wrote countless letters to friends and family, telegrams played an important part in their lives. On 15 January 1879, for instance, Amy Walker wrote 'received a telegram from Mama' (who lived in Hobart) and, on 18 January 1879, she 'sent a telegram to Mama asking for extended leave for Arthur' (her younger brother, who was staying with her) (Walker 1879). Ida McAulay often sent telegrams from her home in Bellerive to people living across the Derwent River in Hobart (McAulay 1897). Few people had telephones at this time, but in April 1904, Ida wrote that a friend 'received a telephone call' (McAulay 1904).

Amy Walker's diary entries mention some of the industrial and agricultural innovations of the time. In March 1882, when visiting Launceston, 'John, Leslie and I went to see the Bischoff Smelting works in the evening after dinner' (Walker 1882). On 17 January 1888, she wrote that 'John, Violet and Maudie went over to French's Forest to see a reaping machine at work on the plains', and on 9 May of that year, 'Our threshing machine arrived in the afternoon' (Walker 1888).

Ida McAulay's diaries talk about the movement of people out of Hobart to the mining towns in the far west of the colony in the final decade of the 19th century. In August 1899, she wrote:

> I went to town to try to get a girl for a fortnight. Impossible to hear of one. Everyone wanting servants and no one can get them. They all go to the West Coast. (McAulay 1899)

The 1880s and 1890s were a time of new ideas for Tasmania and improvements in education opened up people's minds to these ideas; 'reform and progressive legislation characterized the period' (Robson and Roe 1997: 50). For example, the *Women's and Children's Employment (Factories) Act* of 1884 specified that women could not be employed for more than 10 hours a day and children for more than eight (Sprod 1984). The *Public Health Act* came into effect throughout the colony in 1885, leading to the setting up of local health boards, the closure of cesspits and the eradication of typhoid within a short period (Robson and Roe 1997). The 1885 *Education Act* tried to rectify some of the problems of poor school attendance, albeit with limited success. There was also pressure to reform laws related to women, including changing the age at which women could marry from 12 to 16 years (Robson and Roe 1997). In 1896, a bill for female suffrage was passed in the House of Assembly with a large majority but was rejected in the Legislative Assembly (Reynolds 2012). However, women were finally given the right to vote six years later.

As members of the upper class, Amy Walker and Ida McAulay were highly educated women and were interested in life outside the home. Both women went to parliament in Hobart to listen to debates about several matters (McAulay 1897; Walker 1898). Ida McAulay, in particular, was very interested in and receptive to new ideas. She belonged to a reading group and a discussion group. In January 1897, the latter group discussed 'the nationalization of land'; in July 1897, there was a 'discussion of Australia separating from England and becoming a nation itself'; and in October 1899, she took part in a debate on 'woman's suffrage', speaking in favour of the proposal (McAulay 1897, 1899). Before she was married, Ida read Darwin's *On the Origin of Species* and *The Descent of Man* (McAulay 1889).

Infant and child mortality

One element of demographic theory is not supported by the situation in Tasmania—that is, a decline in infant mortality is a necessary condition for fertility to decline. There is no evidence from sources of the period to support theories about the relationship between infant mortality and fertility control. Between 1860 and 1899, the infant mortality rate for Tasmania was relatively flat, despite large annual fluctuations (Kippen 2002c). Infant mortality began to decline in Australia only at the turn of the century—well after fertility had started to decline (McDonald et al. 1987). In Tasmania, infant mortality rates fell from around 100 infant deaths per 1,000 live births in the 1890s to around 55 infant deaths per 1,000 live births in the 1920s.

The 1903 NSW Royal Commission on the Decline in the Birth-Rate investigated the causes of the fall in the birth rate and the high rates of infant mortality but concluded the two were not linked:

> The decrease in infant mortality may be a consequence of the decline in the birth rate, but the converse is not true … there may be a high infant death-rate together with a low birth-rate. (NSW 1904a: 13)

I have not found any historical sources that discuss any link between the fall in child mortality and the fertility decline in Australia. In Tasmania, the mortality of children aged one to 14 years started to decline several years before the decline in infant mortality. 'Male and female child mortality fell by half from 1860–64 to 1895–99' (Kippen 2002c: 239). For both boys and girls, the decline was due mainly to a fall in deaths from epidemic diseases followed by a fall in deaths from accidents. The 'clear downward trend' in the child mortality rate was interrupted in the second half of the 1870s by two epidemics—one of measles and one of scarlet fever (Kippen 2002c: 66). John and Sarah Chick, a couple in the 1870 marriage cohort, lost their four children, aged one to six years, to scarlet fever in the five days between 30 September 1876 and 4 October 1876.

It is probable that most women in 19th-century Tasmania knew someone who had a child die in infancy. In almost all of Amy Walker's diaries, she mentions the death of a baby of a friend or family member. On 30 May 1880, Amy 'wrote to Mrs Milne who has just lost her little baby', while on 23 April 1888, she wrote she had 'heard the sad news of Arthur's little daughter's death this morning at 5 o'clock' and, on 27 July 1898, 'Miss Collier came to see me telling me of the death of Mrs Widdicourse's baby' (Walker 1880, 1888, 1898). Amy's diaries written during her married life do not mention deaths of small children, but her diary written the year before she was married notes, on 29 July 1869: 'Yesterday, poor little Archie was run over in the street and killed' (Walker 1869).

Methods of contraception

Historical sources indicate that, in Australia, the availability and use of artificial methods of contraception increased markedly in the late 19th and early 20th centuries—that is, during the period in which marital fertility started to decline. The methods that were probably used prior to the decline, such as 'withdrawal' and abortion, also became more common.

Although they could not be specific about timing, many witnesses to the 1903 NSW Royal Commission testified that the purchase and use of artificial methods of contraception had greatly increased in the preceding 20 years, as had the practices of 'withdrawal' and abortion. Other evidence shows that, in the late 19th and early 20th centuries, wholesale drug companies imported into New South Wales French letters (condoms), the India rubber *Pessaire Preventif*, Rendell's soluble pessaries and safety sponges (NSW 1904b: 13, 15). Some wholesale druggists and pharmacists also made their own soluble pessaries (NSW 1904b: 15, 20). Enemas, douches and syringes sold by pharmacists were also used for contraceptive purposes.

Witnesses to the royal commission agreed that almost all pharmacists in Sydney stocked contraceptive devices, but this was not the case in the country.[1] Dr Cosby Morton, a general practitioner who had practised in several country areas, said: 'Many country chemists sell them; I would not say all'[2] (NSW 1904b: 27). Preventives were also sold by hawkers, including women, in both the city and the country (NSW 1904b: 18, 24, 27). Some Sydney drug companies and pharmacists sold preventives to country people by mail (NSW 1904b: 21, 44).

Testimony from pharmacists to the royal commission indicates the demand for artificial contraceptives was high, despite the reluctance on the part of a few pharmacists to sell them. Thomas Loney, a pharmacist in William Street, Sydney, said:

> For a great many years, I have absolutely refused to sell those articles at all, but during the last year or two the demand for them has become so imperative that I have been obliged to keep them. (NSW 1904b: 35)

William Park, a pharmacist in Pitt Street, Sydney, was one of the very few pharmacists who refused to stock preventives:

> I don't sell preventives. I don't believe in them. I am asked for these articles every day. The day before yesterday I had four people within an hour ask for these quinine pessaries. (NSW 1904b: 40)

The demand for female preventives was so high that, in the late 1890s, Washington Soul, the largest pharmacy in Sydney, established a 'nurse' in a kiosk in its city store solely to sell articles to women. 'Nurse B' told the commissioners:

> My particular duties are to attend to ladies with articles that are kept in my room—such as enemas, douches, elastic goods, belts, accouchement sheets, sanitary towels, breast pumps, trusses and such articles as those ... I have sold women rubber pessaries or medicated pessaries and safety sponges. (NSW 1904b: 57)

It is not possible to obtain information on the total number of artificial contraceptives sold in New South Wales during this period. However, data provided to the commission from the Customs Department showed the

---

1 'Country' in this Australian context refers to all areas outside the major cities. The 'country' was also referred to as the 'bush'.
2 A 'chemist' was a pharmacist.

number of preventives imported into the state in three sample months in 1903 and 1904 was not large. The October 1903 return shows the highest number of imports: 100 gross French letters (14,400), 212 dozen boxes of Rendell's pessaries, 22 dozen pessaries, 20 gross *Pessaire Preventif* and 10 gross Bandruche Skins (NSW 1904b: 311).

Most artificial contraceptives were relatively expensive in relation to the average wages of working-class and even some middle-class men. The wages of working men ranged from 30s to £2 8s per week, while lower-white-collar workers generally earned from £2 to £3 a week (NSW 1904b: 29, 45, 106, 264–5). India rubber pessaries cost from 8s 6d to £2 2s each, while soluble pessaries cost from 3s a dozen and French letters from 6s a dozen (NSW 1904b: 363–5, 383, 385). Many witnesses told the royal commission it was common for women to use less expensive methods of prevention or to make their own preventives.

Several witnesses testified that the use of syringes, douches and enemas was common practice. William Sharland, representative of the Parke Davis Drug Company, told the commission: 'I think that the latter are the growing class of preventives—that is the douching of the canal with enemas and douches with antiseptic solutions' (NSW 1904b: 24). J.A. Masterton, a pharmacist in Market Street, Sydney, said: 'Others will not go to the expense of anything; they simply use their syringe with an astringent lotion straight away, and that answers the purpose just the same' (NSW 1904b: 30). Dr Robert Scot-Skirving, a physician and surgeon at two major Sydney hospitals, reported that in 'the bush, and among the lower classes generally, the preventive as a rule, is syringing immediately after connection either with hot or cold water' (NSW 1904b: 101).

Many witnesses told the commissioners that women made their own soluble pessaries. J.A. Masterton said:

> Referring to these soluble pessaries, they are made of cocoa butter, which is the vehicle to carry the quinine that is in them and is the sterilising agent. Now a great number of people buy cocoa butter by itself, and they buy quinine by itself. (NSW 1904b: 30)

George Stevens, a pharmacist in a working-class inner-city part of Sydney, reported: 'They come and buy 3d. worth of cocoa butter and some quinine and they mix it up themselves' (NSW 1904b: 43). Dr John Harris, who had been a general practitioner in Newcastle, NSW, for 30 years, said:

> There are a larger percentage of women now who know how to prepare their own pessaries. They use quinine and sulphate of zinc and make them up with cocoa butter themselves. It is common for women to make their own pessaries and introduce them into the vagina and leave them there. (NSW 1904b: 125)

Several witnesses testified that it was common for women to use sponges for preventive purposes, with many women making their own contraceptive sponges. Sir James Graham, who was an honorary surgeon at two major Sydney hospitals, said: 'One frequently finds, in the ordinary outdoor clinic[3] of a woman's hospital, evidence of sponges and the like' (NSW 1904b: 114). J.A. Masterton reported:

> There are sponges used—small sponges. Now these sponges are designed for the same thing. Well, a great number of people will not go [to] the trouble of buying a sponge. They buy the ordinary toilet sponge and cut it into pieces and they tie a tape to them, and they use them themselves. (NSW 1904b: 30)

Several doctors gave evidence to the royal commission that 'withdrawal' was used to prevent conception. Dr Scot-Skirving said: 'I think that withdrawal is practised to a considerable extent' (NSW 1904b: 101). Dr William McKay, medical officer at a suburban Sydney hospital, told the commissioners: 'The main method is the withdrawal of the male organ before the act is completed' (NSW 1904b: 105). Dr Ralph Worrall, senior visiting surgeon to the Sydney Women's Hospital, also thought withdrawal was very common (NSW 1904b: 88).

Some scholars have used this testimony to conclude that withdrawal was the most common method used to prevent conception during the Australian historical fertility decline (Pringle 1973; Quiggin 1988; Bongiorno 2012), but evidence from other witnesses to the NSW royal commission does not support this view. Additionally, when McKay's statement is examined in more detail, it appears he is primarily talking about the use of withdrawal by the middle classes:

> Prevention is more common in the middle classes. I mean men earning say £2 a week in offices … it is not so common among the working classes, because the man will not submit to it. The woman might be quite willing, but the man will not submit. (NSW 1904b: 105)

---

3   An 'outdoor clinic' was an outpatient clinic at a public hospital for poor and working-class women.

Overall, witnesses to the royal commission indicated that female-controlled preventives—that is, soluble pessaries, syringes, douches, enemas and sponges—were commonly used by women of all classes to prevent pregnancy. Soluble pessaries were more popular than French letters, which were used to prevent disease as well as conception (NSW 1904b: 16, 29). Most pharmacists reported the sale of pessaries had overtaken that of French letters in recent years. George Stevens said: 'There is not much sale for the French letters since the pessaries have come into vogue' (NSW 1904b: 43).

Abortion was another method used to limit family size in Australia in the late 19th and early 20th centuries, despite being a criminal offence. Until Federation in 1901, the Australian colonies were subject to the UK *Offences Against the Person Act* of 1861, which made abortion illegal under any circumstances. After Federation, abortion remained a criminal offence under different state legislation.

Most witnesses to the NSW royal commission attributed the decline in the birth rate to both prevention and abortion, with many saying prevention was more commonly used by the middle class to limit family size and abortion more commonly used by the working class (NSW 1904b). Almost all the witnesses—doctors, pharmacists, clergymen, police officers and others—reported that induced abortion was a common practice among both married and unmarried women. Most pharmacists reported a demand for pills that women used to try to procure abortions, such as 'Towle's Pennyroyal and Steel Pills' and 'Dr Boxwell's Silent Pills' (NSW 1904b: 357). Abortifacient pills were sold throughout Sydney and in all country areas (NSW 1904b: 28). They were also available by mail through advertisements in the newspapers (NSW 1904b: 30).

Witnesses to the royal commission reported that there were many abortionists operating in Sydney and some in country areas. These were mainly qualified and unqualified nurses and a very small number of doctors in Sydney, and unqualified midwives in the country areas. James Sawtell, senior sergeant of police in Sydney, thought the procuring of abortions was very prevalent in Sydney: 'I know of 36–38 reputed abortionists, mostly women in my own district. I also know of five legally qualified medical men' (NSW 1904b: 52). Dr Joseph Foreman, senior gynaecological surgeon to the Prince Alfred Hospital, said:

> The prevalence of abortion is almost incredible. The cases that are always coming in and taking up the beds in the hospitals are quite sufficient to show to what extent it prevails. (NSW 1904b: 229)

Most of the witnesses agreed that women of all classes used abortion to limit their families but thought the practice was more common among the working class. Arthur Glover, a general practitioner in a poor working-class district of Sydney, told the commissioners of the desperation of some of his married women patients:

> They are aware that abortion is a criminal act … and several of them, if you tell them how dangerous it is, say they will die before they will have another child. (NSW 1904b: 110)

Many witnesses reported that it was common for country women to come to Sydney to procure an abortion.

McCalman's (1988) study of female patients at a large public hospital in Melbourne shows that abortion was common in Melbourne in the late 19th century. In Adelaide also, several cases of abortion by a well-known abortionist, Madame Harper, were reported in the local newspapers in the late 19th and early 20th centuries (Anderson and Mackinnon 2015).

No data are available on the extent of induced abortion during the fertility decline. Some NSW hospitals provided data to the royal commission on cases of 'abortion or miscarriage' treated in the preceding five years, but it is impossible to separate out the two (NSW 1904b: 297–8, 312–13). In Tasmania, 27 women were recorded as dying from 'abortion' or 'miscarriage' between 1860 and 1899, almost all of them married, with 17 of all deaths occurring in the 1890s (Tasdeaths). Louisa Collings, who was in the 1890 marriage cohort, died from an abortion in May 1901 at the age of 31 years—some 18 months after she had her fifth child. The Tasmanian newspapers in the late 19th and early 20th centuries contain several accounts of women dying in Tasmania from illegal abortions performed by midwives, doctors and other persons (*Daily Telegraph*, [Launceston], 18 January 1890, 5 June 1894; *The Mercury*, [Hobart], 12 March 1879, 26 August 1910; *The Examiner*, [Launceston], 4 November 1891; *The North Western Advocate and the Emu Bay Times*, [Devonport], 19 August 1901).

Almost all the clergymen testifying to the royal commission thought sexual abstinence was the only method people should use to limit their families if this became absolutely necessary—for instance, if the wife's life became endangered by pregnancy (NSW 1904b: 202–26, 275–7). However, none of the evidence to the commission mentioned the use of abstinence as a preventive measure.

Diffusion theory

There is considerable evidence to support diffusion theory as one of the explanations for the historical fertility decline in Australia. Ideas and values about fertility control as well as the knowledge of the methods used to limit fertility clearly spread through Australian society in the late 19th and early 20th centuries.

As noted, Tasmania was not an isolated place in the second half of the 19th century. Communication between Tasmania and the mainland colonies and between Tasmania and English-speaking countries and Western Europe was very good.

Amy Walker's diaries indicate that the upper classes in Tasmania were in constant communication with people living outside Tasmania and they regularly travelled to other colonies and, on some occasions, to other parts of the world. The Walkers often had visitors from Melbourne, Sydney, New Zealand, England and other countries and had friends and family who travelled to these places. Several of Amy Walker's friends, neighbours and family went to stay in England and her brother Arthur went to study medicine in Edinburgh (Walker 1879, 1880). For example, on 12 December 1879, Amy 'wrote to Maria Parsons who has just returned from England with her husband and children'; on 25 May 1881, she went to a reception at Government House and met some of the officers from the Japanese warship *Gingo*; and, on 15 April 1882, she received 'letters from mother and Lilian posted at Honolulu' (Walker 1879, 1881, 1882). Ida McAulay went to Europe in 1889–90 before she was married, visiting cities such as Naples, Paris, Brussels and London (McAulay 1889–90). In 1897, Ida wrote about friends who were travelling to Sydney, Melbourne, the United States, England and South Africa (McAulay 1897).

Lower-class people were also in contact with others outside Australia. On 18 May 1881, Amy Walker wrote that her cook, 'Minnie heard of her sister's death in New Zealand and decided to go there'; and on 13 February 1882, one of the servants, 'Clara went to town for a holiday and to see about some money sent her from England' (Walker 1881, 1882). Several families in the four marriage cohorts of all classes left Tasmania for other colonies or New Zealand and later returned to Tasmania.

Communication between Tasmania and the rest of the world improved dramatically in the 1870s with the establishment of the electric telegraph cable between Tasmania and London. English news could now reach Tasmania in several hours rather than months (Cox 2012) and Tasmanian newspapers could publish news and articles shortly after they appeared in the English newspapers. Some of these articles concerned the trials of people for distributing information about birth control.

The 1903 NSW royal commissioners considered the spread of values regarding fertility limitation and information about fertility control methods was one of the main reasons for the fall in the birth rate from the mid-1880s (NSW 1904a). They reported that, in the final quarter of the 19th century, values about fertility control had spread throughout the 'civilised world' and there was a 'general diffusion of the knowledge of methods by which restriction might be accomplished which was previously wanting' (NSW 1904a: 17).

Some witnesses to the commission reported that the use of prevention first started with the upper classes. Dr Stanley McCulloch, honorary surgeon to the Sydney Women's Hospital, said family limitation was 'first observed by the well to do (I mean the comfortable class). I think it is spreading to the working classes' (NSW 1904b: 71). Most witnesses to the commission agreed that, by 1903, measures to limit the size of their families—either prevention or abortion—were used by people in all classes in New South Wales and by those in the country as well as the towns. However, they thought people in the country were less likely to use these measures. Dr Worrall reported:

> I have observed this tendency [to limit their families] … in every class in the community, but the higher classes resort to prevention of conception more frequently and the lower classes to the induction of abortion. I have noticed it with my patients from the country. They are just as familiar with the methods adopted as the people in the town, but do not practise it as frequently as town folk. (NSW 1904b: 89)

Birth control literature from overseas became available in Australia from the late 1870s. Books and pamphlets about birth control such as Knowlton's *Fruits of Philosophy* (1878), Annie Besant's *The Law of*

Population (1887) and Allbutt's *The Wife's Handbook* (1888) were available in Sydney and Melbourne bookshops and lectures on 'family limitation' were given in Melbourne and Sydney (NSW 1904b; Quiggin 1988; Bongiorno 2012). Brettena Smyth, a widow who ran her own pharmacy, gave frequent women-only lectures in the North Melbourne Town Hall and other locations around Victoria that were attended by hundreds of women at a time (McDonald and Moyle 2018). These lectures were freely advertised and reported on in the leading Melbourne newspapers. Smyth's book *The Limitation of Offspring* (1893), which covered aspects of reproductive health, including the use of contraceptive devices, was based on these lectures.

Many witnesses to the NSW royal commission mentioned *Fruits of Philosophy* and several of them had read it. The commission also heard evidence that pamphlets advertising preventives were in circulation in Sydney. Subinspector of police James Mitchell said of a handbill advertising the French *Pessaire Preventif*:

> Many complaints have been received from citizens that handbills of this character have been left at their houses with their female relatives. They are left door to door and we have had complaints of their being sent to people by post or other means. (NSW 1903b: 51)

It is not clear whether these books and pamphlets were available to the same extent in the country as in the city. The Reverend John Howell-Price, a Church of England clergyman from Richmond, a country area outside Sydney, said 'Bradlaugh's books and Mrs Besant's books and other books which are freely obtainable in Sydney are largely read in country places', but he thought leaflets and pamphlets were not generally distributed in country areas (NSW 1904b: 214).

Amy Walker and Ida McAulay both read for pleasure and for self-edification and they exchanged books of interest with other upper-class women. Neither of them mentioned books about fertility limitation, but on 21 January 1898, Ida wrote in her diary: 'Evening went round to the Victoria Club to take Miss Martin Annie Besant's autobiography to read' (McAulay 1898).

Advertisements in newspapers and journals were a major source of information about fertility control in late 19th and early 20th–century Australia (Quiggin 1988; Bongiorno 2012). The 1903 NSW Royal

Commission found newspapers in metropolitan, suburban and country New South Wales regularly contained advertisements for books and pamphlets providing information about methods of prevention and for the sale of preventives and abortifacients (NSW 1904b: 30, 39, 50, 87, 95, 271–2). Dr Edward Thring, a gynaecologist at a large Sydney hospital, thought:

> The general public are familiarised very much more now than they used to be with the methods by which prevention of pregnancy can be made to take place … and I think that one reason for that is the free advertising—I mean to say, the extensive advertising—[of] the various preventive methods which has taken place during the last, say, 20 years—the knowledge that there are various mechanical means which can be obtained by purchase for the prevention of impregnation. (NSW 1904b: 93)

Tasmanian newspapers such as *The Examiner*, *The Clipper* (Hobart) and *The Mercury* regularly included these types of advertisements:

> Women's Salvation—The wife's welfare within her control. Treatise posted free, sealed. Write to Professor Herman, French Specialist, 41 Collins Place, Melbourne. This treatise will teach you more about prevention in ten minutes than all the years you've lived. (*The Examiner*, [Launceston], 20 September 1894; *The Clipper*, [Hobart], 20 April 1895)

> A Blessing to Womankind, Pessaire Preventif: every mother delicate or otherwise should write for particulars to Dr A.K. Desjardien, Post Office Hobart. (*The Examiner*, [Launceston], 27 September 1885)

> Gents' latest American preventives, simple effective, last for years. 2s 6d posted. Write W.H. GARFIELD, Collins St, Melbourne. (*The Clipper*, [Hobart], 20 July 1895)

> Gents' best made French preventives. 6s per dozen, posted. Write R.R.HERMANN, Collins Place, Melbourne. (*The Clipper*, [Hobart], 20 July 1895)

> Alfaline Quinine Pessaries—A guaranteed harmless Preventative. Posted (from Sydney) … 5/6. (*The Clipper*, [Hobart], 19 August 1902)

> Towle's Pennyroyal and Steele Pills for Females. Quickly correct all irregularities and relieve the distressing symptoms so prevalent with this sex. Boxes 1s 1/2d and 2s 9d of all chemists and patent medicine vendors. (*The Mercury*, [Hobart], 17 March 1888)

> Oriental Female Pills. Triple Power. Restore regularity without fail. Any cause. Sure and Safe. Box posted 5s and 6d. Write, M. Garfield, Agent, West Collins St, Melbourne. (*The Clipper*, [Hobart], 20 April 1895)

Police officers appearing before the NSW royal commission reported that advertisements from well-known abortionists regularly appeared in the newspapers (NSW 1904b: 51–2, 183). However, these advertisements were written in a general way to obscure their true purpose: 'Nurse P. attends ladies during accouchement. Registered lying in home, 550 Cleveland St. Moore Park' (*Sydney Morning Herald*, 24 October 1902, cited in NSW 1904b: 186).

Similar advertisements for 'lying-in homes' appeared in the Tasmanian newspapers in the late 19th and early 20th centuries, and it is likely some of these establishments were also used to procure abortions.

News about the trials of prominent people for obscenity—because they were publishing and/or distributing information about methods of birth control—spread throughout Australia from the late 1870s. The Bradlaugh–Besant trial, which Caldwell (1999) argues was a catalyst for the adoption of birth control, was reported in all the Australian newspapers, including Hobart's *The Mercury* and Launceston's *The Examiner*. *The Mercury* reported on 13 August 1877:

> The trial of Mr Bradlaugh and Mrs Besant, before the Lord Chief Justice and a special jury, lasted five days and in their verdict the jury found the defendants guilty of publishing a work calculated to debase public morals, but exonerated them from all corrupt motives. A new trial will be applied for, and Mr Bradlaugh intends to carry the case to the House of Lords.

The book *Fruits of Philosophy* was again referred to in an article in *The Mercury* on 25 August 1877 reporting proceedings in the British House of Commons, quoted verbatim from the London *Times*. Another article in *The Mercury*, of 26 February 1878, compared an obscene pamphlet published in Melbourne to

> that notorious work 'Fruits of Philosophy' published by Mr Bradlaugh and Mrs Besant, and for which they were deservedly convicted and sentenced to be fined and confined, though the conviction has since been upset in the Supreme Court.

Collins booksellers was tried for obscenity in Sydney in 1888 for selling Annie Besant's book *The Law of Population*, but Judge Windeyer ruled the book was not obscene and Collins had a right to sell it. This judgement was reported in newspapers in all the Australian colonies, including Tasmania:

> In the Banco Court this morning, before the Chief Justice, Mr Justice Windeyer and Mr Justice Stephen judgment was delivered in the appeal of William Whitehouse Collins against his conviction by Mr. Addison, P.M. for offering for sale a certain indecent and obscene book entitled 'The Law of Population'. The Chief Justice reviewed the arguments in connection with the work entitled 'Fruits of Philosophy' ... Justice Windeyer delivered a lengthy opinion and said that it had been admitted that an abstract discussion on the law of population was a fitting one for the philosopher and the student of sociology; His Honor gave it as his opinion that the prohibition should go, as the book did not come under the designation of obscene. Justice Stephen concurred that the prohibition should be ordered to go and the conviction was quashed. (*The Mercury*, [Hobart], 19 December 1888)

The NSW royal commissioners considered that Justice Windeyer's judgement legitimised the practice of fertility control and blamed it for the 'sudden fall in the birth rate' that occurred in New South Wales in 1889 (NSW 1904a: 18). This was disputed by a witness to the commission, Sydney Maxted, who was chief boarding officer for the state Children's Relief Department and also a 'newspaper man'. He thought the Windeyer judgement

> at the time created a sensation, but I think it was less than a 9-days wonder and if you were to ask almost anybody in the street if those remarks were made I do not think you would get an affirmative answer, except from someone who takes a special interest in the question. (NSW 1904b: 96)

Maxted argued instead that midwives read these books and pamphlets and then provided the information to their patients:

> The midwives tell them how to do it. Years ago, they did not know, but of course by the dissemination of this literature that you have just spoken about, the knowledge gets into the minds of the midwives; they study it, and then they tell the people. A woman will attend another woman, and she will say 'Now, I will tell you how to stop having any more children' and she does. (NSW 1904b: 97)

Many witnesses told the commissioners that information about prevention was spread by word of mouth among women. Women discussed ideas and values about prevention with other women and gave them information on how to limit their births. The Reverend Howell-Price said:

> One of the most intelligent ladies that we have in the district is a very keen advocate of prevention, alleging various reasons why prevention should be practiced … This information is communicated to the unmarried and to married persons. (NSW 1904b: 214)

Pharmacist George Stephens reported:

> There is a peculiar thing about women; they will tell one another and they simply come along and ask for them [quinine pessaries] … they spread the information amongst other women … Knowledge travels from one woman to another in the country. (NSW 1904b: 44)

One of the few female witnesses, Witness E, a 47-year-old woman who had borne 16 children, said:

> Ever since my early married life, some of my friends have spoken to me about prevention. They have advocated it … People seem to be well acquainted with the methods of preventing impregnation. I have been spoken to myself by different people about all sorts of ways. They discuss the different methods among themselves openly among women of every class. (NSW 1904b: 189)

Dr Foreman added:

> They acquire the knowledge from the propagandists amongst themselves ... there is one woman ... who goes about telling other women; at all the tea meetings, at all the drawing rooms, it is the subject of conversation. There is not a woman scarcely who comes to me who does not know what to do to prevent conception. (NSW 1904b: 228)

The Reverend Nicholas Hennessy, a Congregationalist clergyman, thought:

> Women themselves have helped to spread the evil ... they are very free (those of them who have either one child or very small families) to tell a woman who has many children the means by which she can prevent the birth of more. (NSW 1904b: 207)

None of the doctors who gave evidence to the commission reported giving information about preventive methods to their patients. However, some doctors were involved in giving their patients access to preventives. Alfred Silly, managing director of the Australian Drug Company, sold preventives to doctors (NSW 1904b: 20), while Lewy Pattinson, a Sydney pharmacist, told the commission that women fairly frequently brought in doctors' prescriptions for preventives: 'I got one this morning from a doctor of good repute—for a box of Rendell's soluble pessaries. He is a leading doctor in Sydney' (NSW 1904b: 37). Nurse B from Washington H. Soul pharmacy in the city reported: 'Medical men of the highest standing have advised women to come to me' (NSW 1904b: 58).

The question of family limitation had become a legitimate topic for public discussion in Australia by the beginning of the 20th century. George Mullins, a Sydney general practitioner, told the commissioners:

> One hears so much about the limiting of families, and the various ailments to which men and women are liable which one did not hear some years ago; these are subjects of ordinary conversation at the present day which were not 10 or 12 years ago. (NSW 1904b: 66)

An analysis by Hicks (1978) of Australian newspapers of the period shows that discussion about the birth rate and family limitation was much more open in the early 1900s than in the 1870s or 1880s. In the early years of the 20th century, there were numerous editorials, articles and letters in the main Sydney, Melbourne and Adelaide newspapers about the fall in the birth rate and the reasons for the decline. During the same period, the Hobart and Launceston and some country newspapers contained articles and letters about the fall in the birth rate and family limitation in Australia and overseas. The Tasmanian newspapers reported on the NSW royal commission's findings in some detail (for example, *Daily Telegraph*, [Launceston], 7 March 1904; *The Mercury*, [Hobart], 7 June 1904). Two country newspapers published articles on a deputation to the Premier of Victoria on 'race suicide', reporting on 'preventive articles' sold by most Victorian pharmacists and 'a wicked and growing traffic in appliances for bringing about abortion' (*Zeehan and Dundas Herald*, 25 July 1909; *The North Western Advocate and the Emu Bay Times*, [Devonport], 27 September 1909).

Economic theories

There is considerable evidence to support economic theories of why fertility declined during this period. While it appears some people were restricting their fertility before the economic depression of the early 1890s, the increase in unemployment and the fall in wages that occurred in Tasmania provided great incentives for couples to adopt fertility control measures. Although conditions had improved by the end of the 19th century, for some groups of workers, wages were not as high as they had been in the 1880s.

Letters published by Sydney, Melbourne and Adelaide newspapers in the first decade of the 20th century show that economic reasons were important in the fertility decline. At least half of those writing to these newspapers about the declining birth rate gave economic factors as the main reason for limiting family size, complaining of unemployment, a lack of regular employment and increases in the cost of living (Hicks 1978).

Australia offered many opportunities for social mobility and this may have encouraged the practice of fertility control. Australian society was less rigid than English society and many people were able to realise their social and economic aspirations—sometimes within one generation (Breward 1988):

> While many of Australia's early migrants were from humble origins, they included many with great natural ability, who were able to use their gifts in the more open-textured Australian communities to achieve a degree of wealth, position and responsibility which would never have been possible in Britain. (Breward 1988: 24)

There are many examples of social mobility in the four marriage cohorts. For example, Samuel Sutton (1860 cohort), who was a baker during the 1860s, became a Member of the Tasmanian Parliament in 1886 (Appendix D: Story 7); David Dally (1870 cohort) was a lime dealer in the early 1870s, but became rich when he and his brothers discovered the famous Tasmanian (gold) Reef in 1877 (Appendix D: Story 8); and Joseph Lyons, the son of Michael Lyons (1870 cohort), a farmer and a butcher, became Premier of Tasmania in 1923 and Prime Minister of Australia in 1932 (Appendix D: Story 9).

In New South Wales in the early 1900s, many witnesses to the royal commission gave economics as one of the main reasons couples wanted to limit their families (NSW 1904b). Several witnesses regarded this as 'selfishness' on the part of these couples.

A continual theme of witness statements to the commission was that couples wanted to limit their families because of the costs of having children—that is, the cost of another child outweighed the benefits of having that child. Implicit in these statements was the view that people in all classes wanted a better future for their children—that is, they had social and material aspirations for their children.

Edmund Fuss, a pharmacist in a working-class area of Sydney, said of the middle and working classes:

> People are trying to acquire knowledge, in my opinion to get means to prevent having large families, for the simple reason that they have not means to support their children or to educate them. (NSW 1904b: 29)

Dr Worrall reported: 'I ask them over and over again and they say they cannot afford to rear and educate their children' (NSW 1904b: 89). Dr Scot-Skirving added:

> A good many of them say 'Well I can afford to educate and take care of two or three children, but I cannot give six a good education': so they say 'Well, I will not have any more than three'. (NSW 1904b: 97)

Many witnesses thought couples in all classes used prevention because they wanted to maintain their standard of living or aspired to a higher standard of living for themselves and/or their children. Dr Mullins reported that people told him 'it is too expensive … in many cases they can afford it, but they want the money for other purposes' (NSW 1904b: 66). Dr McKay said:

> In the majority of cases the reason given is that they have not got the money to support them … If these people have only £2 a week and have good clothes and live in a better class of house, they cannot support a large family. (NSW 1904b: 106)

John West, a master plumber and secretary of the Trades Hall Council, exemplified the situation of a working man with aspirations for his children:

> A working man with 4 or 5 children on £2 per week would exist and manage to get through it very well, but of course he would have to debar himself from luxuries. When I was earning less money I managed to save a little and when I got more my family wanted more. When I was on wages I could not get my daughters taught music. As soon as I was able to get in a bigger way, I let my girls learn the piano. (NSW 1904b: 200)

The aspiration to own their own home became part of the desire for a higher standard of living for working-class and middle-class families in Australia in the final two decades of the 19th century. 'The level of owner-occupation … was unquestionably very high by world standards' (Davison 2004: 219). Between one-third and one-half of homes in Melbourne, Sydney and Adelaide were owned or were being bought by their residents in the late 19th and early 20th centuries. Although we do not have Tasmanian data on home ownership in the late 19th century, the 1911 Australian census shows that 44.7 per cent of private dwellings in Tasmania were occupied by people who owned or were purchasing their home (Commonwealth of Australia 1914a: 419).

Several witnesses to the royal commission labelled the desire for a better standard of living as 'pleasure seeking'. Edmund Fuss thought wealthy people purchased preventives because of the 'desire … to follow their social and pleasurable inclinations' (NSW 1904b: 30). A witness from the Salvation Army said middle-class couples 'desire not to have children in order to have more social pleasure' (NSW 1904b: 187). Some witnesses thought working-class people did not want large families because they wanted to go out dancing, to the theatre and on picnics. John West said:

> Among the working class, the object of lessening their births is very often the fear of poverty, and in others it is on account of curtailing their pleasures and enjoyments. (NSW 1904b: 199)

Edmund Riley, a plasterer and president of the Sydney Labour Council, argued that education had increased working-class people's aspirations:

> If you want people to remain still in their social state you must not give them free education. When people's minds are educated they crave for enjoyments and pleasures … The industrial classes … have as much right to their enjoyment and pleasure as any other class. (NSW 1904b: 196)

Witness statements to the NSW royal commission outlined above clearly show a concern for the 'quality' of children rather than 'quantity'. Dr Grace Russell from the Sydney Women's Hospital considered that, '[w]ith a good many of the thinking women, it is a very strong reason for limitation—the anxiety for the well-being of those children that are born' (NSW 1904b: 110). Books and magazine articles of the time support the view that parents were concerned about the 'quality' of their children. *The Dawn*, a women's journal published monthly in Sydney between May 1888 and July 1905, contained many articles about bringing up children—for instance, 'Sleep' (November 1889), 'About babies' (February 1891) and 'Shall all children learn music' (March 1894) (Lawson 1990). This journal had subscribers across eastern Australia, including Tasmania. Parents focused not only on their children's health and education, but also on their behaviour. A history of manners in colonial Australia cites several magazine articles published in the late 1880s on the need to teach children good manners, and two books on etiquette published at the turn of the century included chapters on children's manners (Russell 2010). Ida McAulay's diaries indicate that theories about child development were in circulation in the late 1890s. On 20 January 1897, she wrote about her young son: 'I almost agree with J.P. Richter that the most important time for training in a child's life is the first year' (McAulay 1897).

We do not know whether the 'opportunity costs' for women of having children were a consideration in family limitation during the historical fertility decline in Tasmania, since there is no information as to whether married women with dependent children worked outside the home other than in the family business or farm. One of the witnesses to the 1903 royal commission, Annie Duncan, an inspector of factories and shops, reported the situation in Sydney, saying:

> I think the proportion of women with very young children is very small. I think the married women who are employed in factories are mostly women whose children are out of hand. (NSW 1904b: 130)

The evidence to support Caldwell's 'wealth flows' theory is not strong but is supportive. Although education became compulsory in Tasmania in 1868, average attendance at government schools was 70–75 per cent throughout the final quarter of the 19th century. Children who were absent regularly from government schools were those of the urban and rural working classes and of smaller farmers. These children helped in the home or on the family farm or were working in paid employment outside the family home to supplement the family income. These families would have been more likely to regard children as 'workers' than 'dependants'.

Most witnesses to the NSW royal commission discussed children in terms of their economic dependency on their parents, although some said the situation was different in the country. Dr Worrall, when asked why women in country districts had more children than those in the towns, replied:

> It is because they are more useful in the country; the children are more useful on the farms … they are equally poor but the children are really a source of wealth to them. (NSW 1904b: 92)

Secularisation

The history of religion in Tasmania and in Australia generally and the historical sources of the time support theories of secularisation and fertility decline. Religion did not have a major effect on people's lives in Australia and did not affect the adoption of ideas and values about fertility control and its practice.

Although many religious denominations became established in the early decades of the colony, Tasmania appears to have been a relatively secular society throughout the 19th and early 20th centuries. Tasmanians generally married in church, had their children baptised and were buried according to religious rites, but in most cases the church did not have a major influence over their lives.

Amy Walker and Ida McAulay were the antithesis of one another regarding religious practices. Walker, the daughter of an Anglican clergyman, participated very actively in the life of St Mary's Gretna, attending every Sunday, playing the harmonium in church, teaching Sunday school and was a member of the church society (Walker 1880, 1881, 1882, 1898). McAulay, on the other hand, had no religious beliefs. In 1900, she discussed evolution with her five-year-old son, gave him a lecture on agnosticism and told him that 'father and I do not believe in God' (McAulay 1900).

Historians generally agree that, in the early decades of the colony, most of the Tasmanian population did not have a strong religious affiliation (Breward 1988, 1993; Robson and Roe 1997; Boyce 2010; Reynolds 2012). Religion was generally not as important to people in Australia as it was in the United Kingdom or the United States (Breward 1988). By the 1850s and 1860s, religious groups in Australia did not have a strong influence on people's political and social attitudes and values. Anglicans, like other religious groups, reflected 'the political and social realities of its community rather than shaping the community' (Breward 1993: 45).

During the 1880s, there were calls for social reform in several areas of Australian life, such as widening the grounds for divorce (Breward 1993). This resulted in a further weakening of the control of religious groups and indicated that 'secular considerations were, by the 1880s, receiving more weight than historic theological ones' (Breward 1993: 83). The testimonies of clergymen of all the main religious denominations to the 1903 NSW Royal Commission show the church was very much opposed to the use of birth control (NSW 1904b), but this had little effect on its practice.

Many witnesses to the commission testified that a weakening of 'religious feeling' was one of the main factors responsible for the adoption of preventives and the subsequent decline in the birth rate (NSW 1904a: 17). Cardinal Patrick Moran, the Catholic Archbishop of Sydney, thought:

> In relation to my own religious people, there has been a marvelous [sic] development of respect for religion and devotion to all exercises of religion … But speaking of the community in general … there is a great decay of religious sentiment and what I would call manifest indifference to religion on the part of a great number of the citizens of New South Wales. (NSW 1904b: 210)

Dr Cosby William Morgan, a general practitioner who had worked in both the country and the city, thought:

> The decay of the religious sense in the people ... has conduced to the causes which bring about the decline in the birth rate. I think that their moral sense is blunted and that they do not care very much about religion at all. (NSW 1904b: 26)

Similarly, police sergeant Sawtell attributed the fall in the birth rate to

> the bad home training of children; both education and religious ... On Sundays you will see our young people in the parks and down the harbour engaged in all kinds of outdoor amusements, instead of being at Sunday school or attending religious instruction of some sort. (NSW 1904b: 136)

Dr Scot-Skirving said:

> The whole of this community, from the highest to the lowest are prone to use preventives. They are simply ordinary worldly people in whom religious sentiment has no very active measure of importance in their daily life and thought. (NSW 1904b: 100)

Even people who had religious views and were regular churchgoers often made their own decisions about what they believed was right rather than taking the church's views. John West told the commissioners he did not think

> religious sentiment has much effect ... I know persons who are very strong attendants at their church who are equally as bad as those who do not go ... My knowledge of the world is that the pocket plays the more important part than religious sentiment with most people in the community. (NSW 1904b: 199–200)

A witness from the Salvation Army testified that '[s]ome people who profess to have strong religious views still carry on these practices' (NSW 1904b: 187), while the Reverend Howell-Price said: 'They only admit the religious sense in as far as it may touch them in other directions—absolutely not in this' (NSW 1904b: 215).

While the clergymen appearing before the commission were very much opposed to fertility control, several thought it too sensitive a subject to bring up in the pulpit. Dr William Mckay, a Presbyterian minister, said:

> There is a natural shrinking from treating of such subjects; and although we clergymen know that such things have been going on yet, either out of a fear of bringing subjects before the young people that should not be brought before them or out of natural delicacy, the matter has been tabooed and not treated from the pulpit. (NSW 1904b: 204)

Other clergymen were afraid to preach against fertility control publicly because they thought they would alienate some of their parishioners, which would reduce their stipend. Dr Howell-Price said:

> I have spoken to the clergy about it and they have given me the answer back that they are afraid to speak of it from the pulpit … lest they should give offence and thus cause the offenders to withdraw their contributions from the churches. (NSW 1904b: 215–16)

The Reverend Howell-Price reported that when he preached against birth control from the pulpit, 'I know it injured myself for awhile' (NSW 1904b: 217). The Reverend Patrick Stephen, a Methodist clergyman, added:

> I have scarcely preached to my congregation upon that subject. I touched upon it in a general way … It is a most difficult thing to handle a delicate subject in public … Sometimes when a clergyman preaches to his congregation on this subject he is called to account by some members of his church … and in consequence of that and of circumstance that he may incur the ill will of his parishioners, he refrains from alluding to it at all. (NSW 1904b: 276)

Dr Howell-Price reported that clergymen who preached against prevention had been ridiculed publicly:

> Canon Potter, of Melbourne was the first, I think in Australia to introduce the matter into the pulpit and he was lampooned afterwards in one of the illustrated papers in Victoria. (NSW 1904b: 215)

Changes in women's roles and status

Historical sources of the time show women played a major role in the historical fertility decline in all the Australian colonies, due to changes in their roles in the family and in society that were occurring at this time. A recent article examining women's roles as agents in fertility decision-making concludes they were central agents in Australia's historical fertility transition (McDonald and Moyle 2018)—an argument also made by Cook (2000) and Anderson and Mackinnon (2015).

The fertility decline in Australia took place during a period in which ideas about women's rights began to spread throughout the colonies (Quiggin 1988; Anderson 1999). Books and pamphlets about women's rights began to circulate from the 1860s. This was followed by various feminist campaigns in the 1880s and 1890s on matters relating to property and child custody reform, public health and universal suffrage (Anderson 1999).

Several laws were enacted in Australia in the late 19th and early 20th centuries relating to women's rights.

Divorce was first made legal in all colonies except New South Wales between 1858 and 1864, with Tasmania enacting divorce laws in 1860 (Finlay 2001). New South Wales enacted a similar divorce law in 1873. Adultery was the only ground for divorce in the first divorce acts, but there was a double standard in that a husband could divorce his wife for adultery, but a wife could only divorce her husband for adultery under limited circumstances. New South Wales, although late to enact the first divorce laws, amended its Act in 1881 to treat husband and wife equally regarding adultery. Desertion, drunkenness and imprisonment were introduced as grounds for divorce in Victoria in 1889 and in New South Wales in 1892, but not until 1919 in Tasmania. The 1919 Tasmanian Act also abolished the double standard relating to adultery.

The *Married Women's Property Act*, which gave women the right to own and control property, was passed in 1884 in Victoria, in New South Wales in 1889 and in the other colonies in the early 1890s, including Tasmania, in 1893 (Cowie 2009).

Australia was one of the first of the English-speaking and European countries to give women the vote. South Australia and Western Australia gave women the right to vote shortly before Federation in 1901 and the other four colonies shortly after.

The feminist reform movement in Australia in the second half of the 19th century was to a large extent the province of elite and middle-class women (Quiggin 1988; Anderson 1999). Feminist writings were read mainly by these women, and the reformers involved in the various campaigns were also middle-class. However, feminist ideas gradually spread throughout the other strata of society. The introduction of compulsory primary education in the colonies from the late 1860s improved both men's and women's literacy, their access to information and their openness to new ideas. Women also began to participate in higher education in the late 1890s and early 1900s (McAulay 1898, 1899, 1904). From the late 1890s, women began to participate in many other areas of society that had formerly been closed to them. For instance, in Tasmania, women rode bicycles and participated in sporting teams, with some of these teams for women only.

Feminist organisations did not openly support the use of artificial means of birth control. However, some individual feminists advocated the use of contraception and a few, such as Brettena Smyth in Melbourne, sold contraceptives (Quiggin 1988; Bongiorno 2012; McDonald and Moyle 2018). Feminists were divided in their views about contraception, with some opposing birth control because they thought it would encourage excessive male sexuality (Bongiorno 2012). The efforts of the feminists, however, led to a society in which all women were increasingly being acknowledged as individuals with rights, and this began to change the concepts of marriage, the family and relations between the sexes (Anderson 1999). Feminism started to change women's position in the domestic sphere and husbands became more concerned about their wives' situation regarding childbearing (Quiggin 1988). Upper-class women were the first to achieve rights within the domestic sphere, as is evident from the diaries of Amy Walker and Ida McAulay.

In the late 19th century, Tasmanian upper-class women ran their own households and led independent lives outside the home. Walker and McAulay chose all the furnishings for their homes and hired and managed the servants (McAulay 1899; Walker 1879). Both women also travelled without their husbands. Amy Walker often travelled on her own or with her small daughter to visit her parents and siblings in Hobart (Walker 1879), while Ida McAulay often travelled on her own within Tasmania and to other colonies (McAulay 1897, 1898, 1899). Both women had extensive social lives. Walker (1879, 1880) went to cricket matches, the theatre, the opera, concerts and balls and 'at homes' at Government House, while McAulay (1897, 1899, 1903) went to the theatre, attended lectures and took part in debating and reading groups. Ida McAulay had her own private income, which she controlled herself. On 30 June 1897, she wrote: 'Got my first quarterly dividend from the Mt Lyell mine'; and, on 26 May 1900, she bought '33 shares in the Sawpit Gully Gold and Silver Mining Company at 6/- per share' (McAulay 1897, 1900).

Both Amy and Ida were interested in issues outside the home. Amy's diaries refer to the capture of the Kelly Gang bushrangers in 1880, the taking of the Tasmanian census in 1881 and the polling for Federation in 1898 (Walker 1880, 1881, 1898). Ida's diaries for 1899 have comments on the progress of the Dreyfus trial in France and, from October, on the war in Transvaal (McAulay 1899). Amy showed a keen interest in her husband's farming of the estate and took over its management when he died in 1906. Ida was a declared feminist, was active in women's clubs and discussion groups and was president of the Tasmanian Women's Suffrage Association (later the Tasmanian Women's Political Organisation) from 1903 to 1905.

The 1903 NSW Royal Commission on the Decline of the Birth-Rate was evidence of resistance to the changes that were occurring in women's lives (NSW 1904a, 1904b). For women, there was nothing more fundamental than having control over their fertility. The commission was overwhelmingly male. All 13 commissioners were well-established professional men and, of the 92 witnesses who were not commissioners, only nine were women. Feminists boycotted the commission. A noted feminist, Rose Scott, refused her invitation to appear before the commission and gave speeches to women's organisations attacking the commissioners for conducting this type of inquiry into women's affairs (Allen 1990).

The commission concluded that women had played a crucial role in the 19th-century fertility decline in New South Wales. They viewed women's 'selfishness' in adopting birth control practices as primarily responsible for the fall of the birth rate in that colony since the 1880s (NSW 1904a: 17). Despite the commissioners' vehement opposition to prevention and to the changes in women's behaviour, attitudes and lives, the commission made very few recommendations to remedy 'the various evils which are indicated by the evidence as the causes of the decline in the birth-rate' (NSW 1904a: 2). While they recommended changes to the sale of abortifacients and to the registration of lying-in homes to prevent them being used by abortionists, it appears they felt powerless to stop the sale and/or use of preventives and to halt or reverse the changes that had and were occurring in women's lives.

Witness statements to the royal commission show women had a very active role in determining the size of their families.

Evidence outlined above shows that many of the artificial contraceptives used were female-controlled and the sale of female-controlled preventives had overtaken the sale of male-controlled preventives in the late 19th and early 20th centuries. A study of birth control practices in Australia from the 1930s until the 1960s similarly found that the use of female-controlled methods of contraception was considerably higher than the use of the male-controlled methods of withdrawal and the condom (Cook 2000). The study also found the use of female-controlled methods was markedly higher in Australia than in England over the same period.

Methods of prevention such as withdrawal required husbands to cooperate with their wives, while female-controlled preventives could be used without a husband's knowledge. Witnesses to the royal commission indicated that some husbands and wives agreed about the use of prevention, whereas others did not. Dr Worrall reported that there was an 'inclination of both husband and wife to limit their families. They generally discuss the matter and make up their minds' (NSW 1904b: 89). Similarly, Witness E, talking about the use of prevention, thought: 'The women are not always the ones to blame, in fact it is sometimes made a sort of agreement on marrying' (NSW 1904b: 189). John West, however, said of the working classes:

> My experience has taught me that there is a great deal of difference between the two parties and very often the husband is opposed to the wife doing this sort of thing and it has caused disagreements. (NSW 1904b: 199)

Abortion was clearly a female-controlled method of limiting family size and one that some women employed without their husband's knowledge and/or consent (Allen 1990).

Many witnesses to the royal commission reported that women were proactive in purchasing preventives and in seeking out ways to procure an abortion. Pharmacists in Sydney said both men and women came into their shops to purchase preventives or to ask for abortifacients.

William Park, the Pitt Street pharmacist, said 'all classes of people, gentlemen, ladies, wives of working men' came in to buy these goods (NSW 1904b: 40). George Stevens, the pharmacist in a working-class district of Sydney, reported: 'Married women come in and ask for them over the counter … Sometimes they ask me for means to procure abortion' (NSW 1904b: 44). As noted above, one of the Sydney city pharmacies had set up a special kiosk staffed by a 'nurse' where women could buy 'female' goods, including preventives.

Several witnesses expressed dismay at the ease with which women publicly spoke about family limitation. Dr Watson-Munro, a surgeon at two large Sydney hospitals, said: 'Many classes of women are pretty free in expressing the desire to evade the pregnant condition' (NSW 1904b: 48). Dr Scot-Skirving reported that he was

> sometimes a little surprised at the casual way in which a woman, practically a stranger, will talk to me of the most inner sexual relations with as much *sangfroid* as if she were talking about having lunch. (NSW 1904b: 98)

As outlined above, women were an important source of information for other women on the ideas and values about family limitation and knowledge about methods of prevention.

One reason put forward by witnesses for the reluctance of women to have large families was their concern about the pain and risks of childbirth. Dr Scot-Skirving thought: 'There are a good number of women who have a weak shrinkage from the pains of maternity and they hate the disagreeables of gestation' (NSW 1904b: 98). Some doctors, however, thought these fears were not justified. Dr Watson-Munro said:

> They may talk about the trouble of the act of parturition or the pain of it, but I do not think that that is a very dreadful thing any more now than at any other time in the history of the world. (NSW 1904b: 80)

At the same time, however, the commissioners expressed grave concerns about 'unduly numerous' deaths of women in childbirth and the effects of childbirth on women's health and subsequent fertility (NSW 1904a: 31). Two witnesses to the commission, pharmacist Edward Fuss and newsagent John Hume, spoke about the ill effects of continual childbearing on women's health, while the Reverend William Rutledge, a Methodist minister, commented: 'Some women have been worn out, almost done to death, by over-bearing of children' (NSW 1904b: 226).

Women's concerns about the risks of childbirth were clearly realistic. 'In 19th century Tasmania, causes of death connected with maternity were the second most common, after tuberculosis, for women of childbearing age' (Kippen 2002c: 173). Using the World Health Organization (WHO) definition of maternal death (WHO 1992, cited in Kippen 2002c), the maternal mortality rate ranged from 3.4 to 7.9 deaths per 1,000 live births over the period 1860–99 (Kippen 2002c: 180). There was a large increase in maternal mortality in the early 1870s, a decline from the late 1870s to the late 1880s and then an increase in the 1890s. The maternal death rate ranged from 0.6 to 1.2 deaths per 1,000 population between 1860 and 1899 and followed the trend in the maternal mortality rate until the 1890s, when it began to fall in relation to the maternal mortality rate. This is undoubtedly due to the fall in fertility during this period. Kippen (2002c: 188–90) also found many 'hidden maternal deaths' in the period 1880–99, with more than one-third of maternal deaths not registered as such. Given these rates, it is highly likely most women in Tasmania of childbearing age would have been acquainted with or have heard of someone who had died in childbirth.

A letter to a newspaper cited in the royal commission's report (NSW 1904b: 282) suggested couples were limiting their fertility because of their concerns about the husband's survival. A male breadwinner's death would leave his wife with the sole responsibility of supporting her dependent children and in many circumstances facing poverty. These concerns were realistic given that, in the four marriage cohorts in this study, the number of husbands who died during their wife's childbearing years was around the same as the number of wives (Appendix A: Table A.16).

Several witnesses to the commission considered one of the main reasons women did not want many children was because of their love of 'pleasure'. Women of all classes wanted a life outside the domestic sphere and did not want to be burdened with a large family. Witness E thought: 'The practice of preventing conception is followed because of the desire of women to have social pleasures' (NSW 1904b: 180); while Dr Creed, a Sydney general practitioner, and Dr Harris, a Newcastle general practitioner, both said women did not want to be 'bothered with children' (NSW 1904b: 124, 138). The Reverend Howell-Price thought the reason women wanted to limit the size of their family was:

> [T]he children tied them too much to the home and they did not wish to become slaves … they want to be free, free from home ties and home duties as far as possible … they desire to have more leisure, apparently for the pursuit of their own pleasure. (NSW 1904b: 214–15)

Although he did not express it in this way, the Reverend Howell-Price thought women's aversion to having a large family was due to the influence of feminism:

> This desire to prevent the birth of children can undoubtedly be taken as a particular instance of a general relaxation of control over women, which has become the general sentiment during the last 30 or 40 years … That relaxation of all control has led them into this particular desire to be free from restriction in that way too. (NSW 1904b: 216)

Women of all classes were expressing feminist sentiments at the turn of the 20th century and standing up for what they perceived as their rights.

Ida McAulay, in her diary, talked about how a working-class woman had confronted her, an upper-class woman, to stand up for her daughter's rights. On 14 November 1899, Ida McAulay wrote that the mother of one of her servants had objected to Ida's treatment of her daughter: 'I got a most impertinent card from Alice's mother saying she would not allow her to come back as this was the second time she had come home ill' (McAulay 1899). On 17 November 1899, Ida wrote that when Alice and her mother came to get Alice's box, 'strong words were exchanged and she was violent and abusive' (McAulay 1899).

The Hobart *Mercury* on 31 December 1900 reported an argument between Emma Dixon and her husband, John (1870 cohort), in which Emma asserted her rights in relation to her husband:

> John Dixon, milkman, residing at the retreat farm, Lower Sandy Bay, deposed that … his wife, left home at 6.20 in a cart to accompany him on his rounds. When about 100 yards from the farm she said she was going to have a new set of harness for the horse they were driving. He replied that they must pay a certain account first. She then said she had earned the money as well as he, that she was going to do as she liked and she would not go with him.

Emma subsequently jumped down from the cart, was run over by the wheels and died later that day. The death was ruled 'accidental' by the coroner.

Conclusion

Overall, the historical sources quoted in this chapter provide support for most theories of why marital fertility declined in the late 19th and early 20th centuries. In the conclusion to this book, I summarise how the quantitative findings from Chapters 6 and 7 and the qualitative findings from this chapter answer the questions of when, how and why fertility declined in Tasmania at this time. I also examine how these findings compare with those from studies of the fertility decline in other English-speaking countries and in Western Europe, discussed in Chapter 1, and from other studies of the historical fertility decline in Australia, discussed in Chapter 2.

9

Conclusion

The quantitative and qualitative evidence presented in this book shows that the historical fertility decline took place in Tasmania about the same time as in the other Australian colonies, in Western Europe and in other English-speaking countries (Jones 1971; Woods 1987; Caldwell 1999; Cleland 2001; Gauvreau and Gossage 2001; Hacker 2003; Bengtsson and Dribe 2014). Fertility started to decline in the late 1880s and the fertility decline became well established during the 1890s. The fertility decline was so entrenched by the early 1900s that people who were opposed to it, such as clergymen and the NSW commissioners into the decline in the birth rate in 1903, recognised they were unable to halt or reverse it.

Quantitative evidence of how fertility declined supports both 'innovation' and 'adjustment' theories, with 'stopping' being an 'innovative' form of behaviour and 'spacing' an 'adjustment' or 'adaptation' to new social and economic circumstances. The fall in fertility in late 19th-century Tasmania was due primarily to the practice of stopping behaviour in the 1880 and 1890 cohorts, as argued by many demographers (Henry 1961; Knodel and van de Walle 1979; Coale 1986). However, as in 19th-century Utah (Anderton and Bean 1985; Bean et al. 1990), in Tasmania, birth spacing was also used as a strategy to limit fertility by the 1890 cohort. In all marriage cohorts, some groups had longer birth intervals than others, suggesting that, as in parts of Western Europe (Van Bavel 2004a; Dribe and Scalone 2010; Tsuya et al. 2010; Van Bavel and Kok 2010; Kolk 2011), these groups were deliberately spacing their births before the fertility decline. Changes in starting behaviour contributed to the fertility decline due to an increase in the age at marriage. The change in the age at marriage is probably related to a change in social values, rather than a change in fertility preferences.

Quantitative and qualitative evidence shown here supports all the individual theories of why fertility fell, apart from many of the theories related to infant and child mortality. Similar to findings from a recent study of the fertility transition in five North American and European countries (Dribe et al. 2014), here both 'innovation' and 'adjustment' factors played a role in the fertility decline. Rather than 'blending' the two sets of theories (Cleland 2001), however, the fertility decline should be viewed in a much broader context. The fertility transition occurred during the broad social and economic revolution that occurred in Tasmania in the final two decades of the 19th century, with an important part of this revolution being changes in the role and status of women. The adoption of ideas and values about fertility limitation and of methods of fertility control can be seen as one of the many social changes that occurred at this time.

Few studies of the historical fertility decline have had access to contemporary literature of the period. Thus, there is little evidence of how ideas and values about fertility control were diffused (Casterline 2001), what types of contraceptives were used or the role played by women in the fertility decline (McDonald 2000). The historical sources used in this study provide valuable information in all these areas.

In Tasmania, the final three decades of the 19th century were a time of economic and social transformation—conditions under which fertility would fall, according to demographic transition theory (Notestein 1945). The colony became more industrialised and urbanised. Agriculture became progressively less important in terms of both employment and its contribution to the colony's economy. Methods of transportation improved with the spread of the railways and, in the final decade of the 19th century, the bicycle became a form of transport for both men and women. Inventions such as the electric telegraph, electric lighting, electric trams and even the telephone were well established in Tasmania by the end of the 19th century and farming became more mechanised. From the late 1860s, schooling became compulsory for both boys and girls, new schools were established across the colony during the final three decades of the 19th century and rates of literacy improved dramatically. In the 1880s and 1890s, a number of significant public health measures were put in place throughout the colony. Studies of the fertility transition in Western European and other English-speaking countries have shown that many of these indicators of social and economic development are associated with the fertility decline (for example, Lee et al. 1994; Schellekens and van Poppel 2012; Dribe et al. 2014).

Although there was a marked improvement in literacy in the late 19th century, similar to Alter's (1988) study of the historical fertility decline in Verviers, Belgium, I did not find any relationship in the quantitative analysis between husbands' and wives' levels of literacy and their fertility. This is possibly because the measure of literacy—that is, whether the husband and/or wife signed the marriage certificate—is a weak measure of literacy levels.

Social and economic development brought new ideas to Tasmania. Improvements in education opened people's minds to these new ideas and allowed them to access information (Cleland 2001). Tasmania was not an isolated place in the second half of the 19th century. There was considerable movement of people between Tasmania and other colonies and countries. Communication within Tasmania, with other colonies and with other countries improved markedly from the 1870s. Written material about fertility limitation became available in the Australian colonies from the late 1870s. Books and pamphlets were available in city bookshops and were advertised for sale by mail in the newspapers, lectures were given on 'family limitation' and pamphlets were circulated in some cities. Newspapers also published articles about the trials of people charged with selling 'obscene' literature pertaining to fertility control. Many of the witnesses to the NSW royal commission spoke about the books' authors and the trial judges with great familiarity.

Unlike in Britain and Western Europe (Seccombe 1993), the 1903 NSW Royal Commission on the Decline of the Birth-Rate indicates that some doctors were a source of information on fertility control for their patients. However, informal sources were much more important in spreading ideas and values about fertility limitation and information about methods of fertility control. Information about prevention was spread by word of mouth among women, including from midwives to their patients. In the Australian colonies, informal sources appear to have been an important source of information for women of all classes. In contrast, for England, evidence of the importance of informal sources relates mainly to the working classes (Llewelyn Davies 1978; Seccombe 1993).

By the beginning of the 20th century, family limitation had become a legitimate topic for public discussion in Australia. People spoke freely about the subject in ordinary conversation and newspapers contained many editorials, articles and letters on the subject.

As argued by Caldwell (1999), the availability and use of artificial methods of contraception increased markedly from the 1880s, as did the use of methods such as 'withdrawal' and abortion, which had been practised before the fertility decline. Several artificial methods of contraception were used in the late 19th and early 20th centuries: French letters, the India rubber *Pessaire Preventif*, soluble pessaries, sponges, syringes, douches and enemas. Artificial contraceptives and pills to procure abortions were sold by pharmacies, hawkers and by mail through advertisements in the newspapers. Some abortionists also advertised discreetly through the newspapers. Most artificial methods of contraception were relatively expensive in relation to middle-class and working men's wages, so many women made their own contraceptives. 'Withdrawal' appears to have been used as a method of prevention mainly by the middle class. Abortion was used to limit family size by married and unmarried women of all classes, but particularly by working-class women. There is no evidence that abstinence was the main method of reducing marital fertility, as argued by Szreter (1996) for England and Wales.

The quantitative analysis shows that, in Tasmania, as in other Australian colonies, parts of Western Europe, Canada and the United States, the upper and middle classes were the first to limit their fertility followed by the other classes, with unskilled workers and farmers the last to adopt fertility control (Jones 1971; Livi-Bacci 1986; Anderson 1999; Schellekens and van Poppel 2012; Bengtsson and Dribe 2014; Breschi et al. 2014; Dribe et al. 2014; Vézina et al. 2014). In the 1890 cohort, white-collar workers also spaced their births, compared with farmers and unskilled workers, possibly for economic reasons. These findings are similar to Larson's (1994) for Melbourne (Victoria) in the late 19th century.

The quantitative data show that couples in urban areas of Tasmania had significantly lower fertility than couples in rural areas, even before the fertility transition. This was similar to the other Australian colonies, parts of Western Europe and Canada (Jones 1971; Larson 1994; Livi-Bacci 1986; Sharlin 1986; Anderson 1999; Gauvreau and Gossage 2001; Vézina et al. 2014). In Tasmania, couples in urban areas were more likely to stop having children and to space their births than couples in rural areas even in the 1860/70 marriage cohorts. The qualitative data indicate that people in urban areas had better access to artificial methods of contraception than those in rural areas at the time of the fertility decline.

Mining grew in importance as an occupation in late 19th-century Tasmania. However, the quantitative analysis shows that, unlike in 19th-century England and Wales (Szreter 1996), Tasmanian miners did not have very high fertility. Miners in Tasmania were very different from those in England. English miners tended to be born in a mining location and worked there as miners all their lives. Tasmanian miners, on the other hand, were highly mobile both occupationally and geographically. In Tasmania, men often worked in other occupations in non-mining areas before they moved to mining localities and took up mining. In later life, they often took up other occupations in the mining area or moved elsewhere.

Opportunities for social mobility were an important feature of the late 19th and early 20th–century social and economic transformation. Australian society was less rigid than English society and there were many opportunities for social mobility, particularly with the growth of more 'modern' occupations. The qualitative evidence shows that many middle and working-class people had high aspirations for themselves and their children and this probably encouraged the practice of fertility control, as argued by some scholars (Banks 1954; Lesthaeghe and Wilson 1986). These couples often aspired to a higher standard of living for themselves, including the opportunity to purchase their own home. As in Britain and Western Europe, a continual theme of witness statements to the 1903 NSW Royal Commission was that couples wanted to limit their families because they could not afford to have large numbers of children. Parents had high aspirations for their children and were concerned with the 'quality' of their children, rather than 'quantity'. They wanted their children to have a good education and to have other opportunities that people of higher socioeconomic status took for granted, such as learning to play the piano. In these circumstances, the demand for children fell because the cost of having another child was greater than the benefit of having that child (Easterlin 1975; Becker 1981; Becker et al. 1990).

Children were generally viewed as 'dependants' rather than 'workers', except in rural areas, where farmers relied to some extent on their children's labour. While education became compulsory in the late 1860s, children of the urban and rural working classes and of smaller farmers were regularly absent from school to help in the home or on the family farm or to go out to work to supplement the family income. The quantitative analysis shows these families had the highest fertility, supporting Caldwell's wealth-flow theories (Caldwell 1976; Caldwell and Ruzicka 1978). This is consistent with Canadian findings that families in Ontario whose children attended school all year had significantly lower fertility than other families (Gauvreau and Gossage 2001).

While Tasmania was undergoing remarkable social and economic change in the final two decades of the 19th century, there was an economic depression in the early 1890s that brought an increase in unemployment and a fall in wages. This probably provided an additional incentive for couples to adopt fertility control measures and may explain why couples in the 1890 cohort were significantly more likely to space their births than those in the 1860/70 cohorts.

Tasmania was a relatively secular society from its earliest days. Religion was generally not as important to people in Australia as it was in Britain or the United States. By the 1880s, religious groups had little influence on political and social attitudes and values. In general, people did not view religion as having importance in their daily lives. Even people who had religious beliefs and went to church regularly often made their own decisions about what was right rather than taking the church's views. Although clergymen were opposed to fertility control, they were unwilling to speak about it publicly for fear of being ridiculed or, worse, of losing some of their stipend through their parishioners leaving the church.

The adoption of fertility control in a secular society such as Tasmania is consistent with the argument that, in late 19th and early 20th–century Western Europe, secularisation was a necessary condition for the spread of fertility control, with the EFP finding that secularised communities tended to adopt fertility control early (Lesthaeghe and Wilson 1986). Other studies have found that, in Western Europe and Canada, 'traditional' religious groups, such as Catholics and orthodox Protestants, had significantly higher fertility than the other more liberal religious groups (Gauvreau and Gossage 2001; Van Bavel and Kok 2005; van Poppel and Derosas 2006). Van Poppel et al. (2012) also suggest that some of the Protestant groups had high levels of literacy because of their emphasis on reading the scriptures. Education gave them access to ideas and information about fertility control and encouraged them to take control over this aspect of their lives.

Consistent with previous Australian analyses outlined in Chapter 2, in Tasmania, the relationship between religious affiliation and fertility was not straightforward. There were no significant differences between religious groups in stopping behaviour, with Catholics no less likely to stop having children than Anglicans. There were, however, significant differences in spacing behaviour, with Other Nonconformists (mainly Baptists and Congregationalists) more likely to space their births than Anglicans in every marriage cohort, indicating that they were deliberately spacing their births before the fertility decline. Congregationalists and Baptists may have had high levels of literacy from the earliest years because of their religion's emphasis on reading the scriptures. Methodists also had significantly shorter birth intervals than Anglicans in the 1880 marriage cohort, but this is difficult to explain. In trying to interpret these quantitative results, it is important to note that the measure of religion used in the analysis—that is, the religious rites according to which the couple was married—is a measure of religious affiliation, not of religiosity. Additionally, some Tasmanians may have changed their religious affiliation during their lifetime.

As noted, one of the major social changes in Tasmania in the late 19th and early 20th centuries was a change in the role and status of women. From the 1880s, women achieved important rights, their position in the family and in the wider society started to change and they began to participate in areas of society that had formerly been closed to them. For women, there was no more fundamental right than controlling their fertility.

Qualitative evidence in this study supports Seccombe's (1993: 168) view that 'women were the driving force' behind the fertility decline. The 1903 NSW Royal Commission on the Decline of the Birth-Rate viewed women as primarily responsible for the fall in the birth rate in the late 19th century and this applied to women of all classes. Women played a very active role in determining the size of their families. Many of the artificial contraceptives used were female-controlled—some of them made by women themselves. Specialist women's sections were established in some retail pharmacies, selling women's goods, including preventives. While some husbands and wives agreed about the use of prevention, some methods of family limitation, such as abortion, could be used without a husband's knowledge and/or consent. Women were proactive in purchasing preventives and in seeking out ways to procure an abortion. They also spoke freely in public about their desire to avoid having large families. Women were an important source of information for other women on the ideas and values about family limitation and knowledge about methods of prevention. Although feminism was originally a movement for elite and middle-class women, feminist ideas gradually spread throughout other strata of society. By the turn of the century, women of all classes were expressing feminist sentiments and standing up for what they perceived as their rights.

The quantitative and qualitative analyses in this study do not provide support for many theories of the relationship between infant and child mortality and fertility decline. Infant mortality in Tasmania was relatively flat between 1860 and 1899 and only started to decline at the turn of the century, well after fertility had begun to decline. Child mortality began to decline from the 1860s, with the decline interrupted by a couple of major epidemics in the 1870s.

Unlike in Western Europe and the United States (Knodel 1978; Alter 1988; Haines 1998; Alter et al. 2010; Schellekens and van Poppel 2012; Breschi et al. 2014; Vézina et al. 2014), the quantitative analysis here does not support the 'replacement' theory of infant mortality. In Tasmania, couples who had a child die in infancy while the mother was not pregnant with another were as likely to stop having children as other couples. Also, unlike in Germany and the United States (Knodel 1978; Haines 1988), the quantitative evidence does not support the 'insurance' theory of infant mortality for Tasmania. Rather than child mortality deterring couples from efforts to limit their fertility, in Tasmania—similar to the Netherlands (Schellekens and van Poppel 2012)—the more infant and child deaths the family experienced, the more likely they were to stop childbearing.

Unlike the Netherlands and Spain (Reher and Sanz-Gimeno 2007; van Poppel et al. 2012), in Tasmania, the number of surviving children had no significant association with the time to the next birth, indicating that couples were not adjusting their birth spacing in relation to the deaths of infants or children. Unlike Utah and Germany (Bohnert et al. 2012; Sandström and Vikström 2015), but similar to Belgium (Alter et al. 2010), in Tasmania, the sex composition of the family also had no significant association with stopping or spacing practices.

However, in Tasmania, there was a 'physiological' relationship between infant mortality and fertility, as also found in England and many parts of Western Europe (Knodel 1978, 1982; Wrigley et al. 1997). Having a child die as an infant when a woman was not pregnant with another significantly reduced the time to the next birth, because of the effect on amenorrhoea of stopping breastfeeding. The survival analysis of parity progression shows that women who had a child die as an infant had a significantly higher risk of having another birth than other women at most parities, but this probably reflects the length of time to the next birth rather than having another birth.

In conclusion, the evidence from historical sources of the period allows the quantitative evidence to be placed in context and the various theories of why fertility declined to be viewed in a coherent framework. Fertility declined in Tasmania in a period of remarkable social and economic transformation. Tasmania became more industrialised and urbanised, there was growth in 'modern' occupations and an increase in opportunities for social and economic mobility. With the introduction of compulsory education, both boys and girls had access to an education and literacy improved markedly. One of the major social changes was in the role and status of women, who became the driving force behind the fertility decline. With the spread of feminism, women of all classes wanted more from their lives than being restricted to the home through constant childbearing. In many ways, the fertility decline can be viewed as a period in which middle and working-class men and women aspired to lead lives like those of upper-class people. They realised they could improve their social and material conditions and give their children a better future through controlling their fertility, as the upper classes had begun to do many years before.

These findings can be applied to other Australian colonies that were also experiencing broad social and economic changes together with a fertility decline in the same period.

Appendix A: Appendix tables

Table A.1 Mean children ever born to married women by birth cohort, Australian censuses, 1911 and 1921

	Australia, 1911 census	Tasmania, 1911 census	Australia, 1921 census	Tasmania, 1921 census
Birth cohort	Children ever born (mean)			
1832–36	6.98	7.48	..	..
1837–41	7.02	7.22	..	..
1842–46	7.03	7.15	6.77	6.49
1847–51	6.75	6.69	6.51	6.42
1852–56	6.44	6.64	6.25	6.32
1857–61	5.92	6.11	5.74	5.97
1862–66	5.25	5.67	5.11	5.48
1867–71	..	..	4.57	4.97
1872–76	..	..	4.19	4.56

.. not applicable
Sources: Commonwealth of Australia (1914c: 1143; 1921: 1926).

Table A.2 Number of children ever born by birth cohort of married women, Australian census, 1921

Birth cohort	1842–46	1847–51	1852–56	1857–61	1862–66	1867–71	1872–76
No. of children	Percentage						
None	10.3	10.8	10.1	10.0	10.8	12.1	12.4
One	3.7	3.6	4.3	4.9	5.9	7.6	9.0
Two	3.8	4.9	5.2	6.2	8.3	10.2	12.4
Three	4.9	5.3	6.5	8.1	10.1	11.8	13.2
Four	6.0	6.9	7.4	9.4	11.1	12.0	12.3
Five	7.1	7.5	8.8	10.1	10.5	10.6	10.5
Six	9.1	8.8	9.0	9.6	9.9	9.1	8.3

Birth cohort	1842–46	1847–51	1852–56	1857–61	1862–66	1867–71	1872–76
No. of children	Percentage						
Seven	8.6	9.1	9.5	9.4	8.5	7.4	6.6
Eight	9.9	9.8	9.0	8.4	7.2	5.9	5.0
Nine	9.2	8.5	8.5	7.4	5.8	4.6	3.8
Ten	9.3	8.4	7.3	6.1	4.4	3.4	2.7
Eleven	7.0	5.9	5.9	4.2	3.0	2.2	1.7
Twelve	4.7	4.8	4.1	2.8	1.0	1.4	1.1
Thirteen	3.4	2.8	2.3	1.7	1.1	0.8	0.6
Fourteen or more	2.9	2.8	2.2	1.6	1.2	0.8	0.3
Total (%)	100.0	100.0	100.0	100.0	100.0	100.0	100.0
Total (no.)	3,512	8,478	18,098	35,383	52,123	69,258	84,264

Source: Commonwealth of Australia (1921: 1926).

Table A.3 Number of children ever born by birth cohort of married women, Australian census, 1911

Birth cohort	1842–46	1847–51	1852–56	1857–61	1862–66
No. of children	Percentage				
None	8.4	8.6	8.1	8.0	8.5
One	3.8	4.1	4.6	5.1	6.4
Two	4.1	4.7	5.3	6.4	8.5
Three	4.8	5.3	6.5	8.2	10.2
Four	5.7	6.8	7.7	9.4	11.3
Five	7.0	7.6	8.5	9.9	10.7
Six	8.5	8.6	8.9	9.7	10.2
Seven	9.2	9.1	9.3	9.5	8.7
Eight	10.0	9.6	9.4	8.8	7.4
Nine	9.3	9.1	8.6	7.7	6.0
Ten	9.5	8.6	7.9	6.4	4.7
Eleven	7.0	6.4	5.8	4.4	3.1
Twelve	5.7	5.1	4.2	3.1	2.0
Thirteen	3.3	2.9	2.5	1.8	1.1
Fourteen or more	1.8	1.6	1.3	0.9	0.6
Total (%)	100.0	100.0	100.0	100.0	100.0
Total (no.)	16,632	24,862	37,585	60,945	81,548

Source: Commonwealth of Australia (1914c: 1143).

APPENDIX A

Table A.4 Net migration, Tasmania, 1861–1900

Years	Net migration
1861–1865	–4,355
1866–1870	–813
1871–1875	–4,416
1876–1880	2,880
1881–1885	2,422
1886–1890	2,606
1891–1895	–4,562
1896–1900	4,914

Source: Borrie (1994: 123).

Table A.5 Female population aged 15–49 years, 1861, 1870, 1881 and 1891, Tasmania

Year	1861	1870	1881	1891
Age	Percentage			
15–19 years	19.2	21.9	25.1	20.6
20–24 years	18.2	17.5	22.3	19.9
25–29 years	16.8	14.1	15.7	18.0
30–34 years	14.9	13.4	11.0	14.7
35–39 years	12.7	12.5	9.1	11.3
40–44 years	10.4	11.1	8.7	8.5
45–49 years	7.9	9.4	8.1	7.1
Total (%)	100.0	100.0	100.0	100.0
Total (no.)	20,454	20,799	26,602	33,136

Source: Kippen (2002b).

Table A.6 Male population aged 15–49 years, 1861, 1870, 1881 and 1891, Tasmania

Year	1861	1870	1881	1891
Age at marriage	Percentage			
15–19 years	13.8	20.1	24.0	18.5
20–24 years	12.1	15.0	21.5	18.7
25–29 years	12.6	11.5	16.1	18.6
30–34 years	15.2	11.7	11.6	15.9
35–39 years	16.5	12.9	9.3	12.4

Year	1861	1870	1881	1891
Age at marriage	Percentage			
40–44 years	16.0	14.2	8.7	9.1
45–49 years	13.8	14.6	8.8	6.9
Total (%)	100.0	100.0	100.0	100.0
Total (no.)	24,505	21,330	27,900	38,229

Source: Kippen (2002b).

Table A.7 Population by occupation, 1842 and 1851, Tasmania

Year	1842	1851	1842	1851
Type of occupation	No.		Percentage	
Occupation specified:	20,594	28,998	35.9	41.3
Landed proprietors, merchants, bankers and professional persons	1,846	1,577	9.0	5.4
Shopkeepers and other retail dealers	802	1,415	3.9	4.9
Mechanics and artificers	3,720	5,687	18.1	19.6
Shepherds and others caring for sheep	879	1,445	4.3	5.0
Gardeners, stockmen and persons employed in agriculture[1]	9,870	12,545	47.9	43.3
Domestic servants	3,477	5,600	16.9	19.3
Seamen, boatmen and whalers[2]	–	729	–	2.5
Convicts employed in public works[3]	9,759	953	17.0	1.4
Military, including wives and children	–	568	–	0.8
All other persons not included above	27,067	39,611	47.1	56.5
Total	57,420	70,130	100.0	100.0

– Not specified

[1] In 1851, includes 'Farmers', 'Market gardeners' and 'Gardeners, stockmen and farm servants'.

[2] Includes 'Licensed boatmen', 'Seamen employed in the coastal and river craft' and 'Whalers'.

[3] In 1842, includes 'Convicts employed on government vessels', 'Convicts employed in public works throughout the colony', 'Convicts at the penal settlements on Tasman's Peninsula' and 'Female convicts in house of corrections, Hobart'. In 1851, includes only 'Convicts employed in public works'.

Sources: TAS (1842, 1851).

APPENDIX A

Table A.8 Population by occupation, Tasmania, 1861 and 1870

Year	1861	1870	1861	1870
Type of occupation	No.		Percentage	
Occupation specified:	27,655	32,398	30.7	32.6
Professionals[1]	1,908	1,725	6.9	5.3
Shopkeepers and other retail dealers[2]	1,267	1,152	4.6	3.6
Mechanics and artificers	5,978	4,473	21.6	13.8
Farmers, stockholders and farm labourers	13,647	15,741	49.3	48.6
Domestic servants	4,372	4,319	15.8	13.3
Licensed victuallers	483	408	1.7	1.3
Other labourers and seamen	–	4,580	–	14.1
All other persons not included above	62,322	66,930	69.3	67.4
Total	89,977	99,328	100.0	100.0

– Not specified

[1] Includes 'Merchants and bankers', 'Legal profession', 'Medical profession', 'Clergymen', 'Army or navy', 'Government employ', 'Schoolmasters' and also, in 1870, 'Schoolmistresses'.
[2] In 1870, includes 'Shopkeepers and other retail dealers' and 'Hawkers'.
Sources: TAS (1861, 1870).

Table A.9 Population by occupation, Tasmania, 1881 and 1891

Year	1881	1891	1881	1891
Type of occupation	No.		Percentage	
Breadwinners	50,071	61,411	43.3	41.9
Professional[1]	2,546	3,918	5.1	6.4
Domestic[2]	4,856	7,180	9.7	11.7
Commercial: Mercantile, general dealers[3]	1,777	3,698	3.5	6.0
Commercial: Transport and communication[3]	2,241	3,267	4.5	5.3
Industrial[4]	14,996	18,644	29.9	30.4
Primary producers: Agricultural[5]	17,699	16,031	35.3	26.1
Primary producers: Pastoral[5]	860	2,447	1.7	4.0
Primary producers: Mineral[5]	3,164	3,988	6.3	6.5
Primary producers: Other[5]	462	1,102	0.9	1.8
Indefinite[6]	1,470	1,136	2.9	1.8
Dependants	65,634	85,256	56.7	58.1
Total	115,705	146,667	100.0	100.0

[1] 'Professional' includes persons mainly 'engaged in the government and defence of the country, and in satisfying the intellectual, moral, and social wants of its inhabitants'.

[2] 'Domestic' includes 'all persons engaged in the supply of board and lodging and in rendering personal services for which remuneration is usually paid'.

[3] 'Commercial' includes 'all persons directly connected with the hire, sale, transfer, distribution, storage, and security of property and materials, and with the transport of persons or goods, or engaged in effecting communication'.

[4] 'Industrial' includes 'all persons principally engaged in various works of utility, or in specialities connected with the manufacture, construction, modification, or alteration of materials so as to render them more available for the various uses of man, but excluding, as far as possible, all who are mainly or solely in the service of commercial interchange'.

[5] 'Agricultural, pastoral, mineral, and other primary producers' includes 'all persons mainly engaged in the cultivation or original acquisition of food products, and in obtaining other raw materials direct from natural sources'.

[6] 'Indefinite' includes 'all persons who derive incomes from services rendered, but the direction of which services cannot be exactly determined'.

Source: TAS (1891: 01_viii).

Table A.10 Population by occupation, Tasmania, 1891, 1901 and 1911

Year	1891	1901	1911	1891	1901	1911
Type of occupation	No.			Percentage		
Breadwinners	60,946	72,586	75,969	41.6	42.1	39.7
Professional	3,918	4,997	5,481	6.4	6.9	7.2
Domestic	7,180	7,937	7,864	11.8	10.9	10.4
Commercial: Mercantile, general dealers	6,326	7,497	8,712	10.4	10.3	11.5
Commercial: Transport and communication	3,267	4,848	4,738	5.4	6.7	6.2
Industrial	16,016	18,750	17,268	26.3	25.8	22.7
Primary producers: Agricultural	16,031	19,422	20,168	26.3	26.8	26.5
Primary producers: Pastoral	2,447	1,881	2,635	4.0	2.6	3.5
Primary producers: Mineral	3,987	5,467	5,631	6.5	7.5	7.4
Primary producers: Other[1]	1,103	1,129	2,593	1.8	1.6	3.4
Independent	671	658	879	1.1	0.9	1.2
Dependants	85,256	98,981	112,801	58.1	57.4	59.0
Unspecified	465	908	2,441	0.3	0.5	1.3
Total	146,667	172,475	191,211	100.0	100.0	100.0

[1] 'Primary producers: Other' includes capture of wild animals and their produce, fisheries, forestry and water conservation and supply.

Source: Commonwealth of Australia (1914d: 1291).

APPENDIX A

Table A.11 Males aged 20 years and older, occupation by class, Tasmania, 1881

Occupation	No.	Percentage
Professional[1]	1,377	4.3
Domestic[2]	996	3.1
Commercial[3]	2,968	9.3
Agricultural[4]	11,776	36.7
Industrial[5]	10,153	31.7
Indefinite and non-productive[6]	4,250	13.3
Not stated	544	1.7
Total	32,064	100.0

[1] 'Professional' includes 'Persons engaged in general or local government, or the defence or protection of the country' and 'Persons engaged in the learned professions, in literature, art, and science'.

[2] 'Domestic' includes 'Persons engaged in the domestic offices or duties of wives, mothers, mistresses of families, children, relatives and visitors' and 'Persons engaged in entertaining and performing personal offices for man'.

[3] 'Commercial' includes 'Persons who buy or sell, keep or lend money, houses, or goods of various kinds' and 'Persons engaged in the conveyance of men, animals, goods and messages'.

[4] 'Agricultural' includes 'Persons possessing, working or cultivating land, raising or dealing in animals'.

[5] 'Industrial' includes 'Persons engaged in working and dealing in art and mechanic productions', 'Persons working and dealing in textile fabrics, in dress, and in fibrous materials', 'Persons working and dealing in food and drinks', 'Persons working and dealing in animal and vegetable substances' and 'Persons dealing in minerals'.

[6] 'Indefinite and non-productive' includes 'Labourers and others', 'Persons of property or rank' and 'Persons supported by the community and of no specified occupation'.

Source: TAS (1881: 02_139).

Table A.12 Males aged 20 years and older, occupation by class, Tasmania, 1891

Occupation	No.	Percentage
Breadwinners	40,194	96.9
Professional[1]	2,408	6.0
Domestic[2]	1,158	2.9
Commercial[3]	6,979	17.4
Industrial[4]	11,664	29.0
Primary producers[5]	17,476	43.5
Indefinite[6]	509	1.3
Dependants[7]	1,290	3.1
Total	41,484	100.0

[1] 'Professional' includes 'Government, law, defence and protection' and 'Religion, charity, health, education, science and amusement'.

[2] 'Domestic' includes 'Board and lodging and personal service'.

[3] 'Commercial' includes 'Property and finance', 'Traders and dealers' and 'Storage, transport, and communication'.

[4] 'Industrial' includes 'Modifiers, manufacturers of materials'.

[5] 'Primary producers' includes 'Agricultural, pastoral, mineral and other primary producers'.

[6] 'Indefinite' includes 'Persons of independent means' and 'Undefined'.

[7] 'Dependants' includes 'Wives, children, and relatives dependent upon natural guardians' and 'Other dependants upon the State or upon public or private support'.

Source: TAS (1891: 04_175, 04_180–81).

Table A.13 Males aged 20 years and older, occupation by class, Tasmania, 1901

Occupation	No.	Percentage
Breadwinners	46,734	97.9
Professional[1]	2,793	6.0
Domestic[2]	1,153	2.5
Commercial[3]	4,912	10.5
Transportation and communication[4]	3,899	8.3
Industrial[5]	13,276	28.4
Primary producers[6]	20,200	43.2
Indefinite[7]	501	1.1
Dependants[8]	991	2.1
Total	47,725	100.0

[1] 'Professional' includes 'Government, law, defence and protection' and 'Religion, charity, health, education, science and amusement'.

[2] 'Domestic' includes 'Board and lodging and personal service'.

[3] 'Commercial' includes 'Property and finance' and 'Traders and dealers'.

[4] 'Transportation and communication' includes 'Carriers and messengers on railways, roads, seas and rivers', 'Postal service' and 'Telegraph and telephone service'.

[5] 'Industrial' includes 'Modifiers, manufacturers of materials'.

[6] 'Primary producers' includes 'Agricultural, pastoral, mineral and other producers'.

[7] 'Indefinite' includes 'Persons of independent means and undefined'.

[8] 'Dependants' includes 'Children and relatives dependent upon natural guardians' and 'Other dependants upon the State or upon public or private support'.

Source: TAS (1901: 05_261, 05_264–67).

APPENDIX A

Table A.14 Females by occupation and marital status, Tasmania, 1911

Marital status	Never married	Married	Widowed[1]	Not specified	Total
Type of occupation					
Breadwinners	11,144	1,473	1,482	24	14,123
Professional	1,760	210	155	6	2,131
Domestic	5,318	552	494	11	6,375
Commercial	1,215	214	239	3	1,671
Transport and communication	168	122	41	0	331
Industrial	2,312	149	96	1	2,558
Primary producers	223	180	208	3	614
Independent	148	46	249		443
Dependants	45,437	30,016	3,612	106	79,171
Not specified	212	84	26	4	326
Total	56,793	31,573	5,120	134	93,620

[1] The category 'Widowed' includes 34 divorced women, 20 of whom were breadwinners.
Source: Commonwealth of Australia (1914d: 1672).

Table A.15 Major towns in Tasmania, 1881, 1891 and 1901

Year		1881	1891	1901
Town	Pursuits connected with	Population (no.)		
Beaconsfield	Mining	455	1,584	2,658
Bothwell	A. and P. farming	454	520	384
Burnie (Emu Bay)	A. farming, mining seaport	305	981	1,548
Campbell Town	P. farming	948	818	735
Carrick	A. farming	282	281	224
Colebrook (Jerusalem)	A. and P. farming, coalmining	194	189	147
Deloraine	A. and P. farming	836	895	949
Derby	Tin mining and agriculture	--	273	587
Devonport E. (Torquay)	Seaport/watering place, A. farming.	370	559	673
Devonport W. (Formby)	Seaport/watering place, A. farming	162	1,246	2,101
Evandale	Farming	564	540	617
Fingal	Dairy farming and coalmining	247	425	372

AUSTRALIA'S FERTILITY TRANSITION

Year		1881	1891	1901
Town	Pursuits connected with	Population (no.)		
Franklin	Fruit growing and timber producing	457	506	765
George Town	Watering place	299	299	274
Glenorchy	Fruit and hop growing	--	588	578
Gormanston	Mining	--	--	1,760
Hamilton	P. farming	387	348	232
Hobart	Metropolis	21,118	24,905	24,654
Bellerive	Suburb of Hobart	--	625	653
Beltana	Suburb of Hobart	--	--	251
Glebeton	Suburb of Hobart	--	643	694
Moonah	Suburb of Hobart	--	--	732
Mt Stuart	Suburb of Hobart	--	--	523
New Town[1]	Suburb of Hobart	1,720	2,288	2,314
Queensborough (Sandy Bay)[2]	Suburb of Hobart	795	1,443	1,821
Wellington Hamlets	Suburb of Hobart	--	704	776
Kempton	A. and P. farming	434	426	288
Kingston	Fruit growing and dairying	171	249	219
Latrobe	A. farming	711	1,560	1,360
Launceston	City	12,752	17,208	18,022
Invermay	Suburb of Launceston	--	882	1,010
Trevallyn	Suburb of Launceston	--	256	529
Lefroy	Mining, gold	436	465	709
Longford	A. and P. farming	1,286	1,084	1,223
Mathinna	Goldmining	--	426	815
New Norfolk	Fruit and hop growing	1,036	1,072	1,151
Oatlands	A. and P. farming	673	731	618
Penguin	A. farming, mining seaport	--	396	540
Perth	A. and P. farming	478	517	442
Pillinger	Mining seaport	--	--	637
Pontville	A. and dairy farming	329	172	114
Queenstown	Mining	--	--	5,051
Richmond	A. and P. farming	448	536	395
Ross	P. farming	353	389	311
St Helens	Dairy and A. farming	257	363	410
Scottsdale	A. farming	--	--	636

Year		1881	1891	1901
Town	Pursuits connected with	Population (no.)		
Sheffield	A. farming	263	429	446
Sorell	A. and P. farming	267	282	245
Stanley	A. farming	332	400	484
Strahan	Mining seaport	--	561	1,504
Swansea	A. farming and fruit growing	244	295	213
Ulverstone	A. farming	--	1,129	1,164
Waratah	Tin mining	874	1,420	1,265
Westbury	A. farming	1,156	1,104	1,027
Wynyard	A. farming	168	621	526
Zeehan	Silver mining	--	1,965	5,014

-- Not included as a town in the 1881 and/or 1891 census tables.

A. farming = Agricultural farming

P. farming = Pastoral farming

[1] New Town was a separate town from Hobart prior to 1891.

[2] Sandy Bay was a separate town from Hobart prior to 1891.

Notes: Comprises the 36 largest of the 45 towns listed in the 1881 census table 'Population of Towns' and all towns of 500 or more people listed in the table 'Population and Dwellings, 1901'. Town names as of 1901. Names in parentheses are the earlier names of these towns.

Sources: TAS (1887: 76; 1892: 90–1; 1902: 86–7); Tasmanian Family History Society (2014).

Table A.16 Marriage outcomes for incomplete group: 1860, 1870, 1880 and 1890 marriage cohorts, Tasmania

Marriage cohort	1860	1870	1880	1890
Marriage outcome	No.			
Separated during wife's childbearing years	14	4	10	9
Wife died during childbearing years	50	60	70	82
Husband died during wife's childbearing years	57	58	76	71
Total	121	122	156	162
	Percentage			
Separated during wife's childbearing years	11.6	3.3	6.4	5.6
Wife died during childbearing years	41.3	49.2	44.9	50.6
Husband died during wife's childbearing years	47.1	47.5	48.7	43.8
Total	100.0	100.0	100.0	100.0

Table A.17 Proportion of families by number of children, complete group: 1860, 1870, 1880 and 1890 marriage cohorts, Tasmania

Marriage cohort	1860	1870	1880	1890
No. of children	Percentage			
1–3	14.5	14.1	14.6	27.6
4–6	20.7	18.0	30.2	37.6
7–9	29.7	30.4	32.1	23.3
10+	35.2	37.5	23.0	11.5
Total (%)	100.0	100.0	100.0	100.0
Total (no.)	256	283	417	529

Table A.18 Infant and child mortality, incomplete group: 1860, 1870, 1880 and 1890 marriage cohorts, Tasmania

Marriage cohort	1860	1870	1880	1890
Infant/child deaths	Per 1,000			
Infant deaths (< 1 year)	105	83	70	82
Child deaths (1–4 years)	42	47	30	36
Total births (no.)	640	651	762	672

Note: Rates for infant deaths calculated per 1,000 live births and for child deaths per 1,000 children reaching age one.

Table A.19 Infant and child mortality, unobserved group: 1860, 1870, 1880 and 1890 marriage cohorts, Tasmania

Marriage cohort	1860	1870	1880	1890
Infant/child deaths	Per 1,000			
Infant deaths (< 1 year)	89	103	66	34
Child deaths (1–4 years)	55	50	53	35
Total births (no.)	259	156	244	149

Note: Rates for infant deaths calculated per 1,000 live births and for child deaths per 1,000 children reaching age one.

Table A.20 Age at last birth by age at marriage, complete group: 1860/70, 1880 and 1890 marriage cohorts, Tasmania

Marriage cohort	1860/70	1880	1890
Age at marriage/Age at last birth	Percentage		
Under 20 years			
< 30 years	11.1	18.9	27.4
30–34 years	9.6	15.4	11.5

APPENDIX A

Marriage cohort	1860/70	1880	1890
Age at marriage/Age at last birth	Percentage		
35–39 years	23.2	28.3	25.7
40+ years	56.1	37.8	35.4
Total (%)	100.0	100.0	100.0
Total (no.)	198	127	113
20–24 years			
< 30 years	8.6	13.6	23.0
30–34 years	11.9	15.4	18.9
35–39 years	31.3	31.7	30.9
40+ years	48.1	39.4	27.2
Total (%)	100.0	100.0	100.0
Total (no.)	243	221	265
25+ years			
< 30 years	4.1	6.1	8.2
30–34 years	13.3	4.5	15.8
35–39 years	33.7	42.4	45.2
40+ years	49.0	47.0	30.8
Total (%)	100.0	100.0	100.0
Total (no.)	98	66	146

Note: There were three women in the 1880 cohort and five in the 1890 cohort for whom age was missing.

Table A.21 Mean birth interval by birth order, complete group: 1860/70, 1880 and 1890 marriage cohorts, Tasmania

Marriage cohort	1860/70	1880	1890
Birth order	Mean birth interval (months)		
1–2	23.0	23.3	24.3
2–3	26.0	25.4	26.1
3–4	27.2	25.9	28.7
4–5	25.8	27.6	28.1
5–6	27.1	28.3	27.4
6–7	26.5	27.5	28.2
7–8	26.1	26.9	27.6
8–9	25.0	27.1	26.9
9–10	25.8	24.5	24.6

Note: Excludes last birth interval.

Table A.22 Distribution of covariates for logistic regression (Table 7.16)

Covariate	No. of births	Percentage
Mother's age at the birth		
< 25 years (ref.)	2,416	24.0
25 to < 30 years	2,663	26.4
30+ years	4,970	49.3
Missing	37	0.4
Mother's age at marriage		
< 20 years (ref.)	3,743	37.1
20 to < 25 years	4,834	47.9
25+ years	1,472	14.6
Missing	37	0.4
Age difference between couple		
Same/Husband up to 5 years older (ref.)	4,432	43.9
Wife older	1,416	14.0
Husband 5+ years older	4,100	40.7
Missing	138	1.4
Marriage cohort		
1860/70 cohort (ref.)	4,215	41.8
1880 cohort	2,921	29.0
1890 cohort	2,950	29.3
Socioeconomic status		
White-collar (ref.)	1,862	18.5
Skilled	1,460	14.5
Farmers	2,861	28.4
Lower-skilled	1,068	10.6
Unskilled	2,806	27.8
Missing	29	0.3
Type of geographic location		
Urban area in Tasmania (ref.)	2,773	27.5
Rural area in Tasmania	6,376	63.2
Another colony	937	9.3
Religion		
Anglican (ref.)	3,634	36.0
Catholic	1,194	11.8
Presbyterian	1,381	13.7
Methodist	2,170	21.5

Covariate	No. of births	Percentage
Other Nonconformist	1,701	16.9
Missing	6	0.1
Literacy status of husband and wife		
Both literate (ref.)	8,483	84.1
Husband and/or wife illiterate	1,603	15.9
Twin birth	99	1.0
Child dies as infant before conception of another	620	6.2
Family composition		
More girls than boys	3,917	38.8
More boys than girls	4,413	43.8
Equal numbers of boys and girls	1,756	17.4
Total births = 10,086		

Table A.23 Predicted probability that a birth is the last by socioeconomic status, complete group: 1860/70, 1880 and 1890 marriage cohorts, Tasmania

Marriage cohort/ Socioeconomic status	Predicted probability	Standard error	Significance
1860/70 cohort			
White-collar	0.14	0.008	0.000
Skilled	0.12	0.009	0.000
Farmers	0.10	0.006	0.000
Lower-skilled	0.13	0.010	0.000
Unskilled	0.10	0.006	0.000
1880 cohort			
White-collar	0.18	0.010	0.000
Skilled	0.16	0.011	0.000
Farmers	0.13	0.008	0.000
Lower-skilled	0.16	0.012	0.000
Unskilled	0.13	0.008	0.000
1890 cohort			
White-collar	0.24	0.012	0.000
Skilled	0.21	0.013	0.000
Farmers	0.18	0.009	0.000
Lower-skilled	0.22	0.014	0.000
Unskilled	0.18	0.009	0.000

Table A.24 Predicted probability that a birth is the last by socioeconomic status for women who married at 20–24 years, gave birth at 30+ years with a husband the same age or 1–4 years older, complete group: 1860/70, 1880 and 1890 marriage cohorts, Tasmania

Marriage cohort/ Socioeconomic status	Predicted probability	Standard error	Significance
1860/70 cohort			
White-collar	0.19	0.013	0.000
Skilled	0.16	0.013	0.000
Farmers	0.13	0.010	0.000
Lower-skilled	0.17	0.015	0.000
Unskilled	0.14	0.010	0.000
1880 cohort			
White-collar	0.24	0.016	0.000
Skilled	0.21	0.017	0.000
Farmers	0.17	0.013	0.000
Lower-skilled	0.22	0.018	0.000
Unskilled	0.18	0.013	0.000
1890 cohort			
White-collar	0.32	0.020	0.000
Skilled	0.28	0.020	0.000
Farmers	0.24	0.015	0.000
Lower-skilled	0.30	0.021	0.000
Unskilled	0.24	0.015	0.000

Table A.25 Predicted probability that a birth is the last by urban/rural location, complete group: 1860/70, 1880 and 1890 marriage cohorts, Tasmania

Marriage cohort/Geographic location	Predicted probability	Standard error	Significance
1860/70 cohort			
Urban	0.13	0.007	0.000
Rural	0.10	0.005	0.000
1880 cohort			
Urban	0.17	0.009	0.000
Rural	0.13	0.006	0.000
1890 cohort			
Urban	0.23	0.011	0.000
Rural	0.18	0.007	0.000

APPENDIX A

Table A.26 Predicted probability that a birth is the last by urban/rural location for women who married at 20–24 years, gave birth at 30+ years with a husband the same age or 1–4 years older, complete group: 1860/70, 1880 and 1890 marriage cohorts, Tasmania

Marriage cohort/Geographic location	Predicted probability	Standard error	Significance
1860/70 cohort			
Urban	0.18	0.012	0.000
Rural	0.13	0.009	0.000
1880 cohort			
Urban	0.23	0.015	0.000
Rural	0.18	0.010	0.000
1890 cohort			
Urban	0.31	0.018	0.000
Rural	0.24	0.013	0.000

Table A.27 Proportion of women who have at least a specific number of surviving children, complete group: 1860/70, 1880 and 1890 marriage cohorts, Tasmania

Marriage cohort	1860/70	1880	1890
No. of surviving children	Percentage		
One	100.0	100.0	100.0
Two	0.95	0.94	0.91
Three	0.90	0.86	0.80
Four	0.84	0.78	0.69
Five	0.76	0.69	0.58
Six	0.69	0.60	0.47
Seven	0.60	0.50	0.37
Eight	0.51	0.41	0.27
Nine	0.43	0.32	0.19
Ten	0.34	0.24	0.13
Eleven	0.26	0.17	0.08
Twelve	0.19	0.11	0.05

Table A.28 Distribution of covariates for survival analysis (Table 7.17)

Covariate	No. of births	Percentage
Mother's age at the birth		
< 25 years (ref.)	2,359	27.4
25 to < 30 years	2,511	29.2
30+ years	3,702	43.0
Missing	29	0.3
Mother's age at marriage		
< 20 years (ref.)	3,305	38.4
20 to < 25 years	4,105	47.7
25+ years	1,162	13.5
Missing	29	0.3
Age difference between couple		
Same age/Husband up to 5 years older (ref.)	3,785	44.0
Wife older	1,174	13.7
Husband 5+ years older	3,529	41.0
Missing	113	1.3
Marriage cohort		
1860/70 cohort (ref.)	3,676	42.7
1880 cohort	2,504	29.1
1890 cohort	2,421	28.2
Socioeconomic status		
White-collar (ref.)	1,510	17.6
Skilled	1,235	14.4
Farmers	2,482	28.9
Lower-skilled	887	10.3
Unskilled	2,461	28.6
Missing	26	0.3
Type of geographic location		
Urban area in Tasmania (ref.)	2,310	26.9
Rural area in Tasmania	5,537	64.4
Another colony	754	8.8
Religion		
Anglican (ref.)	3,105	36.1
Catholic	1,032	12.0
Presbyterian	1,161	13.5
Methodist	1,867	21.7

Covariate	No. of births	Percentage
Other Nonconformist	1,431	16.6
Missing	5	0.1
Literacy status of husband and wife		
Both literate (ref.)	7,196	83.7
Husband and/or wife illiterate	1,405	16.3
Twin birth	72	0.8
Child dies as infant before conception of another	522	6.1
Family composition		
More girls than boys	3,317	38.6
More boys than girls	3,760	43.7
Equal numbers of boys and girls	1,524	17.7
Total birth intervals = 8,601		

Table A.29 Estimated effects (relative risks) of various characteristics on the time to the next birth (closed birth intervals), interaction model, complete group: 1860/70, 1880 and 1890 marriage cohorts, Tasmania

Covariate	Relative risk	Standard error	Significance (p)	
Constant	0.08	0.006	0.000	**
Mother's age at birth of a child				
< 25 years (ref.)	1.00	--	--	
25–29 years	0.74	0.025	0.000	**
30+ years	0.63	0.029	0.000	**
Mother's age at marriage				
< 20 years (ref.)	1.00	--	--	
20–24 years	1.14	0.031	0.000	**
25+ years	1.56	0.075	0.000	**
Age difference between couple				
Same age/Husband up to 5 years older (ref.)	1.00	--	--	
Wife older	1.05	0.038	0.188	
Husband 5+ years older	1.01	0.025	0.576	
Marriage cohort				
1860/70 cohort (ref.)	1.00	--	--	
1880 cohort	0.94	0.075	0.406	
1890 cohort	0.7	0.062	0.000	**

Covariate	Relative risk	Standard error	Significance (p)	
Socioeconomic status				
White-collar (ref.)	1.00	--	--	
Skilled	1.04	0.062	0.515	
Farmers	1.02	0.053	0.649	
Lower-skilled	1.00	0.075	0.985	
Unskilled	0.98	0.051	0.696	
Type of geographic location				
Urban area in Tasmania (ref.)	1.00	--	--	
Rural area in Tasmania	1.04	0.044	0.414	
Another colony	1.03	0.062	0.571	
Religion				
Anglican (ref.)	1.00	--	--	
Catholic	1.00	0.058	0.992	
Presbyterian	1.001	0.053	0.967	
Methodist	1.03	0.049	0.564	
Other Nonconformist	0.91	0.046	0.053	
Literacy status of husband and wife				
Both literate (ref.)	1.00	--	--	
Husband and/or wife illiterate	0.97	0.032	0.428	
Twin birth	1.06	0.128	0.638	
Number of children (crude parity)	1.05	0.018	0.007	**
Number of surviving children	0.99	0.018	0.707	
Child dies as infant before conception of another	1.44	0.067	0.000	**
Ultimate birth interval	0.42	0.014	0.000	**
Sex composition of surviving children				
More surviving girls than boys (ref.)	1.00	--	--	
More surviving boys than girls	1.02	0.025	0.515	
Equal numbers of surviving boys and girls	0.96	0.03	0.196	
Interactions				
Marriage cohort*Socioeconomic status				
1880*Skilled Workers	0.87	0.820	0.143	
1880*Farmers	0.95	0.810	0.556	
1880*Lower-Skilled	0.98	0.103	0.870	

Covariate	Relative risk	Standard error	Significance (p)	
1880*Unskilled	1.06	0.086	0.485	
1890*Skilled workers	1.05	0.102	0.622	
1890*Farmers	1.24	0.107	0.014	*
1890*Lower-skilled	1.03	0.113	0.789	
1890*Unskilled	1.21	0.102	0.024	*
Marriage cohort*Geographic location				
1880*Rural	0.98	0.066	0.762	
1880*Outside Tasmania	0.83	0.092	0.098	
1890*Rural	1.12	0.076	0.108	
1890*Outside Tasmania	1.20	0.133	0.106	
Marriage cohort*Socioeconomic status				
1880*Catholic	1.13	0.098	0.177	
1880*Presbyterian	0.94	0.084	0.458	
1880*Methodist	1.17	0.086	0.028	*
1880*Other Nonconformist	1.07	0.086	0.405	
1890*Catholic	1.01	0.092	0.926	
1890*Presbyterian	1.04	0.088	0.610	
1890*Methodist	0.93	0.068	0.318	
1890*Other Nonconformist	1.03	0.084	0.721	
Number of birth intervals = 8,466				

* p < 0.05
** p < 0.01
-- not applicable for the reference category

Appendix B: Data sources used for family reconstitution

1. Tasbirths Birth registrations for Tasmania, 1838–99; Tasdeaths Death registrations for Tasmania, 1838–99; and Tasmarriages Marriage registrations for Tasmania, 1838–99. Civil register data collected in machine readable form c. 1993 as part of the Nineteenth-Century Household Formation in Tasmania Project by P. Gunn, University of Tasmania. Funded by the Australian Research Council under grants A78715590, A79131567 and A79532723, Australian Data Archive, The Australian National University, Canberra.
2. Kippen, Rebecca. 2013. *Database of deaths registered in Tasmania, 1900–1930*. Melbourne: University of Melbourne.
3. Catholic Church Museums and Registers. Various Tasmanian Catholic parish registers for nineteenth century. Microfilm. Founders and Survivors Project. University of Melbourne, Melbourne.
4. Tasmanian Federation Index. Births, 1900–1919; Deaths and Marriages, 1900–1930. Registry of Births, Deaths and Marriages Tasmania, 2006. CD format. Tasmania.
5. Colonial Tasmanian Family Links Database. Archives Office of Tasmania [Now Tasmanian Archives and Heritage Office]. This database is designed to provide an initial online genealogical research resource. The database is incomplete and the information not always accurate. Available from: portal.archives.tas.gov.au/menu.aspx?search=8.
6. Index to Divorces, 1861–1920. Archives Office of Tasmania [Now Tasmanian Archives and Heritage Office]. Available from: data.gov.au/dataset/ds-dga-1edcd6fb-adec-46c6-9851-e923bc657cd1/details.

7. Index to Wills and Letters of Administration, 1824–1989. Archives Office of Tasmania [Now Tasmanian Archives and Heritage Office]. Available from: data.gov.au/dataset/ds-dga-e897a164-153a-448b-9558-ec0b57079b3d/details.
8. Pioneer Index, Victoria, 1836–1888. Index to births, deaths and marriages in Victoria. CD format. Melbourne: Victorian Registry of Births, Deaths and Marriages.
9. Federation Index, Victoria, 1889–1901. Index to births, deaths and marriage in Victoria. CD format. Melbourne: Victorian Registry of Births, Deaths and Marriages, 1997.
10. Edwardian Index, Victoria, 1902–1913. Index to births, deaths and marriages in Victoria. CD format. Melbourne: Victorian Registry of Births, Deaths and Marriages.
11. Great War Index, Victoria, 1914–1920. Index to births, deaths and marriages in Victoria. CD format. Melbourne: Victorian Registry of Births, Deaths and Marriages.
12. SA births; SA deaths; SA marriages [microform] indexes. South Australia. Births, Deaths and Marriages Division. 1985–1988.
13. NSW births, 1788–1913; NSW deaths, 1788–1983; NSW marriages, 1788–1963. NSW Government Registry of Births, Deaths and Marriages. Sydney: Department of Justice. Available from: www.bdm.nsw.gov.au.
14. Queensland births, 1829–1914; Queensland deaths, 1829–1984; Queensland marriages, 1829–1939. Available from: www.familyhistory.bdm.qld.gov.au.
15. WA births, 1841–1932; WA deaths, 1941–1971; WA marriages, 1941–1936. Government of Western Australia Registry of Births, Deaths and Marriages. Perth: Department of Justice. Available from: www.bdm.dotag.wa.gov.au.
16. NZ births, 1848–1913; NZ deaths, 1848–1963; NZ marriages, 1854–1933. Birth, Death and Marriage Historical Records. Wellington: New Zealand Department of Internal Affairs. Available from: www.bdmhistoricalrecords.dia.govt.nz.
17. FreeBMD UK. (Births, 1837–1939; Deaths, 1837–1968; Marriages, 1837–1951). Civil Registration Index for England and Wales. FreeBMD. Registered charity in UK. Available from: www.freebmd.org.uk.

APPENDIX B

18. Australian Birth Index, 1788–1922; Australian Death Index, 1788–1985; Australian Marriage Index, 1788–1950. Ancestry. Available from: www.ancestry.com.au.
19. Australian Cemetery Index, 1808–2007. Ancestry. Available from: www.ancestry.com.au.
20. Australian Electoral Rolls, 1903–1980. Ancestry. Available from: www.ancestry.com.au.
21. New Zealand Electoral Rolls, 1853–1981. Ancestry. Available from: www.ancestry.com.au.
22. English Censuses, 1871, 1881, 1891, 1901 and 1911. Ancestry. Available from: www.ancestry.com.au.
23. Public Member Family Trees. Ancestry. Available from: www.ancestry.com.au.
24. Trove Digitised Newspapers and More. Canberra: National Library of Australia. Available from: www.trove.nla.gov.au. [For example, for Tasmania, includes newspapers from 1816 to 1954.]
25. *Australian Dictionary of Biography*. Canberra: The Australian National University. Available from: adb.anu.edu.au.
26. Boer War Embarkation Rolls. Canberra: Australian War Memorial. Available from: www.awm.gov.au.
27. World War I Embarkation Rolls. Canberra: Australian War Memorial. Available from: www.awm.gov.au.
28. Mapping Our Anzacs [now Discovering Anzacs]. Canberra: National Archives of Australia. Available from: discoveringanzacs.naa.gov.au/.

Appendix C: Local history museums

I visited the following Tasmanian local history centres:

- Beaconsfield Mine and Heritage Centre, Beaconsfield
- Cygnet Living History Museum, Cygnet
- Deloraine and Districts Folk Museum, Deloraine
- Derby Historical Society and Museum, Derby
- Eric Thomas Galley Museum, Queenstown
- Evandale History Room, Evandale Tourist and Information Centre, Evandale
- Heritage Highway Museum, Campbell Town
- Kentish History Museum, Sheffield
- Oatlands History Room, Oatlands
- St Helens History Room, St Helens
- Stanley Discovery Museum, Stanley
- Ulverstone History Museum, Ulverstone
- Waratah Museum, Waratah
- West Coast Pioneers' Memorial Museum, Zeehan
- Woolmers Estate, Longford, World Heritage Listed Australian Convict Site

Appendix D: Individual stories

Story 1

Thomas Cathcart Archer and Eleanor Harrop (1890 marriage cohort): Landowners, Woolmers Estate

Thomas Cathcart Archer married Eleanor May Harrop on 7 October 1890 in Launceston. They had one child, Thomas Edward Cathcart Archer, born on 24 November 1892. Thomas Cathcart Archer owned Woolmers Estate, a large farming estate near Longford that was founded in 1817 by his great-grandfather Thomas Archer, who was a free settler from England. The house and farm building were built by convict labour.

> Thomas Cathcart Archer (1862–1934) inherited Woolmers on the death of his father, Thomas Chalmers in 1890. He had little interest in farming and chose to remain in Launceston where he could pursue his sporting interest. Thomas Cathcart represented Northern Tasmania in cricket and was patron and commodore of the Tamar Yacht Club and president of the Longford Regatta Association. He chose to live at Woolmers in the late 1890s where he built a nine-hole golf course near the house. This course became the home of the Longford Golf Club between 1902 and 1914. Thomas Cathcart was noted for his interest in public affairs, being a member of the Longford Council from 1902 to 1934. (Noticeboard, Woolmers Estate, near Longford, Tasmania. 9 December 2014)

Story 2

Alfred Gale and Emma Wigg (1890 marriage cohort): Selector in Marrawah, remote north-western Tasmania

Alfred Herbert Gale married Emma Elizabeth Wigg in her father's house in Duck River, Stanley, on 20 August 1890. They had nine children, born between 18 June 1891 and 21 June 1911. Their fifth child died in infancy. Alf Gale was a 'selector' who selected a large area of land at Green Point, near Marrawah, and made it into one of the most productive dairy farms in the district. They established a cheese factory, store and sawmill. For many years, Alf acted as a bush doctor and dentist to the residents of the isolated area.

Story 3

Charles Fleming and Lavinia Rawsley (1870 cohort): 'Modern' occupations

Charles Fleming married Lavinia Jane Rawsley in Oatlands on 8 November 1870. They had eight children, born between April 1871 and January 1888. Charles was a labourer when he married and when the first four children were born, although he also did some farming. By the time the fifth child was born, in 1880, Charles was working as a railway porter. When his last child was born, in 1888, he was also a postmaster and remained in that position until he died in 1908. 'The government has approved of the establishment of a post office at Anthill Ponds Railway Station and of the appointment of Mr Charles Fleming as Post Master' (*Tasmanian News*, [Hobart], 20 September 1887).

Story 4

Richard Fleming and Eliza Barwick (1860 marriage cohort): Emigration from and return to Tasmania

Richard Fleming married Eliza Barwick on 1 August 1860 in Oatlands. The couple had 13 children, born between May 1861 and April 1884. Their twelfth child died in infancy. They had two children in Oatlands, but in March 1863 they left Hobart aboard the vessel *Hargreaves* to travel to the goldfields at Wyndham, New Zealand. They had three children in New Zealand, but by 1869 had returned to Oatlands, where another eight children were born. Richard died in Oatlands and Eliza in Launceston. Richard was a farmer in Oatlands, but towards the end of his life was also running a hotel/public house in Antill Ponds, just outside Oatlands (Oatlands History Room).

Story 5

John Walker and Amy Davenport (1870 marriage cohort): Amy Walker's diaries (Walker 1879, 1880, 1881, 1882, 1888, 1898)

John Fletcher Walker and Amy Clarisse Davenport married in Holy Trinity Church, Hobart, on 3 February 1870. They had one child, a daughter, Violet Hope, born on 6 August 1875.

Amy (1851–1940) was the daughter of the Reverend Arthur Davenport, who was rector of Holy Trinity Hobart for most of Amy's childhood, became Canon of St David's Cathedral, Hobart, in 1872 and then Archdeacon of Hobart. John Walker owned and ran a large number of properties near Gretna (south of Hamilton). Some of these estates were inherited from his father; others he purchased. The Walkers lived at 'Clarendon', which was a few miles from Gretna and about 35 miles (56 kilometres) from Hobart. John Walker was a Justice of the Peace, coroner and warden (that is, mayor) of Hamilton.

Amy was involved in many charitable activities and was very active in church affairs. She took a keen interest in farming during her husband's life and, after his death in 1906, she ran the farming property with the assistance of her manager/overseer (*The Mercury*, [Hobart], 23 November 1906; *The Examiner*, [Launceston], 9 November 1940).

Tasmanian Archives holds diaries written by Amy from when she was a young girl to the month before she was married in 1870 and then annually from 1879 to 1900 inclusive.

Story 6

Ida McAulay nee Butler (1858–1949): Ida McAulay's diaries (McAulay 1889–90, 1890, 1897, 1898, 1899, 1900, 1903, 1904, 1905)

Ida Butler was the daughter of Charles Butler, who was a Hobart solicitor and member of a prominent family in Hobart society. Ida married Alexander McAulay, lecturer and then professor of mathematics and physics at the University of Tasmania, in February 1895. The couple had three children: a son born in November 1895 and twin girls born in September 1898.

> Ida McAulay … was a feminist who rejected the argument of intrinsic differences in 'the mind-stuff of the sexes' and advocated higher education for girls, sex education and family planning. In 1899 she dismissed the claim that women would be drawn out of their sphere by the franchise: 'a woman's sphere is just that which she chooses to make it'. She was active in women's clubs and was president (1903–05) of the Tasmanian Women's Suffrage Association (later the Women's Political Association), resigning after a controversy. (Scott 1986: 203)

Story 7

Edward Sutton and Henrietta Lloyd (1860 marriage cohort): Upward social and economic mobility

Edward Henry Sutton, who was born in Launceston in 1838, was the second of 13 children. Edward worked as a baker in Launceston for several years. He married Henrietta Lloyd in Launceston on 15 November 1860 and they had three sons, in 1862, 1864 and 1870. The family moved to Longford in 1867, where Edward

> identified himself with all local matters, taking special interest in the Poultry and Agricultural Societies and the Library, to the success of which he contributed largely. Mr Sutton had, early in life, a turn for political study, and always manifested a desire to enter Parliament. In the year 1886 he opposed Mr W. St Paul Gellibrand for the Cressy seat in the House of Assembly, and was elected for that constituency, which he represented until the time of his death … Though his oratory was not brilliant, he was practical, and did not throw away many words … Keeping himself closely in touch with passing events, his opinions were formed after due thought, and his expressions in the House were listened to with attention. (*The Examiner*, [Launceston], 25 April 1893)

One of Edward's sons was supervisor of the Tasmanian International Exhibition of 1891–92, a highly prestigious event.

Story 8

David Dally and Maria Cox (1870 marriage cohort): Upward social and economic mobility

David Dally married Maria Cox in Launceston on 14 May 1870. They had five children, born between June 1871 and June 1882. David was a lime dealer during the early years of his marriage; however, in 1877, he and his brother William Dally discovered a huge gold reef, the famous Tasmania Reef, at Beaconsfield. By October 1877, the Dally brothers had sold their claim on the reef to William Grubb and William Hart for £15,000 and a one-tenth share of the Tasmania Gold Mining and

Quartz Crushing Company (Critchett 2012b). David Dally subsequently used his share of the money to acquire a large amount of property. At the time of his death, he owned a lime quarry near Beaconsfield and was a large property owner in Launceston (*North Western Advocate and Emu Bay Times*, [Devonport], 19 February 1913).

Story 9

Michael Lyons and Ellen Carroll (1870 marriage cohort): Parents of a prime minister, Joseph Lyons

Michael Lyons and Ellen Carroll were married in Stanley on 7 September 1870. They had eight children, born between July 1871 and May 1887. Joseph Lyons, their fifth child, was born in Stanley on 15 September 1879. Michael was a farmer when he married, but later also ran a small store. Michael and Ellen had seven children while living in this small house.

The family moved to Ulverstone in late 1884, but in 1887 Michael lost all his money on a bet on the Melbourne Cup horse race and was forced to work as a labourer. Joseph had to attend school part-time so he could work to help the family survive. In 1892, his mother's two sisters, Misses Letitia and Mary Carroll, invited Joseph to return to Stanley to live with them so he could attend school full-time. He attended the local school and eventually became a teacher with the Education Department. Joseph was Premier of Tasmania (1923–28) and later Prime Minister of Australia (1932–39) (Stanley Discovery Museum, 2014).

Bibliography

Abbasi-Shavazi, M.J., P. McDonald and M. Hosseini-Chavoshi. 2009. *The Fertility Transition in Iran: Revolution and reproduction*. Dordrecht: Springer. doi.org/10.1007/978-90-481-3198-3.

Accampo, E.A. 2003. The gendered nature of contraception in France: Neo-Malthusianism, 1900–1920. *The Journal of Interdisciplinary History* 34(2): 235–62.

Alexander, A. 2014. *Tasmania's Convicts: How felons built a free society*. Sydney: Allen & Unwin. 2nd edn.

Allbutt, H.A. 1888 [1886]. *The Wife's Handbook: How a woman should order herself during pregnancy, in the lying-in room, and after delivery, with hints on the management of the baby*. London: Forder. 7th edn. Available from: archive.org/details/39002086320026.med.yale.edu.

Allen, J.A. 1990. *Sex and Secrets: Crimes involving Australian women since 1880*. Melbourne: Oxford University Press.

Alter, G. 1988. *Family and the Female Life Course: The women of Verviers, Belgium, 1849–1880*. Madison: University of Wisconsin Press.

Alter, G. 1992. Theories of fertility decline: A non-specialist's guide to the current debate, in J.R. Gillis, L.A. Tilly and D. Levine (eds), *The European Experience of Declining Fertility, 1850–1970—The quiet revolution*. Cambridge, MA: Blackwell, pp. 13–27.

Alter, G., M. Neven and M. Oris. 2010. Economic change and differential fertility in rural eastern Belgium, 1812 to 1875, in N.O. Tsuya, W. Feng, G. Alter and J.Z. Lee (eds), *Prudence and Pressure: Reproduction and human agency in Europe and Asia, 1700–1900*. Cambridge, MA: Massachusetts Institute of Technology, pp. 195–216.

Anderson, M. 1999. No sex please, we're demographers: Nineteenth century fertility decline revisited, in J. Damousi and K. Ellinghaus (eds), *Citizenship, Women and Social Justice: International historical perspectives*. Melbourne: Department of History, University of Melbourne and Australian Network for Research in Women's History, pp. 251–64.

Anderson, M. and A. Mackinnon. 2015. Women's agency in Australia's first fertility transition: A debate revisited. *The History of the Family* 20(1): 9–23. doi.org/10.1080/1081602X.2014.990479.

Anderton, D.L. 1989. Comment on Knodel's 'Starting, stopping, and spacing during the early stages of fertility transition'. *Demography* 26(3): 467–70. doi.org/10.2307/2061605.

Anderton, D.L. and L.L. Bean. 1985. Birth spacing and fertility limitation: A behavioral analysis of a nineteenth century frontier population. *Demography* 22(2): 169–83. doi.org/10.2307/2061176.

Australian Bureau of Statistics (ABS). 2008. *Australian Historical Population Statistics, 2008*. Cat. No. 3105.0.65.001. Canberra: ABS. Available from: www.abs.gov.au/AUSSTATS/abs@.nsf/Lookup/3105.0.65.001Explanatory %20Notes12008.

Australian Bureau of Statistics (ABS). 2011. *2011 Census QuickStats*. Canberra: ABS. Available from: quickstats.censusdata.abs.gov.au/census_services/get product/census/2011/quickstat/0.

Baizán, P. and E. Camps. 2007. The impact of women's educational and economic resources on fertility: Spanish birth cohorts, 1901–1950, in A. Janssens (ed.), *Gendering the Fertility Decline in the Western World*. Bern: Peter Lang, pp. 25–58.

Banks, J.A. 1954. *Prosperity and Parenthood: A study of family planning among the Victorian middle classes*. London: Routledge & Kegan Paul.

Barnes, G. and T. Guinnane. 2012. Social class and the fertility transition: A critical comment on the statistical results reported in Simon Szreter's 'Fertility, class and gender in Britain, 1860–1940'. *The Economic History Review* 65(4): 1267–79. doi.org/10.1111/j.1468-0289.2011.00631.x.

Bean, L.L., G.P. Mineau and D.L. Anderton. 1990. *Fertility Change on the American Frontier: Adaptation and innovation*. Berkeley, CA: University of California Press.

Bean, L.L., G.P. Mineau and D.L. Anderton. 1992. High-risk childbearing: Fertility and infant mortality on the American frontier. *Social Science History* 16(3): 337–63. doi.org/10.1017/S0145553200016539.

Becker, G.S. 1981. *A Treatise on the Family*. Cambridge, MA: Harvard University Press.

Becker, G.S., K.M. Murphy and R. Tamura. 1990. Human capital, fertility and economic growth. *Journal of Political Economy* 98(5), Part 2: S12–S37. doi.org/10.1086/261723.

Bengtsson, T. and M. Dribe. 2014. The historical fertility transition at the micro level: Southern Sweden 1815–1939. *Demographic Research* 30(17): 493–534. doi.org/10.4054/DemRes.2014.30.17.

Berger, S., E. Merchant and J.M. Puerta. 2009. Responding to fertility shocks: Twins as a window into the demographic transition at the family level. Poster presented at the annual meeting of the Social Science History Association, Chicago, November.

Besant, A. 1887 [1877]. *The Law of Population: Its bearing and its consequences upon human conduct and morals*. London: Freethought Publishing Company. Available from: catalogue.nla.gov.au/Record/6499607.

Bland, L. 1995. *Banishing the Beast: English feminism and sexual morality, 1885–1914*. London: Penguin.

Bohnert, N., L.L. Jastad, J. Vechbanyongratana and E. Walhout. 2012. Offspring sex preference in frontier America. *Journal of Interdisciplinary History* 42(4): 519–41. doi.org/10.1162/JINH_a_00303.

Bolger, P. 1978. The changing image of Hobart, in J.W. McCarty and C.B. Schedvin (eds), *Australian Capital Cities: Historical essays*. Sydney: Sydney University Press, pp. 159–70.

Bongiorno, F. 2012. *The Sex Lives of Australians: A history*. Melbourne: Black Inc.

Borrie, W.D. 1994. *The European Peopling of Australia: A demographic history, 1788–1988*. Canberra: The Australian National University.

Boyce, J. 2010. *Van Diemen's Land*. Melbourne: Black Inc.

Branca, P. 1975. *Silent Sisterhood: Middle class women in the Victorian home*. London: Croom Helm.

Breschi, M., S. Mazzoni, M. Esposito and L. Pozzi. 2014. Fertility transition and social stratification in the town of Alghero, Sardinia (1866–1935). *Demographic Research* 30(28): 823–52. doi.org/10.4054/DemRes.2014.30.28.

Breward, I. 1988. *Australia: The most godless place under heaven?* Melbourne: Beacon Hill Press.

Breward, I. 1993. *A History of the Australian Churches*. Sydney: Allen & Unwin.

British Medical Journal (BMJ). 1899. The traffic in abortifacients. *British Medical Journal*, 14 January.

Brodie, J.F. 1994. *Contraception and Abortion in 19th Century America*. Ithaca, NY: Cornell University Press.

Brown, J.C. and T.W. Guinnane. 2002. Fertility transition in a rural Catholic population: Bavaria, 1880–1910. *Population Studies* 56: 35–50. doi.org/10.1080/00324720213799.

Bumpass, L., R. Rindfuss and R. Janosik. 1978. Age and marital status at first birth and the pace of subsequent fertility. *Demography* 15: 74–86. doi.org/10.2307/2060491.

Burnley, I.N. 1980. *The Australian Urban System: Growth, change and differentiation*. Melbourne: Longman Cheshire.

Caldwell, J.C. 1976. Toward a restatement of demographic transition theory. *Population and Development Review* 2(3–4): 321–66. doi.org/10.2307/1971615.

Caldwell, J.C. 1999. The delayed Western fertility decline: An examination of English-speaking countries. *Population and Development Review* 25(3): 479–513. doi.org/10.1111/j.1728-4457.1999.00479.x.

Caldwell, J.C. and P. McDonald. 1982. Influence of maternal education on infant and child mortality: Levels and causes. *Health Policy and Education* 2(3): 251–67. doi.org/10.1016/0165-2281(82)90012-1.

Caldwell, J.C. and L. Ruzicka. 1978. The Australian fertility transition: An analysis. *Population and Development Review* 4(1): 81–103. doi.org/10.2307/1972148.

Caltabiano, M. and G. Dalla Zuanna. 2015. The fertility transition in north-east Italy. *European Journal of Population* 31(1): 21–49. doi.org/10.1007/s10680-014-9328-7.

Carlile, F. 1828. *Every Woman's Book or What is Love? Containing most important instructions for the prudent regulation for the principle of love and the regulation of a family*. London: Carlile R. Available from: digital.library.lse.ac.uk.

Carlsson, G. 1966. The decline of fertility: Innovation or adjustment process? *Population Studies* 20: 149–74. doi.org/10.1080/00324728.1966.10406092.

Carmichael, G.A. 1996. From floating brothels to suburban semi-respectability: Two centuries of non-marital pregnancy in Australia. *Journal of Family History* 21(3): 281–315. doi.org/10.1177/036319909602100303.

Casterline, J.B. 2001. Diffusion processes and fertility transition: Introduction, in J.B. Casterline (ed.), *Diffusion Processes and Fertility Transition: Selected perspectives*. Washington, DC: National Academy Press, pp. 1–38.

Casterline, J.B., L. Williams and P. McDonald. 1986. The age differences between spouses: Variations among developing countries. *Population Studies* 40(3): 353–74. doi.org/10.1080/0032472031000142296.

Cho, L.J., R.D. Retherford and M.K. Choe. 1986. *The Own-Children Method of Fertility Estimation*. Honolulu: University of Hawai`i Press.

Cleland, J. 2001. Potatoes and pills: An overview of innovation–diffusion contribution to explanations of fertility decline, in J.B. Casterline (ed.), *Diffusion Processes and Fertility Transition: Selected perspectives*. Washington, DC: National Academy Press, pp. 39–65.

Cleland, J. and C. Wilson. 1987. Demand theories of the fertility transition: An iconoclastic view. *Population Studies* 41(1): 5–30. doi.org/10.1080/0032472031000142516.

Cleves, M., W. Gould, R.G. Gutierrez and Y.V. Marchenko. 2010. *An Introduction to Survival Analysis Using Stata*. College Station, TX: Stata Press. 3rd edn.

Coale, A.J. 1973. The demographic transition reconsidered, in *International Union for the Scientific Study of Population (IUSSP): Proceedings of the International Population Conference 1973. Volume 1*. Liège, Belgium: Editions Ordina, pp. 53–73.

Coale, A.J. 1986. The decline of fertility in Europe since the 18th century as a chapter in demographic history, in A.J. Coale and S.C. Watkins (eds), *The Decline of Fertility in Europe*. Princeton, NJ: Princeton University Press, pp. 1–30. doi.org/10.1515/9781400886692-006.

Coale, A.J. and R. Treadway. 1986. A summary of the changing distribution of overall fertility, marital fertility, and the proportion married in the provinces of Europe, in A.J. Coale and S.C. Watkins (eds), *The Decline of Fertility in Europe*. Princeton, NJ: Princeton University Press, pp. 31–181. doi.org/10.1515/9781400886692-007.

Coale, A.J. and T.J. Trussell. 1974. Model fertility schedules: Variations in the age structure of childbearing in human populations. *Population Index* 40(2): 185–258. doi.org/10.2307/2733910.

Coale, A.J. and T.J. Trussell. 1978. Technical note: Finding the two parameters that specify a model schedule of marital fertility. *Population Index* 44(2): 203–13. doi.org/10.2307/2735537.

Coale, A.J. and S.C. Watkins (eds). 1986. *The Decline of Fertility in Europe*. Princeton, NJ: Princeton University Press.

Coghlan, T.A. 1903. *The Decline in the Birth-Rate of New South Wales and Other Phenomena of Child-Birth: An essay in statistics*. Sydney: Government Printer.

Commonwealth of Australia. 1914a. *Census of the Commonwealth of Australia Taken for the Night between the 2nd and 3rd April, 1911. Volume I: Statisticians report*. Melbourne: McCarron, Bird & Co.

Commonwealth of Australia. 1914b. *Census of the Commonwealth of Australia Taken for the Night between the 2nd and 3rd April, 1911. Volume II, Part 1: Ages*. Melbourne: McCarron, Bird & Co.

Commonwealth of Australia. 1914c. *Census of the Commonwealth of Australia Taken for the Night between the 2nd and 3rd April, 1911. Volume III, Part X: Families*. Melbourne: McCarron, Bird & Co.

Commonwealth of Australia. 1914d. *Census of the Commonwealth of Australia Taken for the Night between the 2nd and 3rd April, 1911. Volume III, Part XII: Occupations*. Melbourne: McCarron, Bird & Co.

Commonwealth of Australia. 1921. *Census of the Commonwealth of Australia Taken for the Night between the 3rd and 4th April, 1921. Part XXVIII: Families*. Melbourne: H.J. Green.

Cook, H. 2000. Unseemly and unwomanly behaviour: Comparing women's control of their fertility in Australia and England from 1890 to 1970. *Journal of Population Research* 17(2): 125–41. doi.org/10.1007/BF03029461.

Cowie, A. 2009. A history of married women's real property rights. *Australian Journal of Gender and Law* 1: 1–21.

Cox, P. 2012. The electric telegraph, in A.M. Bartlett (ed.), *Way Back When … People, Places and Events: Contributed stories about the early days of settlement in northern Tasmania*. Launceston, Tas.: West Tamar Historical Society Inc., George Town and District Historical Society Inc. and Launceston Historical Society Inc., pp. 73–4.

Critchett, J. 2012a. West Tamar welcomes Methodism, in A.M. Bartlett (ed.), *Way Back When … People, Places and Events: Contributed stories about the early days of settlement in northern Tasmania*. Launceston, Tas.: West Tamar Historical Society Inc., George Town and District Historical Society Inc. and Launceston Historical Society Inc., pp. 76–7.

Critchett, J. 2012b. Beaconsfield Mine: One of Australia's greatest, in A.M. Bartlett (ed.), *Way Back When … People, Places and Events: Contributed stories about the early days of settlement in northern Tasmania*. Launceston, Tas.: West Tamar Historical Society Inc., George Town and District Historical Society Inc. and Launceston Historical Society Inc., pp. 87–8.

David, P.A. and W.C. Sanderson. 1988. Measuring marital fertility control with CPA. *Population Index* 54(4): 691–713. doi.org/10.2307/3645101.

David, P.A., T.A. Mroz, W.C. Sanderson, K.W. Wachter and D.R. Weir. 1988. Cohort parity analysis: Statistical estimates of the extent of fertility control. *Demography* 25(2): 163–88. doi.org/10.2307/2061287.

Davison, G. 2004. *The Rise and Fall of Marvellous Melbourne*. Melbourne: Melbourne University Press. 2nd edn.

Derosas, R. 2006. Between identity and assimilation: Jewish fertility in nineteenth-century Venice, in R. Derosas and F. van Poppel (eds), *Religion and the Decline of Fertility in the Western World*. Dordrecht, Netherlands: Springer, pp. 176–205. doi.org/10.1007/1-4020-5190-5.

Dribe, M. and F. Scalone. 2010. Detecting deliberate fertility control in pre-transitional populations: Evidence from six German villages, 1766–1863. *European Journal of Population* 26(4): 411–34. doi.org/10.1007/s10680-010-9208-8.

Dribe, M. and F. Scalone. 2014. Social class and net fertility before, during and after the demographic transition: A micro-level analysis of Sweden 1880–1970. *Demographic Research* 30(15): 429–64. doi.org/10.4054/DemRes.2014.30.15.

Dribe, M., J.D. Hacker and F. Scalone. 2014. The impact of socio-economic status on net fertility during the historical fertility decline: A comparative analysis of Canada, Iccland, Sweden, Norway, and the USA. *Population Studies* 68(2): 135–49. doi.org/10.1080/00324728.2014.889741.

Drysdale, G.R. 1861 [1854]. *The Elements of Social Science: Or physical, sexual or natural religion*. London: Truelove. 3rd edn. Available from: books.google.com.au/books/about/The_Elements_of_Social_Science.html?id=KG17KV1ezZMC.

Easterlin, R.A. 1975. An economic framework for fertility analysis. *Studies in Family Planning* 6(3): 54–63. doi.org/10.2307/1964934.

Easterlin, R.A. and E.M. Crimmins. 1985. *The Fertility Revolution: A supply–demand analysis*. Chicago: University of Chicago Press.

Elderton, E.M. 1914. *Report on the English Birthrate*. Cambridge: Cambridge University Press. Available from: openlibrary.org/works/OL202885W/Report_on_the_English_birthrate.

Evans, R. 2005. *Evangelism and Revivals in 19th Century Australia, 1880 to 1914 (First Volume)*. Hazelbrook, NSW: Research in Evangelistic Revivals. Available from: www.revivals.arkangles.com.

Ewbank, D.C. 1989. Estimating stopping and spacing behaviour. *Demography* 26(3): 473–83. doi.org/10.2307/2061607.

Fahy, K. 2007. An Australian history of the subordination of midwifery. *Women and Birth* 20(1): 25–9. doi.org/10.1016/j.wombi.2006.08.003.

Famour, A. and G. Withers. 2014. Australian wages, 1850–1900. Unpublished ms.

Feng, W., J.Z. Lee, N.O. Tsuya and S. Kurosu, in collaboration with M. Oris, M. Dribe and M. Manfredini. 2010. Household organization, co-resident kin, and reproduction, in N. Tsuya, W. Feng, G. Alter and J.Z. Lee (eds), *Prudence and Pressure: Reproduction and human agency in Europe and Asia, 1700–1900*. Cambridge, MA: Massachusetts Institute of Technology, pp. 67–95.

Finch, B.E. and H. Green. 1963. *Contraception Through the Ages*. London: Peter Owen.

Finlay, H. 1999. Lawmaking in the shadow of the empire: Divorce in colonial Australia. *Journal of Family History* 24(1): 74–109. doi.org/10.1177/036319909902400105.

Finlay, H. 2001. Divorce and the status of women: Beginnings in 19th century Australia. Presentation to the Australian Institute of Family Studies, Melbourne, 20 September.

Finnas, F. and J.M. Hoem. 1980. Starting age and subsequent birth intervals in co-habitational unions in current Danish cohorts, 1975. *Demography* 17(3): 275–95. doi.org/10.2307/2061104.

Folbre, N. 1983. Of patriarchy born: The political economy of fertility decisions. *Feminist Studies* 9(2): 261–84. doi.org/10.2307/3177490.

Foster, Frank M.C. 1982. The Collins prosecution, the Windeyer judgement and early publications in Australia on birth control. *Bicentennial History Bulletin: Australia 1888* 10: 76–86.

Freedman, R. 1962. The sociology of human fertility: A trend report and bibliography. *Current Sociology* 11: 35–119. doi.org/10.1177/001139216201100202.

Freedman, R. 1963. Norms for family size in underdeveloped areas. *Proceedings of the Royal Society B: Biological Sciences* 159: 220–45. doi.org/10.1098/rspb.1963.0074.

Galloway, P.R., E.A. Hammel and R.D. Lee. 1994. Fertility decline in Prussia, 1875–1910: A pooled cross-section time series analysis. *Population Studies* 48(1): 135–58. doi.org/10.1080/0032472031000147516.

Galloway, P.R., R.D. Lee and E.A. Hammel. 1998. Infant mortality and the fertility transition: Macro evidence from Europe and new findings from Prussia, in M.D. Montgomery and B. Cohen (eds), *From Death to Birth: Mortality decline and reproductive change*. Washington, DC: National Academy Press, pp. 182–226.

Garrett, E., A. Reid, K. Schürer and S. Szreter. 2001. *Changing Family Size in England and Wales: Place, class and demography, 1891–1911*. Cambridge: Cambridge University Press. doi.org/10.1017/CBO9780511495816.

Gauvreau, D. 1992. Nuptialité et industrialization: Éléments de comparaison entre l'ancien et le nouveau monde [Marriage and industrialisation: Elements of comparison between the old and the new world], in R. Bonnain, G. Bouchard and J. Goy (eds), *Transmettre, Hériter, Succéder: La Reproduction Familiale en Milieu Rural, France-Québec, XVIIIe–XXe siècles* [*Transmit, Inherit, Succeed: Family reproduction in rural areas, France–Québec, 18th–20th centuries*]. Lyon: Presses universitaires de Lyon, pp. 27–41.

Gauvreau, D. and P. Gossage. 2001. Canadian fertility transitions: Quebec and Ontario at the turn of the twentieth century. *Journal of Family History* 26(2): 162–88. doi.org/10.1177/036319900102600202.

Gray, E., A. Evans, J. Anderson and R. Kippen. 2010. Using split-population models to examine predictors of the probability and timing of parity progression. *European Journal of Population* 26(3): 275–95. doi.org/10.1007/s10680-009-9201-2.

Grimshaw, P., C. McConville and E. McEwen (eds). 1985. *Families in Colonial Australia*. Sydney: George Allen & Unwin.

Grundy, D. and F.F.F. Yuan. 1987. Education and science, in W. Vamplew (ed.), *Australians: Historical statistics*. Sydney: Fairfax, Syme & Weldon, pp. 328–46.

Gunn, P. and R. Kippen. 2008. Household and family formation in nineteenth-century Tasmania, dataset of 195 thousand births, 93 thousand deaths and 51 thousand marriages registered in Tasmania, 1838–1899. *Australian Data Archive*. Canberra: The Australian National University.

Gutmann, M.P. and G. Alter. 1993. Family reconstitution as event-history analysis, in D.S. Reher and R. Schofield (eds), *Old and New Methods in Historical Demography*. Oxford: Clarendon, pp. 159–77.

Hacker, J.D. 2003. Rethinking the 'early' decline of marital fertility in the United States. *Demography* 40(4): 605–20. doi.org/10.1353/dem.2003.0035.

Hacker, J.D. and R. Kippen. 2007. A comparison of historical trends in marriage and fertility in the United States and Australia. Paper presented at the annual meeting of the Social Science History Association, Chicago, November.

Haines, M.R. 1989. Social class differentials during fertility decline: England and Wales revisited. *Population Studies* 43(2): 305–23. doi.org/10.1080/0032472031000144136.

Haines, M.R. 1998. The relationship between infant and child mortality and fertility: Some historical and contemporary evidence for the United States, in M.D. Montgomery and B. Cohen (eds), *From Death to Birth: Mortality decline and reproductive change*. Washington, DC: National Academy Press, pp. 227–53.

Hall, E.S. 1872. Climate and vital statistics of Tasmania, in F. Abbott (ed.), *Results of Five Years' Meteorological Observations for Hobart Town*. Hobart Town: Government Printer, pp. 11–37.

Haynes, E.F. 1976. Edward Swarbreck Hall: Medical scientist and social reformer in colonial Tasmania. Master of Arts thesis, University of Tasmania, Hobart.

Henry, L. 1961. Some data on natural fertility. *Eugenics Quarterly* 9(2): 81–91. doi.org/10.1080/19485565.1961.9987465.

Henry, L. and A. Blum. 1988. *Techniques d'Analyse en Demographie Historique [Historical Demography Analysis Techniques]*. Paris: INED. 2nd edn.

Hicks, N. 1978. *'This Sin and Scandal': Australia's population debate 1891–1911*. Canberra: Australian National University Press.

Himes, N.E. 1963. *Medical History of Contraception*. New York: Gamut Press.

Hionidou, V. 1998. The adoption of fertility control on Mykonos, 1879–1959: Stopping, spacing or both. *Population Studies* 52(1): 67–83. doi.org/10.1080/0032472031000150186.

Hirschman, C. 1994. Why fertility changes. *Annual Review of Sociology* 20: 203–33. doi.org/10.1146/annurev.soc.20.1.203.

Historical International Standard Classification of Occupations (HISCO). 2013. *History of Work Information System*. Available from: historyofwork.iisg.nl/.

Hitchcock, N.E. 1990. Infant feeding in Australia: An historical perspective. Part 1: 1788–1900. *Breastfeeding Review* 2(1): 17–22.

Jones, E.F. 1971. Fertility decline in Australia and New Zealand 1861–1936. *Population Index* 37(4): 301–38. doi.org/10.2307/2733841.

Kellaway, R. 1999. Tasmania and the Otago gold rush 1861–1865. *Tasmanian Historical Research Association Papers and Proceedings* 46(4): 213–29.

Kippen, R. 2002a. An indispensable duty of government: Civil registration in nineteenth-century Tasmania. *Tasmanian Historical Studies* 8(1): 42–58.

Kippen, R. 2002b. *Annual Tasmanian Population by Age and Sex, 1860–99: Calculations from census and vital-registration data*. Canberra: The Australian National University.

Kippen, R. 2002c. Death in Tasmania: Using civil death registers to measure nineteenth-century cause-specific mortality. PhD thesis, The Australian National University, Canberra.

Kippen, R. 2013. *Database of Deaths Registered in Tasmania, 1900–1930*. Melbourne: University of Melbourne.

Kippen, R. and P. Gunn. 2011. Convict bastards, common-law unions and shotgun weddings: Premarital conceptions and ex-nuptial births in nineteenth-century Tasmania. *Journal of Family History* 36(4): 387–403. doi.org/10.1177/0363199011412720.

Knodel, J. 1978. European populations in the past: Family-level relations, in S. Preston (ed.), *The Effects of Infant and Child Mortality on Fertility*. New York: Academic Press, pp. 21–45.

Knodel, J. 1982. Child mortality and reproductive behaviour in German village populations in the past: A micro-level analysis of replacement effect. *Population Studies* 36(2): 177–200. doi.org/10.1080/00324728.1982.10409027.

Knodel, J. 1987. Starting, stopping, and spacing during the early stages of fertility transition: The experience of German village populations in the 18th and 19th centuries. *Demography* 24(2): 143–62. doi.org/10.2307/2061627.

Knodel, J. and E. van de Walle. 1979. Lessons from the past: Policy implications of historical fertility studies. *Population and Development Review* 5(2): 217–45. doi.org/10.2307/1971824.

Knodel, J. and E. van de Walle. 1986. Lessons from the past: Policy implications of historical fertility studies, in A.J. Coale and S.C. Watkins (eds), *The Decline of Fertility in Europe*. Princeton, NJ: Princeton University Press, pp. 390–419. doi.org/10.1515/9781400886692-015.

Knowlton, C. 1878 [1834]. *Fruits of Philosophy, or the Private Companion of Young Married People*. Melbourne: Asher. Available from: catalogue.nla.gov.au/Record/2692604.

Kolk, M. 2011. Deliberate birth spacing in nineteenth century northern Sweden. *European Journal of Population* 27(3): 337–59. doi.org/10.1007/s10680-011-9228-z.

Larson, A. 1994. *Growing Up in Melbourne: Family life in Melbourne in the late 19th century*. Canberra: The Australian National University.

Lawson, O. (ed.). 1990. *The First Voice of Australian Feminism: Excerpts from Louisa Lawson's The Dawn 1888–1895*. Sydney: Simon & Schuster.

Lee, R.D., P.R. Galloway and E.G. Hammel. 1994. Fertility decline in Prussia: Estimating influences on supply, demand, and degree of control. *Demography* 31(2): 347–73. doi.org/10.2307/2061889.

Lesthaeghe, R.J. 1977. *The Decline of Belgian Fertility, 1800–1970*. Princeton, NJ: Princeton University Press.

Lesthaeghe, R. and C. Wilson. 1986. Modes of production, secularization, and the pace of fertility decline in Western Europe, 1870–1930, in A.J. Coale and S.C. Watkins (eds), *The Decline of Fertility in Europe*. Princeton, NJ: Princeton University Press, pp. 261–92. doi.org/10.1515/9781400886692-011.

Livi-Bacci, M. 1986. Social-group forerunners of fertility control in Europe, in A.J. Coale and S.C. Watkins (eds), *The Decline of Fertility in Europe*. Princeton, NJ: Princeton University Press, pp. 182–200. doi.org/10.1515/9781400886692-008.

Llewelyn Davies, M.L. (ed.). 1978 [1915]. *Maternity: Letters from working women collected by the Women's Cooperative Guild*. London: Virago.

Lundh, C. and S. Kurosu. 2014. Challenging the East West binary, in C. Lundh and S. Kurosu (eds), *Similarity in Difference: Marriage in Europe and Asia, 1700–1900*. Cambridge, MA: MIT Press. doi.org/10.7551/mitpress/9780262027946.001.0001.

McAulay, I. 1889–90. *Diaries of Mrs Ida McAulay (nee Butler)*. NS 1077/1/2. Hobart: Tasmanian Archives.

McAulay, I. 1890. *Diaries of Mrs Ida McAulay (nee Butler)*. NS 1077/1/3. Hobart: Tasmanian Archives.

McAulay, I. 1897. *Diaries of Mrs Ida McAulay (nee Butler)*. NS 1077/1/4. Hobart: Tasmanian Archives.

McAulay, I. 1898. *Diaries of Mrs Ida McAulay (nee Butler)*. NS 1077/1/5. Hobart: Tasmanian Archives.

McAulay, I. 1899. *Diaries of Mrs Ida McAulay (nee Butler)*. NS 1077/1/6. Hobart: Tasmanian Archives.

McAulay, I. 1900. *Diaries of Mrs Ida McAulay (nee Butler)*. NS 1077/1/7. Hobart: Tasmanian Archives.

McAulay, I. 1903. *Diaries of Mrs Ida McAulay (nee Butler)*. NS 1077/1/10. Hobart: Tasmanian Archives.

McAulay, I. 1904. *Diaries of Mrs Ida McAulay (nee Butler)*. NS 1077/1/11. Hobart: Tasmanian Archives.

McAulay, I. 1905. *Diaries of Mrs Ida McAulay (nee Butler)*. NS 1077/1/12. Hobart: Tasmanian Archives.

McCalman, J. 1988. *Sex and Suffering: Women's health and a women's hospital*. Melbourne: Melbourne University Press.

McCarty, J.W. 1974. Australian capital cities in the nineteenth century, in C.B. Schedvin and J.W. McCarty (eds), *Urbanisation in Australia: The nineteenth century*. Sydney: Sydney University Press, pp. 9–39.

McDonald, P. 1974. *Marriage in Australia: Age at first marriage and proportions marrying, 1860–1971*. Australian Family Formation Project Monograph No. 2. Canberra: Department of Demography, The Australian National University.

McDonald, P. 1981. Social change and age at marriage, in *International Union for the Scientific Study of Population (IUSSP): Proceedings of the International Population Conference 1981. Volume 1*. Liège, Belgium: Editions Ordina, pp. 413–32.

McDonald, P. 1984. *Nuptiality and Completed Fertility: A study of starting, stopping and spacing behaviour*. World Fertility Survey Comparative Studies No. 35. Voorburg, Netherlands: International Statistical Institute.

McDonald, P. 2000. Gender equity in theories of fertility transition. *Population and Development Review* 26(3): 427–39. doi.org/10.1111/j.1728-4457.2000.00427.x.

McDonald, P. 2001. Theory pertaining to low fertility. Paper presented at the International Union for the Scientific Study of Population (IUSSP) Seminar on International Perspectives on Low Fertility: Trends, Theories and Policies, Tokyo, March.

McDonald, P. and J. Knodel. 1989. The impact of changes in birth spacing on age at last birth: A response to Anderton. *Demography* 26(3): 471–2. doi.org/10.2307/2061606.

McDonald, P. and Moyle, H. 2018. Women as agents in fertility decision-making: Australia 1870–1910. *Population and Development Review* 44(2): 203–30. doi.org/10.1111/padr.12140.

McDonald, P. and P. Quiggin. 1985. Lifecourse transitions in Victoria in the 1880s, in P. Grimshaw, C. McConville and E. McEwen (eds), *Families in Colonial Australia*. Sydney: Allen & Unwin, pp. 64–82.

McDonald, P., L. Ruzicka and P. Pine. 1987. Marriage, fertility and mortality, in W. Vamplew (ed.), *Australians, Historical Statistics*. Sydney: Fairfax, Syme & Weldon Associates, pp. 42–61.

Mackinnon, A., C. Batson and J. Petersen-Gray. 2007. 'But I'm so embarrassed, I said if it's another baby!': Schooling, girls and declining fertility in urban South Australia in the late nineteenth and early twentieth century, in A. Janssens (ed.), *Gendering the Fertility Decline in the Western World*. Bern: Peter Lang, pp. 205–35.

McLaren, A. 1990. *A History of Contraception: From antiquity to the present day*. Oxford: Basil Blackwell.

MaHood, J. and K. Wenburg (eds). 1980. *The 'Mosher' Survey: Sexual attitudes of 45 Victorian women/Clelia Duel Mosher*. New York: Arno Press.

Malthus, T. 1798. *An Essay on the Principle of Population*. London: Johnson.

Mason, K.O. 1997. Gender and demographic change: What do we know?, in G.W. Jones, R.M. Douglas, J.C. Caldwell and R.M. D'Souza (eds), *The Continuing Demographic Transition*. Oxford: Clarendon Press, pp. 158–82.

Matras, J. 1965. The social strategy of family formation: Some variations in space and time. *Demography* 2(1): 350–1. doi.org/10.2307/2060123.

Matthiessen, P.D. and J.C. McCann. 1978. The role of mortality in the European fertility transition: Aggregate-level relations, in S. Preston (ed.), *The Effects of Infant and Child Mortality on Fertility*. New York: Academic Press, pp. 47–67.

Meikle, B. 2010. Hard times in the golden age: The long depression of Tasmania, 1857–75. *Tasmanian Historical Studies* 15: 39–70.

Meikle, B. 2011. Squatters and selectors: The Waste Lands Acts of Tasmania, 1858–68. *Tasmanian Historical Studies* 16: 1–24.

Menken, J., J. Trussell and U. Larsen. 1986. Age and infertility. *Science* 233: 1389–94. doi.org/10.1126/science.3755843.

Mineau, G.P., K.R. Smith and L.L. Bean. 2002. Historical trends of survival among widows and widowers. *Social Science and Medicine* 54(2): 245–54. doi.org/10.1016/S0277-9536(01)00024-7.

Moyle, H. 2012. The historical decline of marital fertility in Tasmania, Australia: The role of occupational status. Paper presented for the Seminar on Socioeconomic Stratification and Fertility Before, During and After the Demographic Transition, International Union for the Scientific Study of Population (IUSSP) Scientific Panel on Historical Demography, Alghero, Sardinia, September.

Moyle, Helen. 2015. The fall of fertility in Tasmania in the late 19th and early 20th centuries. PhD thesis, The Australian National University, Canberra. Available from: openresearch-repository.anu.edu.au/handle/1885/16176.

New South Wales (NSW). Legislative Assembly. 1904a. *Royal Commission on the Decline of the Birth-Rate and on the Mortality of Infants in New South Wales. Volume I: Report and statistics*. Sydney: NSW Government Printer.

New South Wales (NSW). Legislative Assembly. 1904b. *Royal Commission on the Decline of the Birth-Rate and on the Mortality of Infants in New South Wales. Volume 2: Minutes, evidence, exhibits, index*. Sydney: NSW Government Printer. [Microfilm. Canberra: National Library of Australia.]

New South Wales (NSW) Bureau of Statistics and Economics. 1912. *Report on the Vital Statistics of New South Wales, 1911*. Sydney: Government Printer.

Notestein, F.W. 1945. Population: The long view, in T.W. Schultz (ed.), *Food for the World*. Chicago: University of Chicago Press, pp. 36–57.

Notestein, F.W. 1983. Frank Notestein on population growth and economic development. *Population and Development Review* 9(2): 345–60. doi.org/10.2307/1973057.

Okun, B. 1994. Evaluating methods for detecting fertility control: Coale and Trussell's model and cohort parity analysis. *Population Studies* 48(2): 193–222. doi.org/10.1080/0032472031000147766.

Okun, B. 1995. Distinguishing stopping behavior from spacing behavior with indirect methods. *Historical Methods: A Journal of Quantitative and Interdisciplinary History* 28(2): 85–96. doi.org/10.1080/01615440.1995.9956357.

Pink, K. 1990. *And Wealth for Toil: A history of north-west and western Tasmania, 1825–1900*. Burnie, Tas.: Advocate Marketing Services.

Preston, S. 1978. Introduction, in S. Preston (ed.), *The Effects of Infant and Child Mortality on Fertility*. New York: Academic Press, pp. 1–18.

Pringle, R. 1973. Octavius Beale and the ideology of the birth-rate: The royal commissions of 1904 and 1905. *Refractory Girl* 3: 19–27.

Quiggin, P. 1988. *No Rising Generation: Women and fertility in late nineteenth century Australia*. Australian Family Formation Project Monograph No. 10. Canberra: Department of Demography, The Australian National University.

Rao, T.V. 1978. Maternal age, parity and twin pregnancies. *Progress in Clinical Biological Research* 24(B): 99–103.

Reher, D.S. and A. Sanz-Gimeno. 2007. Rethinking historical reproductive change: Insights from longitudinal data for a Spanish town. *Population and Development Review* 33(4): 703–27. doi.org/10.1111/j.1728-4457.2007.00194.x.

Reynolds, H. 1969. Men of substance and deservedly good repute: Tasmanian gentry 1856–1875. *Australian Journal of Politics and History* 15(3): 61–72. doi.org/10.1111/j.1467-8497.1969.tb00957.x.

Reynolds, H. 2012. *A History of Tasmania*. Melbourne: Cambridge University Press.

Robson, L. 1983. *A History of Tasmania. Volume 1: Van Diemen's Land from the earliest times to 1855*. Melbourne: Oxford University Press.

Robson, L. and M. Roe. 1997. *A Short History of Tasmania*. Melbourne: Oxford University Press. New edn.

Robson, S.L. and K.R. Smith. 2011. Twinning in humans: Maternal heterogeneity in reproduction and survival. *Proceedings of the Royal Society B: Biological Sciences* 278: 3755–61. doi.org/10.1098/rspb.2011.0573.

Robson, S.L. and K.R. Smith. 2012. Parity progression ratios confirm higher lifetime fertility in women who bear twins. *Proceedings of the Royal Society B: Biological Sciences* 279: 2512–14. doi.org/10.1098/rspb.2012.0436.

Rogers, E.M. 1983. *Diffusion of Innovations*. New York: Free Press. 3rd edn.

Ruggles, S. 1992. Migration, marriage and mortality: Correcting sources of bias in English family reconstitution. *Population Studies* 46(3): 507–22. doi.org/10.1080/0032472031000146486.

Russell, P. 2010. *Savage or Civilised? Manners in colonial Australia*. Sydney: UNSW Press.

Ruzicka, L.T. and J.C. Caldwell. 1977. *The End of the Demographic Transition in Australia*. Australian Family Formation Project Monograph No. 5. Canberra: Department of Demography, The Australian National University.

Sandström, G. and L. Vikström. 2015. Sex preference for children in German villages during the fertility transition. *Population Studies* 69(1): 57–71. doi.org/10.1080/00324728.2014.994667.

Santow, G. 1995. Coitus interruptus and the control of natural fertility. *Population Studies* 49(1): 19–43. doi.org/10.1080/0032472031000148226.

Schellekens, J. and F. van Poppel. 2012. Marital fertility decline in the Netherlands: Child mortality, real wages and unemployment, 1860–1939. *Demography* 49(3): 965–88. doi.org/10.1007/s13524-012-0112-1.

Scott, B. 1986. Alexander McAulay (1863–1931), in *Australian Dictionary of Biography. Volume 10*. Melbourne: Melbourne University Press, pp. 202–4.

Scrimshaw, S. 1978. Infant mortality and behaviour in the regulation of family size. *Population and Development Review* 4(3): 383–403. doi.org/10.2307/1972856.

Seccombe, W. 1993. *Weathering the Storm: Working-class families from the Industrial Revolution to the fertility decline*. London: Verso.

Sharlin, A. 1986. Urban–rural differences in fertility in Europe during the demographic transition, in A.J. Coale and S.C. Watkins (eds), *The Decline of Fertility in Europe*. Princeton, NJ: Princeton University Press, pp. 234–60. doi.org/10.1515/9781400886692-010.

Smith, K.R., G.P. Mineau and L.L. Bean. 2002. Fertility and post-reproductive longevity. *Social Biology* 49(3): 185–205. doi.org/10.1080/19485565.2002.9989058.

Smyth, B. 1893. *The Limitation of Offspring: Being the substance of a lecture delivered in the North Melbourne Town Hall and elsewhere, to large audiences of women only*. Melbourne: Rae Brothers.

Sohn, A. 1996. *Chrysalides: Femmes dans la vie privée (XIXe-XXe siècles)*. Publications de la Sorbonne, 1, 2 volumes.

Spengler, J.J. 1968. Demographic factors and early modern economic development. *Daedalus* 97(2): 433–46.

Sprod, M.N. 1984. The old education: Government schools in Tasmania 1839–1904. *Historical Research Association Papers and Proceedings* 31(2): 18–36.

Swain, S. and R. Howe. 1995. *Single Mothers and their Children: Disposal, punishment and survival in Australia*. Melbourne: Cambridge University Press.

Switzerland. 1878. *Statistiques de la Suisse, movement de la population en Suisse en 1876, livraison 35* [*Statistics from Switzerland: Population movement in Switzerland in 1876, Delivery 35*]. Bern: Federal Assembly of Switzerland.

Szreter, S. 1996. *Fertility, Class and Gender in Britain, 1860–1940*. Cambridge: Cambridge University Press. doi.org/10.1017/CBO9780511582240.

Szreter, S., R.A. Nye and F. van Poppel. 2003. Fertility and contraception during the demographic transition: Qualitative and quantitative approaches. *The Journal of Interdisciplinary History* 34(2): 141–54. doi.org/10.1162/002219503322649453.

Tasmania (TAS). 1842. Census of Tasmania 1842. *Australian Data Archive*. Canberra: The Australian National University. Available from: hccda.ada.edu.au/documents/TAS-1842-census.

Tasmania (TAS). 1851. Census of Tasmania 1851. *Australian Data Archive*. Canberra: The Australian National University. Available from: hccda.ada.edu.au/documents/TAS-1851-census.

Tasmania (TAS). 1857. Census of Tasmania 1857. *Australian Data Archive*. Canberra: The Australian National University. Available from: hccda.ada.edu.au/documents/TAS-1857-census.

Tasmania (TAS). 1861. Census of Tasmania 1861. *Australian Data Archive*. Canberra: The Australian National University. Available from: hccda.ada.edu.au/documents/TAS-1861-census.

Tasmania (TAS). 1870. Census of Tasmania 1870. *Australian Data Archive*. Canberra: The Australian National University. Available from: hccda.ada.edu.au/documents/TAS-1870-census.

Tasmania (TAS). 1881. Census of Tasmania 1881. *Australian Data Archive*. Canberra: The Australian National University. Available from: hccda.ada.edu.au/pages/TAS-1881-census.

Tasmania (TAS). 1887. *Statistics of Tasmania, 1887*. Hobart: Government Printer.

Tasmania (TAS). 1891. Census of Tasmania 1891. *Australian Data Archive*. Canberra: The Australian National University. Available from: hccda.ada.edu.au/documents/TAS-1891-census.

Tasmania (TAS). 1892. *Statistics of Tasmania, 1892*. Hobart: Government Printer.

Tasmania (TAS). 1895. *An Act to Consolidate and Amend the Law Relating to the Registration of Births and Deaths in Tasmania (1895)*. 59 Victoria, No. 9.

Tasmania (TAS). 1901. Census of Tasmania 1901. *Australian Data Archive*. Canberra: The Australian National University. Available from: hccda.ada.edu.au/documents/TAS-1901-census.

Tasmania (TAS). 1902. *Statistics of Tasmania, 1902*. Hobart: Government Printer.

Tasmania (TAS). 1905. *The Women's and Children's Employment Act 1905*. 5 Edw. VII, No. 5.

Tasmanian Archive and Heritage Office (TAHO). 2014. *Registrar General's Department Pre-1900 Birth, Death and Marriage Records*. Hobart: TAHO.

Tasmanian Family History Society. 2014. *Tasmanian Place Names and Changes*. [Online.] Available from: www.hobart.tasfhs.org/changed_places.php.

Thompson, T.P. 1826. *The True Theory of Rent*. [Extract reprinted as Thomas Perronet Thompson on the force of habit and opinion on family size, *Population and Development Review* 37(4): 785–8 (December 2011).]

Tsuya, N., C. Campbell and W. Feng. 2010. Reproduction: Models and sources, in N.O. Tsuya, W. Feng, G. Alter and J.Z. Lee (eds), *Prudence and Pressure: Reproduction and human agency in Europe and Asia, 1700–1900*. Cambridge, MA: Massachusetts Institute of Technology, pp. 39–64. doi.org/10.7551/mitpress/8162.001.0001.

Van Bavel, J. 2004a. Deliberate birth spacing before the fertility transition in Europe: Evidence from nineteenth-century Belgium. *Population Studies* 58(1): 95–107. doi.org/10.1080/0032472032000167706.

Van Bavel, J. 2004b. Detecting stopping and spacing behaviour in historical demography: A critical review of methods. *Population* 59(1): 117–28. doi.org/10.3917/pope.401.0117.

Van Bavel, J. 2004c. Diffusion effects in the European fertility transition: Historical evidence from within a Belgian town. *European Journal of Population* 20(1): 63–85. doi.org/10.1023/B:EUJP.0000014572.66520.0d.

Van Bavel, J. and J. Kok. 2004. Birth spacing in the Netherlands: The effects of family composition, occupation and religion on birth intervals, 1820–1885. *European Journal of Population* 20(2): 119–40. doi.org/10.1023/B:EUJP.0000033860.39537.e2.

Van Bavel, J. and J. Kok. 2005. The role of religion in the Dutch fertility transition: Starting, spacing, and stopping in the heart of the Netherlands, 1845–1945. *Continuity and Change* 20(2): 247–63. doi.org/10.1017/S0268416005005473.

Van Bavel, J. and J. Kok. 2010. A mixed effects model of birth spacing for pre-transition populations: Evidence of deliberate fertility control from nineteenth century Netherlands. *History of the Family* 15(2): 125–38. doi.org/10.1016/j.hisfam.2009.12.004.

Van Bavel, J., S. Moreels, B. van de Putte and K. Matthijs. 2011. Family size and intergenerational social mobility during the fertility transition: Evidence of resource dilution from the city of Antwerp in nineteenth century Belgium. *Demographic Research* 24(14): 313–44. doi.org/10.4054/DemRes.2011.24.14.

van de Kaa, D.J. 1996. Anchored narratives: The story and findings of half a century of research into the determinants of fertility. *Population Studies* 50(3): 389–432. doi.org/10.1080/0032472031000149546.

van de Walle, F. 1986. Infant mortality and the European demographic transition, in A.J. Coale and S.C. Watkins (eds), *The Decline of Fertility in Europe*. Princeton, NJ: Princeton University Press, pp. 201–33.

Van Leeuwen, M. and I. Maas. 2005. A short note on HISCLASS. *History of Work Information System*. Leuven: Leuven University Press. Available from: historyofwork.iisg.nl/docs/hisclass-brief.doc.

van Poppel, F. and R. Derosas. 2006. Introduction, in R. Derosas and F. van Poppel (eds), *Religion and the Decline of Fertility in the Western World*. Dordrecht, Netherlands: Springer, pp. 1–19. doi.org/10.1007/1-4020-5190-5_1.

van Poppel, F., D.S. Reher, A. Sanz-Gimeno, M. Sanchez-Dominguez and E. Beekink. 2012. Mortality decline and reproductive change during the Dutch demographic transition: Revisiting a traditional debate with new data. *Demographic Research* 27(11): 299–338. doi.org/10.4054/DemRes.2012.27.11.

Vézina, H., D. Gauvreau and A. Gagnon. 2014. Socioeconomic fertility differentials in a late transition setting: A micro-level analysis of the Saguenay region in Quebec. *Demographic Research* 30(38): 1097–128. doi.org/10.4054/DemRes.2014.30.38.

Walker, A. 1869. *Diaries of Amy Clarisse Walker*. NS144/2/1/30. Hobart: Tasmanian Archives.

Walker, A. 1879. *Diaries of Amy Clarisse Walker*. NS144/2/1/31. Hobart: Tasmanian Archives.

Walker, A. 1880. *Diaries of Amy Clarisse Walker*. NS144/2/1/31. Hobart: Tasmanian Archives.

Walker, A. 1881. *Diaries of Amy Clarisse Walker*. NS144/2/1/31. Hobart: Tasmanian Archives.

Walker, A. 1882. *Diaries of Amy Clarisse Walker*. NS144/2/1/31. Hobart: Tasmanian Archives.

Walker, A. 1888. *Diaries of Amy Clarisse Walker*. NS144/2/1/38. Hobart: Tasmanian Archives.

Walker, A. 1898. *Diaries of Amy Clarisse Walker*. NS144/2/1/46. Hobart: Tasmanian Archives.

Woods, R.I. 1987. Approaches to the fertility transition in Victorian England. *Population Studies* 41(2): 283–311. doi.org/10.1080/0032472031000142806.

World Health Organization (WHO). 1992. *International Statistical Classification of Diseases and Related Health Problems. Tenth Revision. Volume 1*. Geneva: WHO.

Wrigley, E.A. 1966. Family reconstitution, in E.A. Wrigley (ed.), *An Introduction to English Historical Demography: From the sixteenth to the nineteenth century*. New York: Basic Books, pp. 44–95.

Wrigley, E.A. 1978. Fertility strategy for the individual and the group, in C. Tilly (ed.), *Historical Studies of Changing Fertility*. Princeton, NJ: Princeton University Press, pp. 135–54.

Wrigley, E.A., R.S. Davies, J.E. Oeppen and R.S. Schofield. 1997. *English Population History from Family Reconstitution: 1580–1837*. Cambridge: Cambridge University Press. doi.org/10.1017/CBO9780511660344.

Yerushalmy, J., M. Kramer and E.M. Gardiner. 1940. Studies in childbirth mortality: Puerperal fatality and loss of offspring. *Public Health Reports* 55(23): 1010–27. doi.org/10.2307/4583317.

Index

abortifacients 9, 19, 22, 195, 200, 216
abortion 10, 205, 224
    as contraception 24, 191, 195, 198, 216–17, 224
    legality of 195, 196
    rates of 19, 195–6, 198
abortionists 195, 196, 201, 216, 224
abstinence 19, 20, 22, 196, 197, 224
Adelaide 43, 196, 204, 205, 207
'adjustment' theory 22–3, 181, 221, 222
advertising, of contraceptives 9, 18, 19, 22, 107, 108, 195, 199–201, 223, 224
Allbutt, Dr Henry 8–9, 10, 199
Anglicans 89, 90, 210
    birth intervals 244, 250
    dominance in Tasmania 52, 53
    family size 38, 137, 138, 139, 141, 166, 173, 180, 244, 248
    see also Church of England, Protestants, religion
Archer, Thomas Cathcart 103, 259
Asia 145
Australian Cemetery Index 68, 74, 75, 81

Baptists 38, 52, 53, 54, 90, 182, 227
    see also Protestants, religion
Barwick, Eliza 70, 261
Beaconsfield 45, 70, 97, 239, 263, 264

Belgium 2, 6, 7, 8, 13, 16, 223, 228
Besant, Annie 8–9, 18, 107, 108, 198–9, 201, 202
birth control, *see* fertility control
birth intervals 76, 163, 174, 181, 243, 249, 250, 251
    and breastfeeding 24, 150, 153
    and fertility decline 154, 221
    and infant mortality 15, 16, 159, 163–4, 174, 175
    measuring 148, 150–5, 156, 157–9, 160–2, 171–4
    and religion 74, 174, 175–6, 182, 227
    and socioeconomic status 36, 174, 175–6
    see also spacing behaviour
Bradlaugh, Charles 9, 199, 202
Bradlaugh–Besant trial 9, 201–2
breastfeeding 15, 16, 18, 24, 150, 153, 183, 229
Brisbane 43
Britain 44, 51, 55, 66, 69, 190, 197–8, 202, 205, 223, 225
    abortion 19
    abstinence 19, 224
    birth control information 8, 9, 10, 18, 19, 22, 223
    feminism 21
    fertility decline 2, 4, 6–7, 11–12, 13, 21, 40
    fertility rates 21, 39, 167, 225
    mortality 4, 228

religion 53, 54, 210, 226
sale of contraceptives 19
socioeconomic status 6, 7, 21, 205, 225
women and fertility control 20, 21, 22, 216
see also London
British
in Tasmania 41–2, 43, 47, 48, 51–2, 186
British Isles 51, 52
Buddhists 53, 54
Burnie 60, 239

Calvinism 14
Campbell Town 59, 60, 239
Canada 2, 5, 6, 7, 8, 11, 14, 87, 224, 226
see also Ontario, Quebec
Carroll, Ellen 264
Catholics 186, 210
birth registration 74, 78
classification of 89, 90
education 8, 56
fertility decline 123, 143
fertility rates 14, 37, 38–9, 123, 137–40, 143, 166, 173, 226, 227
in Tasmania 52, 53, 54, 90–1
see also religion
chemist shops, *see* pharmacies
China 24, 51
Church of England 38–9, 52, 53, 54, 89, 199
see also Anglican, Protestants, religion
Church of Scotland 54, 89, 123
coitus interruptus (withdrawal) 17, 18, 19
see also withdrawal
Collins booksellers 202
Colonial Tasmanian Family Links Database 67, 68, 74, 253

condoms 18, 191, 193, 195, 200, 216, 224
Congregationalists 37, 38, 52, 53, 90, 182, 204, 227
see also Protestants, religion
contraception 10
acceptance of 19
advertising of 9, 18, 19, 22, 107, 108, 195, 199–201, 223, 224
availability 17–19, 191–3, 224–5
demand for 19, 192
female control of 22, 195, 216, 227
feminist support for 214
and fertility decline 25, 185
and gender power relations 21, 22
historical use of 4, 17–18
information about 10, 109, 199, 222
morality of 18, 19
and stopping behaviour 24
use in Australia 191, 192
use in Britain 10, 19, 22
use in United States 20, 22
women as information vectors 10, 22
women making own 194, 224, 227
see also condoms, douching, fertility control, *Pessaire Preventif*, pessaries, prevention, sponges
Cox, Maria 263
Creed, Dr 218

Dally, David 206, 263–4
Darwin, Charles 190
Davenport, Amy Clarisse *see* Walker, Amy
death, *see* mortality
Deloraine 45, 239
demographic transition theory 1, 4–5, 14, 16, 142, 181, 185, 187, 222

Devonport 45, 60, 97, 106, 196, 205, 239, 264
diffusion theory 4, 6–8, 10, 22, 23, 142, 143, 181–2, 185, 197–8
    evidence to royal commission 198–202, 203–4, 223
    and fertility control 6–10, 22, 25, 185, 198, 199, 222, 223, 226
    and spacing behaviour 181
Dixon, Emma 219
douching 18, 20, 191, 192, 193, 195, 224
Duncan, Annie 208
Dutch, *see* Netherlands

Eastern European 4
economic demand theory 11, 12
economic theories 4, 10–13, 142, 181, 185, 205–9
Egypt 18
England, *see* Britain
Europe 43, 188, 197
    demographic transition 1, 4
    fertility control 6, 10, 12, 17, 18, 19, 20, 21–2, 23, 145, 216
    fertility decline 2, 4, 7, 11, 14, 18, 21, 24, 25, 40, 160, 220, 221, 222, 223
    fertility rates 39, 221
    fertility transition 5, 6, 22, 222, 223
    infant mortality 5, 15, 228
    infanticide 17
    information diffusion 10
    religion 14, 54, 226
    rural–urban divide 7, 224
    secularisation 13, 14, 226
    socioeconomic status 6, 12, 224, 225
    spacing behaviour 25
    stopping behaviour 24
    see also individual countries

feminism 21, 22, 187, 213, 214, 215, 219, 228, 229, 262
fertility control 2, 4, 12, 15, 19, 25, 149, 216
    accessibility of 12, 19, 185
    adoption of 156, 158, 186, 201, 222, 226
    attitudes towards 6, 185, 197, 198
    birth intervals 154, 172
    child mortality 5, 15–16, 190
    education levels 8, 14, 21, 182
    in Europe 6, 10, 17, 18, 19, 20, 21–2, 216
    female control of 195, 200, 215, 216, 227
    and feminism 21, 214, 219
    and information diffusion 6–10, 22, 25, 185, 198, 199, 222, 223, 226
    legality of 9, 201, 202, 223
    male-controlled methods 22, 216
    and medical profession 10, 223
    motivation for 10, 12–13, 20, 205, 226
    opposition to 9, 186, 215
    and religion 38, 209, 210, 212, 226
    and secularisation 13, 14, 209, 210, 226
    and socioeconomic status 10, 12, 13, 35, 142, 182, 224, 225, 229
    spacing behaviour 25, 149, 151, 154, 162
    starting behaviour 145
    stopping behaviour 24, 25, 149, 154, 162
    urban–rural divide 143, 182
    see also contraception, prevention, spacing behaviour, starting behaviour, stopping behaviour
fertility transition 156, 162
    in Australia 30, 213
    in Canada 5, 6, 7, 8, 222

among Catholics 14
among Protestants 14
and child mortality 5, 16
in Europe 1, 5, 6, 7, 8, 11, 13, 16, 21, 222, 223
and gender relations 20, 21, 22, 213, 222
and religion 14
in Scandinavia 5, 8
in Tasmania 2, 64, 222, 224
in United States 5, 6, 8, 154, 222
and use of birth control 19–20, 156
Fleming, Charles 260
Fleming, Richard 70, 261
Foreman, Dr Joseph 195–6, 204
France 1, 215
Franklin, John 41
Freethinkers 18
French letters, *see* condoms
Fuss, Edmund 206, 207, 217

Gale, Alfred ('Alf') 101, 260
George Town 44, 240
Germany 5, 15, 16, 51, 160, 228
Glamorgan 70, 79
Glenorchy 97, 240
Glover, Arthur 196
Graham, Sir James 194

Harris, Dr John 193–4, 218
Harrop, Eleanor 259
Hennessy, Reverend Nicholas 204
Hobart 42, 43, 44, 45, 46, 70, 76, 187, 188, 189, 190, 261
births 70, 79–80, 97, 98, 121
demographics 48, 51, 59, 60
education 57
newspapers 196, 200, 201, 202, 205, 219
religion 52–3
Howell-Price, Reverend Dr John 199, 203, 211, 212, 218, 219
Hume, John 217
Huon Valley 44, 45

Iceland 5, 8
Indigenous 47
'innovation' theory 22–3, 25, 181, 221, 222
'insurance' effect theory 14, 15, 16, 182, 228
see also 'replacement' effect theory
Islam, *see* Mahommedans
Italy 8, 14, 18, 21

Japan 24, 197
Jews 14, 37, 38–9, 54
see also religion

Knopwood, Robert 52

Launceston 42, 43, 44, 45, 46, 70, 76, 188, 189, 259, 261, 263, 264
births 97, 98, 121
demographics 59, 60, 188
newspapers 201, 205
Lloyd, Henrietta 263
London 44, 197, 198
see also Britain
Loney, Thomas 192
Lutherans 37, 38
see also religion
Lyons, Joseph 103, 206, 264
Lyons, Michael 103, 206, 264

McAulay, Ida 187, 188–90, 197, 199, 208, 210, 214–15, 219, 262
McCulloch, Dr Stanley 198
McKay, Dr William 194, 207, 212
Mahommedans 53, 54
Malthusian League 9
Marrawah 60, 101, 260
Masterton, J.A. 193, 194
Maxted, Sydney 202–3
Melbourne 43, 45, 70, 197, 207, 214, 264
abortion 196
fertility levels 27, 36, 204, 205, 224
information about birth control 199, 200, 201, 202, 212

Methodists 52–3, 54, 89–90, 212, 217
  fertility rates 37, 38–9, 123, 137–9, 141, 143, 175, 176, 182, 227
  see also Protestants, religion, Wesleyan
Midlands 42, 60, 94, 97–8
midwives 10, 59, 195, 196, 203, 223
Mitchell, James 199
Moran, Cardinal Patrick 210
Morgan, Dr Cosby William 211
mortality, infant and child 68, 74, 79,
  decline in 4, 5, 15, 16, 17, 115, 185, 190–1, 228
  impact on fertility 3, 5, 14–17, 117, 182–3, 190, 222, 228
  rates of 1, 4, 16–17, 190
  trends in 4, 111, 115–17, 159, 165, 166, 167, 242
mortality, intrauterine 150
mortality, maternal 196, 217, 218
Morton, Dr Cosby 192
Mount Lyell 45–6, 215
Mullins, Dr George 204, 206–7

Neale, Thomas 55
Netherlands 6, 16, 41, 228
New South Wales (NSW) 3, 42, 70, 116, 213
  abortion 196, 198
  birth registrations 69, 78
  contraceptive sales 191, 192–3
  death registrations 69, 74, 75
  fertility control 186, 198, 200, 206
  fertility rates 27, 29, 30, 37, 38, 186, 202, 215
  links with Tasmania 186–7
  religion 38, 53, 186, 210
  see also Royal Commission on the Decline of the Birth-Rate and on the Mortality of Infants in New South Wales, Sydney

New Zealand 2, 43, 49, 52, 67, 69, 70, 77, 78, 81, 197–8, 261
non-Christian 53
Nonconformists 52, 53, 90, 123, 137, 138, 141, 142, 143, 174, 175, 182, 227
  see also Protestants, religion
North America, *see* Canada, United States
Northern Territory 70
Norway 8
NSW, *see* New South Wales

Oatlands 60, 70, 102, 240, 260, 261
obscenity 9, 201, 202, 223
Ontario 11, 226

Park, William 192, 217
Parke Davis Drug Company 193
Pattinson, Lewy 204
Pessaire Preventif 18, 191, 199, 200, 224
pessaries 18, 107, 191, 192, 193–4, 195, 201, 203, 204, 224
pharmacies
  and abortions 195, 216–17, 224
  and sale of contraceptives 19, 191–2, 195, 205, 224, 227
pharmacists 199
  testimony to royal commission 192–3, 195, 203–4, 206, 216 17
'physiological' effect 14, 15, 183, 228
Presbyterians 38–9, 52, 53, 54, 89, 90, 123, 137–41, 143, 212
  see also Protestants, religion
prevention 20, 194, 216, 224
  and decline in birth rate 195
  information on 199, 200–1, 203, 204, 206, 217, 223, 228
  opposition to 212, 215
  and religion 210–11, 212
  and socioeconomic status 194, 198, 206, 207, 211, 224

use of 194, 195, 198, 211, 216, 218, 219, 227
see also abstinence, contraception, fertility control
preventives
advertisements for 199, 200–1
homemade 18, 191, 193–4, 224, 227
sales of 192–3, 204–5, 216, 217, 227
see also coitus interruptus, condoms, contraception, douching, *Pessaire Preventif*, pessaries, sponges, withdrawal
Protestants 14, 16, 38, 53, 54, 123, 137, 143, 226
see also individual religions

Quebec 8, 11, 87
Queensland 37, 67, 69, 74, 75
see also Brisbane
Queenstown 44, 45–6, 54, 60, 104, 105, 106, 240

Rawsley, Lavinia Jane 260
religion 18, 78, 83, 186, 209–11, 226
and birth intervals 74, 174, 175–6, 182, 227
in Britain 53, 54, 226
and fertility control 14, 210, 211, 212
and fertility decline 14, 37, 40, 41, 118, 123, 125, 143, 163
and fertility rates 16, 34, 37–9, 127, 137, 138, 139, 165, 167, 178, 227
and marriage 89–90, 182, 209, 227
and spacing behaviour 175, 182, 227
and stopping behaviour 182
in Tasmania 52–4, 61
see also individual religions, Protestants, secularisation

Rendell, Walter 18, 107, 191, 193, 204
'replacement' effect theory 14, 15, 16, 182, 228
see also 'insurance' effect theory
Riley, Edmund 208
Royal Commission on the Decline of the Birth-Rate and on the Mortality of Infants in New South Wales 3, 30, 186
commissioners 186, 215, 221
evidence on abortion 191, 195, 196, 198, 201, 216, 217
evidence on contraception 191–7, 206, 216
evidence on economics 206–9, 225
evidence on fertility control 186, 198–200, 202–4, 207, 216, 218, 225
evidence on infant mortality 190
evidence on information diffusion 198–202, 203–4, 223
evidence on morality of birth control 210, 211–12, 215, 217
evidence on prevention 195, 198
evidence on role of women 215, 216, 217, 218–19, 227
findings 186, 190, 205, 215–16
opposition to birth control 186, 215–16
testimony from clergy 196–7, 199, 203, 204, 210–12, 217, 218–19
testimony from doctors 193–4, 195–6, 198, 200, 204, 206–7, 208, 209, 211, 216, 217, 218
testimony from pharmacists 192–3, 195, 203–4, 206, 216–17
testimony from police 195, 199, 201, 211
Russell, Dr Grace 208
Rutledge, Reverend William 217

Salvation Army 53, 54, 207, 211
Sawtell, James 195, 211
Scot-Skirving, Dr Robert 193, 194, 206, 211, 217
Scotland 39, 51
Scott, Rose 215
Scottsdale 45, 240
secularisation 4, 13–14, 143, 182, 185–6, 209–12, 226
Sharland, William 193
Silly, Alfred 204
Smyth, Brettena 109, 199, 214
South Australia 27, 33, 34, 35, 37, 67, 69, 87, 214
   see also Adelaide
spacing behaviour
   as adaptation 221
   analysis of 78, 82
   and demographic transition theory 181
   and diffusion theory 181
   and fertility decline 2, 4, 23–25, 145, 147, 154, 181
   and geographic location 182, 224–5
   and infant mortality 15, 16, 183, 228
   and 'insurance' effect 182
   measuring 147–51, 154, 155–8, 160, 162–3, 171, 172, 175, 176
   rates of 36, 221
   and religion 175, 182, 227
   and 'replacement' effect 182
   and socioeconomic status 36, 175, 181–2, 226
   and use of withdrawal 18
   see also birth intervals
Spain 5, 8, 16, 228
sponges 18, 191, 192, 194, 195, 224
starting behaviour 2, 23–4, 82, 145, 160, 181, 221–2
Stephen, Mr Justice 202

Stephen, Reverend Patrick 212
Stevens, George 193, 195, 217
stopping behaviour 2, 4, 23–5, 30, 82, 113, 145, 147–9, 154–8, 160, 162–5, 167–8, 170–1, 176, 181–2, 221, 227, 228
Strahan 45, 241
Sutton, Edward Henry 263
Sutton, Samuel 206
Swansea 70, 241
Sweden 2, 8
Switzerland 2, 17
Sydney 42, 70, 187, 199, 202, 207
   abortion 195–6, 200, 216, 217
   birth rate 204–5, 206, 208–9, 210, 218
   connections with Tasmania 43, 45, 186, 197
   contraceptives 192, 193–4, 198, 200, 201, 204, 217

Tasmanian Women's Suffrage Association (Tasmanian Women's Political Organisation) 215, 262
Thompson, Thomas Perronet 12
Thring, Dr Edward 200

Ulverstone 60, 241, 264
United Kingdom, *see* Britain, London
United States 116, 197, 210, 226
   contraceptive use 9, 19–20, 22, 200
   fertility decline 7, 8
   fertility rate 2, 224
   fertility transition 5, 6, 222
   and 'insurance' effect 16, 228
   and 'replacement' effect 15, 228
   see also Utah
urbanisation 4, 41, 59–60, 187, 188, 222, 229
Utah 7, 16, 17, 25, 33, 112, 114, 154, 156, 221, 228

Victoria 2, 37, 44, 48, 51, 70, 72, 75, 87, 199, 213, 224
　abortion 205
　birth registrations 73, 78
　goldrush 48, 64
　infant mortality 116
　preventives 205, 212
　see also Melbourne

Walker, Amy 187, 188–91, 197, 199, 210, 214, 215, 261–2
Walker, John Fletcher 189, 261
Watson-Munro, Dr 217
Wesleyan 52, 54, 89, 175
　see also Methodists, Protestants, religion
West, John 207–8, 211, 216
Western Australia 2, 37, 45, 49, 69, 78, 214
Western Europe, *see* Europe
Wigg, Emma 260
Windeyer, Mr Justice 202
withdrawal (*coitus interruptus*) 17, 19, 20, 22, 24, 191, 194, 216, 224
　see also *coitus interruptus*
Women's Guild 10, 22
Worrall, Dr Ralph 194, 198, 206, 209, 216

Zeehan 44, 45, 46, 54, 57, 60, 105, 205, 241

www.ingramcontent.com/pod-product-compliance
Lightning Source LLC
Chambersburg PA
CBHW050849240426
43667CB00032B/2960